UNDER THE WEATHER

MCGILL-QUEEN'S/BRIAN MULRONEY INSTITUTE OF GOVERNMENT
STUDIES IN LEADERSHIP, PUBLIC POLICY, AND GOVERNANCE

Series editor: Donald E. Abelson

Titles in this series address critical issues facing Canada at home and
abroad and the efforts policymakers at all levels of government have
made to address a host of complex and multifaceted policy concerns.
Books in this series receive financial support from the Brian Mulroney
Institute of Government at St Francis Xavier University; in keeping with
the institute's mandate, these studies explore how leaders involved in
key policy initiatives arrived at their decisions and what lessons can be
learned. Combining rigorous academic analysis with thoughtful recommendations, this series compels readers to think more critically about
how and why elected officials make certain policy choices, and how, in
concert with other stakeholders, they can better navigate an increasingly
complicated and crowded marketplace of ideas.

1 Braver Canada
   Shaping Our Destiny in a
   Precarious World
   Derek H. Burney and
   Fen Osler Hampson

2 The Canadian Federal Election
   of 2019
   Edited by Jon H. Pammett and
   Christopher Dornan

3 Keeping Canada Running
   Infrastructure and the Future of
   Governance in a Pandemic World
   Edited by G. Bruce Doern,
   Christopher Stoney, and Robert
   Hilton

4 The Age of Consequence
   The Ordeals of Public Policy
   in Canada
   Charles McMillan

5 Government
   Have Presidents and Prime Ministers
   Misdiagnosed the Patient?
   Donald J. Savoie

6 Cyber-Threats to Canadian
   Democracy
   Edited by Holly Ann Garnett and
   Michael Pal

7 The Canadian Federal Election
   of 2021
   Edited by Jon H. Pammett and
   Christopher Dornan

8 CETA Implementation and
   Implications
   Unravelling the Puzzle
   Edited by Robert G. Finbow

9 Multilateral Sanctions Revisited
   Lessons Learned from Margaret
   Doxey
   Edited by Andrea Charron and
   Clara Portela

10 Booze, Cigarettes, and Constitutional
   Dust-Ups
   Canada's Quest for Interprovincial
   Free Trade
   Ryan Manucha

11 NORAD
   In Perpetuity and Beyond
   Andrea Charron and James Fergusson

12 Under the Weather
   Reimagining Mobility in the Climate
   Crisis
   Stephanie Sodero

Under the Weather

Reimagining Mobility in the Climate Crisis

STEPHANIE SODERO

McGill-Queen's University Press
Montreal & Kingston • London • Chicago

© McGill-Queen's University Press 2022

ISBN 978-0-2280-1462-1 (cloth)
ISBN 978-0-2280-1597-0 (paper)
ISBN 978-0-2280-1574-1 (ePDF)
ISBN 978-0-2280-1575-8 (ePUB)

Legal deposit fourth quarter 2022
Bibliothèque nationale du Québec

Printed in Canada on acid-free paper that is 100% ancient forest free
(100% post-consumer recycled), processed chlorine free

Funded by the   Financé par le
Government   gouvernement   Canada Council   Conseil des arts
of Canada   du Canada   for the Arts   du Canada

We acknowledge the support of the Canada Council for the Arts.
Nous remercions le Conseil des arts du Canada de son soutien.

Library and Archives Canada Cataloguing in Publication

Title: Under the weather : reimagining mobility in the climate crisis /
  Stephanie Sodero.
Names: Sodero, Stephanie, 1978– author.
Series: McGill-Queen's/Brian Mulroney Institute of Government studies in
  leadership, public policy, and governance ; 12.
Description: Series statement: McGill-Queen's/Brian Mulroney Institute of
  Government studies in leadership, public policy, and governance ; 12 |
  Includes bibliographical references and index.
Identifiers: Canadiana (print) 20220273383 | Canadiana (ebook) 20220273782
  | ISBN 9780228014621 (cloth) | ISBN 9780228015970 (paper) | ISBN
  9780228015741 (ePDF) | ISBN 9780228015758 (ePUB)
Subjects: LCSH: Human ecology. | LCSH: Severe storms. | LCSH: Climatic changes.
  | LCSH: Hurricanes—Nova Scotia—Case studies. | LCSH: Hurricanes—
  Newfoundland and Labrador—Case studies. | LCGFT: Case studies.
Classification: LCC GF41.S63 2022 | DDC 304.2—dc23

This book was typeset in 10.5/13 Sabon.

To

Mom and Dad

&

Amntu'kati / Point Pleasant Park

Contents

Figures and Tables | ix

Preface | xi

Acknowledgments | xiii

Introduction | 3

1 Setting Sail | 17

2 Ecological Mobilities | 30

3 Hurricane Juan | 56

4 Charismatic Mobilities | 79

5 Hurricane Igor | 98

6 Running on Fumes | 123

7 Transport Resilience | 145

8 Climate Routing | 159

9 Changing Course | 183

Notes | 193

Bibliography | 229

Index | 245

Figures and Tables

FIGURES

1.1 *Family and Rainstorm*, Alex Colville, 1955
     Credit: A.C. Fine Art Inc. | 19
3.1 Fallen trees and power lines, Halifax, 2003
     Credit: Paul Chiasson/The Canadian Press | 64
3.2 Damage to containers, Halifax Port Authority, 2003
     Credit: Laflamme/Percy (Environment Canada,
     Halifax, Nova Scotia) | 72
3.3 Washed-out train tracks with fuel tankers, 2003
     Credit: Laflamme/Percy (Environment Canada,
     Halifax, Nova Scotia) | 74
9.1 *Woman, Dog and Canoe*, Alex Colville, 1962
     Credit: A.C. Fine Art Inc. | 188

TABLES

2.1 Comparison of transport planning, sustainable mobility,
     and an ecological approach to mobilities | 49
3.1 Disruptive events impacting Nova Scotia, 1996–2004 | 69
5.1 Newfoundland and Labrador weather events that triggered
     federal Disaster Financial Assistance Arrangements
     program, 2000–10 | 117
7.1 Measures for managing mobility before, during, and after
     Hurricanes Juan and Igor | 147
8.1 Climate routing measures with select examples | 160

Preface

This book is ten years in the making. Since starting this project, the Earth's climate is different, with global average concentrations of carbon dioxide increasing from 391 to 417 parts per million, nudging the climate closer to a critical threshold of 1.5°C of heating. Another key shift since I started this project is an expanding awareness of the structural injustices imposed on Indigenous communities through the violence of settler colonialism in Canada.

When I started this research, I chose two case studies – one based in my home of Mi'kma'ki/Nova Scotia and one based where I was studying in Ktaqmkuk/Newfoundland. It would not have occurred to me ten years ago to acknowledge this fact in my writing. Now I appreciate that that my research is based in Mi'kma'ki, the ancestral and unceded territory of the Mi'kmaq People, and in the ancestral homelands of the Mi'kmaq and Beothuk, and home of the Inuit of Nunatsiavut and NunatuKavut and the Innu of Nitassinan, and their ancestors, as the original people of Labrador. Further, Mi'kma'ki, which includes Nova Scotia and southwestern Newfoundland, is covered by the "Treaties of Peace and Friendship" first signed by Mi'kmaq and Wolastoqiyik (Maliseet) with the British Crown in 1725; "these did not deal with surrender of lands and resources but recognized ... title and established the rules for what was to be an ongoing relationship between nations."[1] Today I recognize that I benefited from conducting my research on the territory of the Mi'kmaq and Beothuk, and that "we are all treaty people."[2]

My book is about reconceptualizing the relationship between the social and the ecological, namely mobility and the climate. Though this is not a frame I use in the book, I am in fact reflecting on the human relationship with the land. And the land exists in complex and long-standing relationship with diverse peoples, including Indigenous communities, Black settlers, and Acadian communities subject to unequal power relations that shape dominant attitudes about how to live with the land. Max Liboiron's comments on my doctoral dissertation and their book, *Pollution Is Colonialism*, were key interventions in shifting my understanding of how my positionality as a fifth-generation settler-descendant inflects my research.[3] Another key intervention was an article in *Mobilities* journal by Kyle Whyte, Jared Talley, and Julia Gibson titled "Indigenous Mobility Transition, Colonialism and the Anthropocene." To some extent, I feel my learning curve is dampened by living outside of Canada since 2016. However, living in the United Kingdom has exposed me to different expressions of racism as well as pro-colonial views that shed light on the violence and pervasiveness of settler colonialism.[4]

Given that my (un)learning is an ongoing project, I am confronted with how to reflect the process in this book. I opted to make four interventions. First, I include this reflection on my own evolving understanding of my privilege and positionality as a white settler-descendant who calls K'jipuktuk/Halifax home. Next, in the first chapter I reflect on the uneven power dynamics embedded in my research methods. In chapter 4, I reflect on my emerging intellectual and emotional engagement in a discussion of climate mobilities. Finally, upon their first use in a given chapter, I include Indigenous and settler place names.

How this approach will sit with me or others in one or five years, only time will tell. What I know, and what I continue to learn in different depths and facets, is that climate change is about human relationship with the environment. Consequently, meaningful climate action requires acknowledging settler colonial practices in relation to the land and Indigenous communities. Anti-colonization and reconciliation are integral to climate justice.

Acknowledgments

Writing a book is a marathon. Three conversations got me to the start line: thank you to my doctoral supervisor, Dr Mark CJ Stoddart at Memorial University; to my postdoctoral mentor, Dr Jacob Copeman at the University of Edinburgh; and my friend and disabilities scholar, Magda Szarota at Lancaster University. A special thanks to Mark Stoddart, who promptly responds to my out-of-the-blue requests with sage guidance that helps me navigate my next steps with confidence – a practice I now aim for with my students.

Casting back to my PhD, many thanks to my research participants for sharing your experience, time, and energy, which shaped my thinking about mobility and community resilience in the climate emergency. Thanks to the organizers and participants of the University of Oslo doctoral course on the Politics of Mobility – an invaluable experience. Thank you to the Institute for Public Knowledge at New York University and International House, an oasis for high flyers on the Upper West Side (traditional territory of the Lenape). Thanks to Professor Barb Neis for engaging me in the Marine Environmental Observation, Prediction and Response Network and the On the Move project, and to Norm Catto for strengthening my understanding of the physical dimensions of disaster. Thanks to my doctoral committee, Dr Nicole Power and Dr Natalie Slawinski, as well as my examining committee – Dr Tim Cresswell, Dr Kelly Vodden, and Dr Max Liboiron – for getting me to and through my doctoral defence.

Friends from my time in Ktaqmkuk/Newfoundland, Jon Parsons and Erika Steeves, run a writing course that provided the ideal structure to transform my doctoral dissertation into a book. Thank you both for getting me off to a strong start. There are many readers to thank. First and foremost, Professor Jim Conley of Trent University. I attended Trent as an undergrad and was so pleased when I encountered Jim again during my doctoral studies in Environmental Sociology. It takes courage and sensitivity to comment on a first draft, and Jim, your comments energized me to continue. I am so fortunate to have a plethora of friends and colleagues who answered questions, commented on proposals, read chapters, and provided support: Dave Alders, Sharon Bala, Zofia Bednarowska, Angela Birch, Eva Bogdan, Rachel Bower, Maggy Burns, Linda Cohen, Pablo Crespo, Sameena Eidoo, Kathy Fitzpatrick, Laena Garrison, Jon Gibson, Anne Graham, Jen Graham, Julia Hildebrand, Christine Knott, Debora Niermann, Didem Oral, Nicholas Scott, Carly Spornaski, Phillip Vannini, Matt Wyman-McCarthy, and Pinar Zubaroglu. Special thanks to Paula Graham, who provided a second set of eyes on my sprint to the finish line of a first draft.

I want to express gratitude to the global mobilities community. I could not have hoped to find a warmer intellectual home. Thank you particularly to my postdoctoral mentor Monika Büscher at Lancaster University's Centre for Mobilities Research for your creativity and spark. Tim Cresswell noted that being an external examiner is an enduring commitment, and I appreciate the guidance and kindness you have offered along the way. Thank you to Pete Adey for his inspiring work on emergency mobilities and engagement with my research, and to Pennie Drinkall, CeMoRe administrator, *Mobilities* editor, provider of a cozy home, and dedicated attendee of my weekly yoga class.

I knew McGill-Queen's University Press was the right fit when I learned my acquisitions editor, Mark Abley, is a poet who also wrote about the North American ice storm. Thank you, Mark, for your clarity and efficiency, and your receptivity to a less conventional approach to an academic book. Khadija Coxon took over the reins during the height of COVID, guiding the project to completion through numerous twists and turns – thank you. I am grateful to four reviewers for thoughtful and constructive comments that transformed and strengthened the final book. Also at McGill-Queen's, I want to thank Lisa Aitken, Paloma Friedman, Kathleen Fraser, Jennifer Roberts, and Paula Sarson. I want to express appreciation to Sue Goyette and Gaspereau Press for permission to reprint excerpts from *Ocean*; to Tim Cresswell and Penned in the Margins Press for permission to reprint excerpts from *Plastiglomerate*; to Ann (Colville) Kitz for permission to reproduce images of the Alex Colville paintings; and to photographers Bob Ayer, Paul Chiasson, Bob Guscott, Tim Krochak, André Laflamme, and Roger Percy, and especially Colin Peddle for use of photos (available on companion project website).[1]

Months after submitting my manuscript for review, I received an encouraging email from McGill-Queen's that signalled this trek might end in success. I had just spent the morning with my parents, Peter and Elizabeth Sodero, walking with alpacas at Malin Head, the northernmost point of Ireland. Being with them in this place with this news, I was on top of the world – a writer's high. My brilliant niece, Isabelle Melanson, assisted me with formatting endnotes and bibliography, as well as tracking down permissions for quotes and images. And thank you to the Steele family and friends – Aunt Jane, Uncle Geoffrey, Suzanne Steele, Marg Dunphy, Catherine Perry – for providing a home away from home at Winter Place.

Thank you to colleagues at my new intellectual home and dream job with the Humanitarian and Conflict Response Institute at the University of Manchester who encouraged and supported me in this project, including Larissa Fast, Stephanie Rinaldi, Bertrand Taithe, Mandy Turner, Birte Vogel, and Darren Walter. Thank you to my students in *Disaster Mobilities of Climate Change* and *Vital Mobilities: Delivering Health Care in a Changing Climate* for your thoughtful engagement, and to Liam O'Brien for compiling the index.

The time and space to write was made possible by a Banting postdoctoral award and a Social Sciences and Humanities Research Council of Canada postdoctoral award. I conducted the research on which this book is based with the financial support of the Joseph-Armand Bombardier Canada Graduate Doctoral Scholarship, the Harris Centre Student Research Fund Strategic Partnership, a Transportation Association of Canada Award, a Memorial University Dean's Doctoral Award, and a Women's Association of Memorial University of Newfoundland Graduate Student Scholarship. My Visiting Scholarship at New York University was made possible through the Canada Graduate Scholarship Michael Smith Foreign Study Supplement, the Scotiabank Bursary for International Study, and International House of New York. Thank you to Melanie Caines (Nova Yoga), Crystal Chafe, and Beth Whalen, among many others, who kept my mind and body in tune.

Parts of this book draw on work I published elsewhere. In chapter 2, "Ecological Mobilities," I cite "Greenhouse Gases, Pine Beetles, and Humans: The Ecologically-Mediated Development of British

Columbia's Carbon Tax," *Canadian Journal of Sociology* 40, no. 3 (2015): 309–30 (University of Alberta). In chapter 5, "Hurricane Igor," and co-authored with Mark CJ Stoddart, I cite "A Typology of Diversion: Legitimating Discourses of Oil Extraction, Tourism Attraction and Climate Action," *Environmental Sociology* 1, no. 1 (2015): 59–68 (Taylor & Francis). Chapter 8, "Climate Routing," draws on publications I co-authored with Richard Rackham, a chapter on "Vital Mobilities" in *Handbook on Methods and Applications for Mobilities Research* (Edward Elgar) edited by Monika Büscher, Malene Freudendal-Pedersen, Sven Kesselring, and Nikolaj Grauslund Kristensen; and an article, "Blood Drones: Using Utopia as Method to Imagine Future Vital Mobilities," in a special issue on Mobile Utopia in *Mobilities* 15, no. 1 (2020): 11–24 (Taylor & Francis).

Writing a book is a marathon. I hope you enjoy the encapsulated journey and are inspired to reimagine mobility in the climate emergency.

UNDER THE WEATHER

Introduction

When Hurricane Juan hit Mi'kma'ki/Nova Scotia in 2003, twenty-metre waves snapped the moorings of weather buoys in Halifax Harbour. Millions of trees across the province fell. Blocked streets made travel treacherous for emergency and power crews. Already lengthy wait times for medical services increased.[1] When Hurricane Igor hit the neighbouring island of Ktaqmkuk/Newfoundland in 2010, road and bridge washouts isolated more than one hundred communities. People struggled to access food, fuel, and medical supplies.[2] A damaged fish processing plant was closed rather than repaired. While most North Atlantic hurricanes dissipate in the open ocean, Juan and Igor made landfall. Juan was a Category 2 hurricane, and Category 1 Igor measured 1,500 kilometres across, making it the largest storm ever recorded in the Atlantic Basin, until Hurricane Sandy hit the Northeastern United States two years later. Lives were lost. Provincial governments declared states of emergency. Meteorologists retired the names *Juan* and *Igor*.

Solar-powered movements of wind and water collided with the fossil-fuelled movement of people, goods, and services. Transport systems exposed to extreme coastal conditions were tested by these storms. In some cases, alternate transport modes and routes emerged. In others, immobility was the only option. Extreme weather is occurring more frequently in the climate crisis. Strong winds, intense rainfall, and storm surges – all worsened by rising sea levels – highlight societal reliance on movement and the resultant vulnerability when people, supplies, and services fail to move.

Fossil-fuelled mobility contributes to climate change; severe weather, intensified by climate change, disrupts mobility. This cycle needs to be a central consideration in policy-making. Instead, the instinct is to re-establish mobility systems, which through their reliance on fossil fuels, exacerbate the extreme weather that disrupts these systems in the first place. I delve into this relationship in three ways. First, my approach offers a way of conceptualizing a practical problem: the dynamic relationship between disruptions to the climate caused by fossil-fuelled mobility on the one hand, and disruptions to human mobility caused by severe weather on the other hand. The dynamism of this cyclical, ever-changing social-ecological relationship is critical; the social and ecological aspects are inseparable. Second, through the concept of an *ecological approach to mobilities* I reframe and reimagine social-ecological relationships broadly, and the human relationship with mobility specifically. Third, through a suite of measures I include under the umbrella term *climate routing*, I introduce ideas on how to operationalize that reconceptualization beyond decreasing emissions. While a shift to zero-emission vehicles is essential, it is insufficient to meet emission reduction targets within the transport sector or prepare communities for the disruption of severe weather.[3]

I tell the tales of Hurricanes Juan and Igor to describe and theorize the intersection of human mobility and fossil fuels with severe weather and climate change. While hurricanes can be catastrophic, they are also windows of opportunity to enact systemic mobility transformations. I introduce concepts and measures to provide analytical and practical leverage needed to alter course, emphasizing integrated ecological and social approaches to mobility. I argue that given the dangerous circular relationship between mobility and climate change, there are concepts and measures that support shifting out of this cycle, as well as preparing for impacts of a post-normal climate in ways that benefit communities beyond climate change, including health care, education, and economy. Two linked concepts frame this book, an *ecological approach to mobilities* and *climate routing*. The former emphasizes that environmental dynamics, including the climate, need to be considered in lockstep with human mobility. The latter is an overarching concept for shifts in thinking and acting that align with an ecological mobilities approach: *revolutionize mobility, prioritize vital mobility, embrace green and blue, rebrand redundancy*, and *think flex*.

Western society is attuned to thinking about how to minimize cost and time. In the climate emergency, this emphasis needs to shift to minimizing carbon emissions and maximizing climate justice. Grounded in the mobilities paradigm, which highlights the role of movement in everyday life, I bring diverse fields into dialogue: contingency planners, disaster managers, environmental sociologists, geographers, mobilities scholars, municipal politicians, transport managers, urban planners – and even poets. I introduce concepts to assist researchers and practitioners in thinking and feeling through the realities and meanings of mobility in an era of climate change.

Mobilities is an approach to social science that focuses on the implications of movement – of people, things, and ideas – across space and time. Where transport refers to structures and systems that permit movement, like a public transit network, mobility refers to how people use and experience transport, including related meanings and power dynamics. The mobilities approach shines a light on profound mobility dependency, disparities in social distributions of movement, and the significance of disruptions.

The contemporary trend of extreme human reliance on fossil-fuelled mobility disrupts ecological movements. An increasing indication of this pattern is weather disasters (e.g., hurricanes) that, in turn, disrupt human mobility. I argue, perhaps counter-intuitively, that disaster-induced disruptions to human mobility contain potential for positive social change. Locally, they can serve as tipping points in the pernicious cycle between fossil-fuelled movement and the now chronically under-the-weather climate. Much more broadly, the stories from Nova Scotia and Newfoundland and Labrador offer transferable lessons for planners, policy-makers, and community advocates about how to move in ways that support, rather than undermine, the global climate. In each case, the nature of disruption to mobility was particular to local transportation systems and geography. And in each case, disruption to mobility was a central factor in defining the hurricane as an emergency. I highlight how human reliance on mobility intensifies emergencies related to severe weather. This dynamic applies to and intersects with other phenomena, such as the role of global mobilities in spreading the COVID pandemic.

I expand on sociologist Ulrich Beck's emancipatory catastrophism – the idea that the bad of a disaster sometimes leads to good social change.[4] For example, in response to lack of roads and fuel in the aftermath of Hurricanes Juan and Igor, alternate mobilities emerged (e.g., helicopters, quads, boats) and unused infrastructure was activated (e.g., old cabin roads, logging bridges).[5] When dominant mobilities experience significant disturbance, alternate mobilities emerge. An ecological approach to mobilities is a way of thinking about the movement of humans in relation to the movement of the environment, including rivers, animals, and carbon emissions in the context of the climate emergency. It is an overarching concept that highlights the reliance of mobility on the environment, emphasizing that human mobility is not conducted in isolation but in coordination with extensive webs of people, things, and ecologies. I argue that, although Hurricanes Juan and Igor include plenty of bad, they also offer lessons for change. There is a need now – weeks, months, or years before the next disaster in any given region – to prepare for how disruption might be leveraged to benefit communities. This needs to be the focus of robust public input and debate. Severe disruption provides a tipping point to implement systemic change, not only much discussed measures such as switching to zero-emission vehicles but also increasing local preparedness, reconfiguring health care, and ensuring that the most vulnerable are supported.

HURRICANES JUAN AND IGOR

Hurricanes Juan and Igor stand among the worst disasters to impact Nova Scotia and Newfoundland and Labrador in recent decades. They indicate the scale of disruption that the region is experiencing as part of the climate emergency, and subsequent events, such as Hurricane Dorian (Nova Scotia, 2019) and Snowmageddon (Newfoundland and Labrador, 2020), uphold this. While unlikely to be forgotten by Atlantic Canada residents who lived through them, the storms are little-known elsewhere. In contrast, there is extensive literature examining the devastating social disparities exposed by storms such as Hurricane Katrina: a catastrophic disaster that impacted the southern United States (2005). However, there is also a need to tell stories of smaller scale but still momentous events, like Hurricanes Juan and Igor, that impact less densely populated and more geographically peripheral regions.

I bring together the fields of mobility, disruption, and climate change to understand social-ecological responses to severe weather in Atlantic Canada. This triad brings key disciplines into conversation to deepen understanding of how fossil-fuelled mobility impacts the climate and, in turn, how society deals with disrupted mobility. The intersection of mobility and disaster is a growing field, and

I offer a key contribution to theorizing the links between mobility, disruption, and climate change. I contribute to environmental studies by offering concepts and practices for understanding and grappling with the significance of human and non-human mobility in the climate emergency, and I contribute to broader cultural and policy discussions by centring conceptual and practical tools for how mobility can be rethought and reorganized to work with rather than against the environment.

Nova Scotia and Newfoundland and Labrador, though both in Atlantic Canada, illustrate key differences in how transport and geography are impacted by storms. Juan was primarily defined by an urban epicentre subjected to high winds, Igor by extensive flooding of rural areas. Despite these differences, important parallels exist, suggesting a commonality of social response to disasters exacerbated by climate change. For example, in both cases officials observed that it felt like the storms tracked over key infrastructure: the backbone of the electrical transmission system in Nova Scotia and the main highway in Newfoundland. The overlap was so uncanny that infrastructure managers in both provinces perceived it to be intentional, as if the environment targeted critical infrastructure. In reality, the storms reveal the vulnerability of systems upon which communities rely. However, politicians, policy-makers, and the media interpreted the larger significance of hurricane impacts differently. In Newfoundland, the hurricane was viewed as an isolated event that was over as soon as the road network was restored. In Nova Scotia, it was viewed as a part of a changing disaster landscape and prompted climate action. The two cases offer lessons and concepts transferable to communities big and small, near and far. These insights will only increase in relevance as the climate crisis intensifies, demonstrated, for example, by the 2021 heat dome, floods, and landslides residents of British Columbia (traditional territories of diverse groups) experienced.

About Me

My research is shaped by my environment. Nova Scotia is my home, and I completed my doctoral degree at Memorial University in Newfoundland. The seeds for this research were planted in 2003, when I was an intern for the United Nations Children's Fund in Kazakhstan. Canada and Kazakhstan have a long-standing trading relationship that centres on energy, with Canada exporting oil extraction equipment and importing oil.⁶ While overseas for five months, I heard only two references to Canada in the news. Both stories related to states of emergency declared not in the global cities of K'emk'emeláy/Vancouver, Tkaronto/Toronto, or Tiohti/Montreal, but in K'jipuktuk/Halifax: Hurricane Juan in September and a blizzard nicknamed White Juan in February. Upon returning to Canada, the effects hit home: I saw how Hurricane Juan impacted Amntu'kati/Point Pleasant Park, one of my favourite places. To this day, every time I go for a walk or see a Shakespeare by the Sea performance in the park, I notice changes in the forest canopy and am reminded of the storm.

In following years, I worked for the Ecology Action Centre, an environmental organization in Nova Scotia. With my colleagues and friends Laena Garrison, Maggy Burns, and Jen Powley, we collaborated with urban and rural communities around the province. Our goal was to work with community members to learn about their mobility needs and identify opportunities to decrease environmental impact while increasing accessibility. This resulted in a *Green Mobility Strategy* launched in 2008.⁷ In 2011, the year after Hurricane Igor hit, I landed in Newfoundland ready to start my doctoral program, where I undertook the primary research on which this book is based. It's been a long journey, but the concepts and recommendations that emerged from my research are only more relevant as the impacts of the climate emergency are increasingly apparent in Canadian communities.

During the time it took to research, write, and revise this book, I lived in Newfoundland; Manhattan (Lenape Territory); Nova Scotia; Lancaster, UK; Edinburgh, Scotland; and Manchester, UK. This is a typical experience for academics who move to study, conduct research, and take up postdoctoral positions. I now work at the Humanitarian and Conflict Response Institute at the University of Manchester, an ocean away from home. While my mobility carbon footprint is low in each place, with cycling my preferred way of getting around and train travel so easy in the United Kingdom compared to Canada, living away from Nova Scotia means that mobility and carbon emissions are not only what I research but also embedded in my lifestyle.

The precarities entailed in mobility are reflected in my own poetry. From sensations of space and speed,

tin can slingshot
hurtling across
fisheye horizon

to a lack of control,

if the motors were to sputter and
halt

this plane would
not waft
gracefully like
an autumn
leaf
coming to rest
mutely
exhilarated

Perhaps surprisingly, given the themes of these poems, I am not fearful of flying but am conscious of physical and even climatic precarity entailed in air travel. These poems take an ecological angle, imagining the perspective of fish and leaves, water and earth infusing my experiences of flight.

About My Research

My research is empirically grounded and conceptually oriented, allowing me to develop a unique and timely approach to understanding disruption in the climate emergency – not as an aberration that sometimes affects static things or smoothly flowing systems, but as a typical and intense friction or turbulence that constitutes a new social-ecological paradigm. If everything is in movement and flux, even the climate, and everything exists in dynamic relationship, communities need to expect increased disruption.

As part of fieldwork undertaken between 2013 and 2015, I analyzed media articles, legislative transcripts, and policy documents, as well as conducted interviews. Further, I volunteered with the Canadian Red Cross to deepen my research experience, providing phone support to households impacted by Hurricane Arthur, which hit New Brunswick (home of the Wolastoqiyik, Mi'kmaq, and

Peskotomuhkati peoples) in 2014. I participated in a disaster simulation involving a plane crash and hostage-taking as a member of
the Red Cross Personal Disaster Assistance Team. I was a visiting
scholar at New York University, an experience which infuses the
book due to the impacts of Hurricane Sandy (2012). I compare and
juxtapose a range of Atlantic hurricanes, such as Hurricane Sandy in
New York (Lanape territory), Hurricane Katrina in Bulbancha/New
Orleans, and Hurricane Maria in Boriken/Puerto Rico (2017), to draw
attention to surprising similarities and important differences. I focus
on local impacts of hurricanes from the Caribbean to the Labrador
Sea, guided not by national borders but the weather itself.

In combination, I used document analysis, interviews, and historical awareness, as well as ongoing environmental and social ethical
engagement to contribute to robust case construction exploring
the social-ecological dynamics related to mobility, disruption, and
climate change. Through analysis of the two cases, I developed conceptual and strategic tools for rethinking and reorganizing human
mobility, focusing on how to work with, rather than against, the
climate. To make for more varied reading, I intersperse the case
chapters among more conceptual chapters.

Media analysis is valuable in disaster research for its timely coverage. I analyzed news media to determine what practical responses
and rhetorical frames emerged in terms of hurricanes and mobility
in the days leading up to and following the hurricanes.[8] To complement the short-term focus of media coverage, I reviewed provincial
legislative transcripts for the year following each hurricane to gain
a sense of the issues raised by elected officials. Likewise, I analyzed
provincial government documents informed by the hurricanes,
focusing on areas of community vulnerability and resilience, where
vulnerability refers to susceptibility to disruption and resilience is
the capacity to withstand, rebound from, or transform after a disruption. I conducted interviews with professionals who, through
their work, have specialized knowledge of mobility and climate
change in the context of Hurricanes Juan and Igor. Within government, I interviewed transport managers, environmental officials,
emergency services providers; outside government, I interviewed
fuel providers, environmental advocates, and aid providers. I focus
my research on how government officials and transport managers
tackled what Nova Scotian poet Sue Goyette describes as a "tidal

wave of disruption."[9] How did officials and managers understand and act on hurricanes as a proxy for climate change–induced disasters? Specifically, how was the relationship between hurricanes and mobility discussed before and after the arrival of the storms? What was planned, and what was done, to mitigate impacts on human mobility? How do the responses and discussions in the two regions compare? And what theoretical insights and practical lessons do these cases provide for mobility in a changing climate?

I analyzed the data – media articles, legislative transcripts, policy documents, and interview transcripts – based on disaster response measures, experiences of the hurricane, impacts on policy and practice, as well as claims, silences, and tensions related to resilience and vulnerability, and the relationship between the social and ecological. This analysis is the basis for the Hurricane Juan (chapter 3) and Igor (chapter 5) case studies, with each chapter structured around the most salient themes and quotes that emerged in the data sets. For example, the chapter on Hurricane Juan includes a section on the entanglement of trees and power lines that blocked roads, an issue discussed by most research participants. These chapters contain details that may be of particular interest to those living in Atlantic Canada, but the broader experiences and lessons are transferable to other communities.

The strengths of this research approach are the robustness offered by the range of data sets and the balancing of documented and remembered accounts. Limitations of this approach include the exclusion of diverse lived experiences. Due to a focus on mobility and climate governance, I did not interview transport users, who are demographically diverse and include senior citizens, teenagers, low-income earners, new Canadians, individuals with specific mobility needs, commuters, individuals who identify as LGBTQIA2+,[10] and individuals who belong to ethnic minorities, such as the Mi'kmaq people. Further, the lived experience of the professionals I interviewed and the perspectives captured in media, legislative transcripts, and policy documents, appeared to be predominately older, white males. This is a by-product of societal power structures that privilege certain perspectives, resulting in the marginalization of other experiences. How people with diverse experiences understand and respond to the relationship between mobility and climate is a critical area for more research.

BOOK STRUCTURE

Under the Weather has nine chapters. In chapter 1 I detail the ways
in which mobility, disruption, and climate change are entangled,
emphasizing the interconnectedness of mobility and the environment. To explore this relationship, I draw on the interdisciplinary
mobilities paradigm and its understanding of the movements, moorings, and frictions entailed in both the human and non-human environment. I examine risks and opportunities for change presented
by disasters, incorporating the work of environmental sociologist
William Freudenburg on the social construction of disaster.

In chapter 2 I delve deeper, introducing an *ecological approach to
mobilities* as a core concept, which emphasizes that human movement relies upon and impacts the non-human environment, and
that full appreciation of this fact necessarily entails challenging the
mobilities status quo. I bring together the ecological, social, and
physical dimensions of movement, extending the work of sociologist John Urry on the relationship between mobility, peak oil, and
climate change. This new concept captures the tight coupling of
human movement, fuel, and the environment: changes in one impact
the others. Human mobility is not conducted in isolation but in
coordination with extensive networks or ecosystems of people,
infrastructures, and environments. This lens highlights the reciprocal relationship between mobility and climate change: disasters
lay bare the interlocked nature of humanity's relationship with the
environment, causing profound disruption, but also, just as with
ecological disturbances such as forest fires, sparking diversity and
reordering that indicates different ways of doing things. To this end,
I trace an evolution from car-centred traffic planning, to sustainable mobility, to an ecological approach to mobilities. Traditional
traffic planning operates on the scale of the private car, identifying
how to move traffic efficiently: the car is king. In recent decades,
sustainable transport has challenged traditional traffic planning by
focusing on the movement of people rather than cars, addressing
issues of environmental sustainability and social justice. An ecological mobilities approach takes this further, considering human and
non-human mobilities in tandem.

In chapter 3 I describe the impacts of Hurricane Juan on Nova
Scotia, such as entanglements of trees and power poles that hindered
movement of ambulances, utility crews, and public transit. Residents

successfully, if somewhat precariously, governed their own mobility, navigating significant disruption.[11] Hurricane Juan was one of many complex events impacting mobility in the province, from invasive beetles to avian flu, from the Swissair crash to 9/11. These contributed to increased disaster awareness that, in turn, facilitated climate action. In Nova Scotia, a key source of vulnerability remains the entanglement of trees and power lines.

In chapter 4 I describe *charismatic mobilities* as an undercurrent of human engagement with mobility disruption. Building on sociologist Max Weber's work on human charisma and geographer Jamie Lorimer's work on charismatic animals, I introduce the concepts of charismatic and catastrophic mobilities. Charismatic mobilities are impressive ecological movements, such as winds and waves that appeal to humans, disrupt human mobility, and can be leveraged to enact shifts in relationship between mobility and climate. The term highlights a particular dynamic within ecological mobilities, namely the appeal of fossil-fuelled mobility, fascination with severe weather, and the need to make alternative approaches to mobility compelling. In day-to-day life, it is easy to forget humans are part of, and vulnerable to, the larger environment. For some, approaching storms and the resulting damage are charismatic: they are drawn to experience first-hand the force of the weather. For others, from housebound senior citizens without electricity to those permanently displaced by severe weather, charismatic mobilities can tip into catastrophic mobilities: sources of exhaustion, loss, and trauma.

In chapter 5 I detail aspects of Hurricane Igor that relate to mobility in Newfoundland, including extensive road and bridge washouts and resulting community isolation. Sources of community resilience included co-operation between government, media, and communities that allowed the road network to be restored to basic functionality within ten days. In the interim, residents stepped up to support community members in need of assistance. Newfoundlanders used quads and boats and hiked through the woods to carry out essential mobilities.[12] When the dominant mobilities of roads and cars failed, a robust spectrum of alternatives and the necessary skills and know-how to operate them materialized: ferries, helicopters, boats, and more. These *scrambled mobilities*, to use a term coined by sociologist Satya Savitzky, illustrate how disrupted mobilities are reconfigured or adapted, demonstrating latent possibilities for alternate reconfigurations. In

Newfoundland, key sources of vulnerability that remain are a limited road network susceptible to large-scale road washouts, limited transport modes, as well as limited fuel storage.

Chapter 6 focuses on the experience and implications of fuel immobilities following disruption. There are surprising parallels between the aftermath of Hurricanes Juan and Igor with Hurricane Sandy (New York, 2012) and Hurricane Maria (Puerto Rico, 2017). I then look at a 2015 fuel shortage that impacted Nova Scotia; though its origins were far less dramatic than a hurricane, it illustrates the lean supply chains upon which communities often unwittingly rely. Finally, I extend the work of geographers Peter Adey and Ben Anderson on the governance of emergency mobilities to juxtapose the interrelated emergencies of fuel, health, and climate, highlighting the deep interconnections encompassed by an ecological approach to mobilities, and the disjuncture between ensuring fossil fuel flows and the need to transition to a post-carbon paradigm.

In chapter 7 I examine the field of transport resilience, which aims to minimize disruption, differentiating it from an all-encompassing ecological mobilities approach, thus questioning the mobility status quo. I first detail a suite of measures used for managing mobility before, during, and after Hurricanes Juan and Igor, as well as in the longer term. Then, I describe three established and interrelated types of resilience: transport, social-ecological, and infrastructure. Transport resilience focuses on ensuring continual circulation of people, goods, and services in the face of disruption, aiming to quickly restore everyday mobility and economic flows. Social-ecological resilience originates in population dynamics and is useful in conceptualizing an ecological approach to mobilities. Infrastructure resilience entails creating systems where both human and ecological needs are accommodated and future-proofed to survive a changing climate. Such next-generation infrastructure reflects changing conditions, including extreme weather, carbon constraint, and limited financial resources. While all three types of resilience have merits, none sufficiently questions the mobility status quo, a project to which I turn in the next chapter.

In chapter 8 I adapt the marine navigation concept of weather routing – altering a ship's course to take advantage of tide, current, and wind conditions to minimize fuel costs – to introduce the concept of climate routing. Building on the work of geographers Tim Schwanen, David Banister, and Jillian Anable who contest the mobility status quo and sociologist Mimi Sheller's work on mobility justice, climate routing interrogates and reimagines the role of mobility in society. Primary considerations include questioning status quo mobility practices, increasing social and ecological resilience, and improving quality of life. Shaped by the Nova Scotian and Newfoundland case studies, climate routing is an umbrella term for a suite of practical measures that reduce the contribution of mobility to the climate emergency and adapt mobility to the consequences of that emergency. I introduce five measures to reduce community reliance on mobility and to let mobility work with, rather than against, the environment: *revolutionize mobility, prioritize vital mobility, embrace green and blue, rebrand redundancy,* and *think flex.*

Revolutionizing mobility entails fundamentally rethinking human mobility in relation to ecological limits, namely restricting global heating to 1.5°C as advocated by the international scientific community. Prioritizing vital mobilities that enable life and health – such as movement of food, pharmaceuticals, and medical supplies – needs to be a central consideration in the face of increasingly frequent disruption. Planning for green and blue means creating mobility systems that work with the environment, rather than trying to stifle or dominate it. Rebranding redundancy refers to embracing the idea that having backup mobilities, as well as the materials and services upon which communities rely every day, is not wasteful but wise. Lastly, think flex means accepting and adapting to the reality that disruption, from hurricanes to heat waves, will shape daily life and mobility decisions.

In chapter 9 I compare my experience at international climate negotiations (COP26) with recent severe weather in Nova Scotia and Newfoundland. I elaborate on an ecological approach to mobilities and reflect on an ethic of care for the climate and each other.

Poetry and Paintings

Informed by the work of anthropologist Anna Lowenhaupt Tsing and historian Rebecca Solnit, among others, I intersperse academic text, quotes from residents and poetry, as well as photos and paintings. My goal is to accentuate the care, precarity, and anxiety entailed in living with and by the ocean as illustrated in the cases, concepts, and practical measures. Creative responses are needed to meet the challenges of climate change, and, to this end, I aim to stimulate the imagination

and make the material personal. *Under the Weather* is bookended
by two Alex Colville (1920–2013) paintings. Colville is known for
his unsettling modernist depictions of daily life in Nova Scotia – the
subject's gaze often turns away from the viewer or is blocked, creating
a sense of intimacy, anonymity, and voyeurism. Each chapter begins
with an excerpt from Sue Goyette's *Ocean*, a biography of the North
Atlantic that is "part cautionary tale, part creation myth and part
urban legend."[13] When I heard Sue Goyette (1964–) read her work
on CBC Radio one morning, it was like listening to the themes that
emerged in my research in poetic form. I also include poetry by geographer Tim Cresswell (1965–), and my own poetry in which mobility
and the environment are common themes.

Setting Sail

And what a hurricane of a question!
What a tidal wave of disruption. It got worse

when we walked into it and let it taste us ...

When we wrote our names in the soft sand of its back,
we didn't know the first thing about commitment

or about being out of our depths.

Sue Goyette, "One," in *Ocean*

MOBILITY AND THE CLIMATE CRISIS

Navigating mobility disruption caused by severe weather is a "hurricane of a question," bringing together in new ways the spheres of climate change, mobility, and disaster. Two significant intersecting trends confront our society: intensification of mobility and severe weather. Movement is central to our lives: like air, we simultaneously rely upon it and take it for granted. If one could ask a fish to describe its experience of the world, the last thing it would mention is water; so too, for humans and mobility.[1] From commuting to shipping, from school buses to ambulances, from destination weddings to international conferences, mobility permeates the story of our lives. Almost all global transport energy, 95 per cent, is derived from fossil fuels.[2] This chapter has three parts. First, I provide an overview of the impact of a changing climate on hurricane activity. Next, I describe the mobilities paradigm in which I ground my research. Last, I reflect on the risks and opportunities presented by disruptive events, such as extreme weather.

The atmospheric accumulation of greenhouse gases released by fossil-fuelled mobility, like driving and flying, increases global temperatures. This triggers a cascade of climatic changes, such as intensifying weather, rising sea levels, and acidifying oceans. The energetic boomerang comes full circle when severe weather disrupts the complex mobility systems upon which societies rely, threatening livelihoods and life, both human and non-human.[3] "Disasters," writes sociologist Mimi Sheller, "bring to the fore the astounding interdependence and fragility of the complex mobility systems and infrastructural moorings that make up contemporary transnational geographies."[4] Extreme weather and associated risks are more prevalent in daily life. The International Federation of Red Cross and Red Crescent Societies warn that today 100 million people a year rely on aid due in part to climate change and that this figure could double by 2050, rising to a cost of US$20 billion per year. However, if adaptation measures to increase disaster preparedness and reduce vulnerability are implemented quickly just 10 million people a year would require aid by 2050.[5]

Mobility overloads global carbon cycles via the emission of carbon dioxide, one of six greenhouse gases that heats the planet and alters the climate.[6] Climatic disruption causes mobility disruption. Sociologist Ulrich Beck uses the image of a double helix to describe the interconnected production of societal "goods and bads," practices that both benefit and damage society.[7] Alex Colville's painting *Family and Rainstorm* is yet another way to represent the human relationship with the non-human environment. Though painted in 1955, long before climate change was part of public consciousness, it includes key elements: the ocean, a storm, a fossil-fuelled car, and present and future generations. Seeing warning signs of a storm on the horizon, the family retreats, a trip to the beach cut short by the threat of bad weather. The car, powered by fossil fuel, contributes to climate change, and in turn, the climate crisis disrupts human mobility. Together, these interactions form a dynamic and cyclic relationship.

The positive feedback loops of climate change impacts and fossil-fuelled mobility are densely interconnected. Warmer temperatures accelerate the melting of polar ice. Dark ocean water absorbs more

Figure 1.1 *Family and Rainstorm*, Alex Colville, 1955

solar radiation than white ice, accelerating global heating. In this and many other ways, warming causes more warming. Likewise, mobility causes more mobility. Geographer Thomas Birtchnell and sociologist Monika Büscher state that "needs and desires to be somewhere else are never sated." Mobile society is "eternally stranded in mobility."[8] Anthropologist Ghassan Hage describes an existential compulsion toward mobility driven by social and material sensations of moving, advancing, and progressing.[9] Geographer Tim Cresswell, writing before the COVID pandemic, concludes that "mobility is both the lifeblood of modernity and the virus that threatens to undo it."[10] The momentum of global heating and the appetite for movement are interrelated trajectories: one cannot be curtailed without affecting the other.

While I focus on Atlantic Canada, the impacts of climate change are felt across Canada and around the world. On its current emission trajectory, Canada is set to experience ten times as many heat waves and twice as many extreme rainstorms in coming years.[11] In 2021, there was extensive flooding in Ktaqmkuk/Newfoundland and Mi'kma'ki/ Nova Scotia, widespread wildfires in central and western Canada, and a heat wave, landslide, and flooding in British Columbia, among numerous other events heightened by global heating.

HURRICANES AND CLIMATE CHANGE

In short, it is "unequivocal" that human activity is changing the climate. The Intergovernmental Panel on Climate Change (IPCC), the United Nations body that assesses and reports on global climate science, concludes that human activity, not natural climatic variability, is the dominant cause of global heating since the mid-twentieth century.[12] Global average temperature has increased about 1°C since the Industrial Revolution.[13] While a degree or two is an unremarkable increase in daily temperature, at a global scale it is extreme. The IPCC identifies heating of 1.5°C as a threshold beyond which the risks associated with climate change significantly increase, including shortages of water and food, increases in heat waves, and changes in disease ranges. For example, at 1.5°C the likelihood of extreme heat events increases by 14 per cent; at 2.0°C this escalates to almost 40 per cent, reaching critical thresholds for human health.[14] Many around the world who rely directly on the land are already experiencing devastating impacts on health, livelihoods, and well-being. To avoid catastrophic heating, global society has less than a decade to halve carbon emissions, and three decades to decarbonize.

The scale of the challenge is formidable: following current trends, carbon pollution is projected to double by 2050 due to growth in the passenger and freight transport sectors alone.[15] In Canada, transport – excluding aviation – accounts for one-quarter of total emissions and, of that, cars and trucks account for half.[16] While switching to zero-emission vehicles is key to decarbonizing society – Canada aims for 100 per cent of all new vehicles sold by 2035 to be zero-emission – in the face of increasing and intensifying severe weather events that result in disruption, communities need to rethink their overall relationship with mobility.[17] When a road is washed out and a family needs to get a loved one to hospital, the fact that they own an electric vehicle will be of limited advantage. This said, there is an emerging literature on the role of electric vehicles as a secondary communication and power grid in the context of disaster.[18] However, despite potential advantages, there are circumstances such as evacuating and seeking emergency medical care that require physical movement from point to point.

There is high scientific confidence regarding specific impacts of climate change, such as more intense precipitation and more frequent heat waves. In Canada, these effects include more extreme heat, rising sea levels, and longer growing seasons, as well as less extreme cold, thawing permafrost, receding glaciers, and shorter snow seasons.[19] Changing one aspect of the climate – global average temperature – yields complex and far-reaching knock-on impacts for every facet of life, from food prices to mental health. Establishing a link between hurricanes such as Juan and Igor – or, for that matter, any other individual severe weather event – and climate change is more challenging. The IPCC notes the difficulty in assessing long-term variations in hurricane frequency and severity due to a lack of historical data, changing monitoring technology, and confounding meteorological events, such as El Niño and the North Atlantic Oscillation. It is challenging to determine if recent hurricanes are par for the course or made worse by climate change.[20] This also applies to cyclones in the Northwest Pacific Ocean and typhoons in the South Pacific and Indian Oceans – different names for the same meteorological phenomenon.[21]

In aggregate, climate models predict more intense hurricanes due in part to higher water temperatures. Atlantic hurricanes originate in the warm water of the tropics when clusters of thunderstorms coalesce and rotate, reaching minimum sustained wind speeds of 119 kilometres per hour.[22] Starting from 1958, there is a trend of more extreme storms between October and December over marine areas in Atlantic Canada.[23] Looking forward, there is evidence that hurricane activity will shift northward, toward regions like Atlantic Canada: warm ocean water is fuel for hurricanes, propelling them into higher latitudes.[24] There is also evidence that hurricane frequency may decrease, but that hurricane intensity – both wind speed and rainfall – will increase.[25] In other words, there may be a small reduction in overall number of storm frequencies, but extreme storms may be even more intense.[26] Research also finds that active hurricane seasons are on the rise with "extremely active Atlantic hurricane seasons" now twice as likely as forty years ago. For example, in 2020 there were a record thirty named Atlantic hurricanes.[27] Compounding this trend, global average sea level is projected to rise about one metre by 2100,[28] intensifying the impact of all storms.[29] This means that Atlantic Canada needs to prepare for more frequent and intense hurricanes.

Humanity is experiencing profound changes. The term *Anthropocene* describes the current geological epoch, defined as the point at which humans have a discernible impact on the global environment.[30] "Atmospheric warming, ocean warming, ocean acidification, sea-level rise, deglaciation, desertification, eutrophication," writes journalist Elizabeth Kolbert, "these are just some of the byproducts of our species' success."[31] Further, climate change combined with habitat loss, overfishing, pollution, and invasive species threaten the survival of animal, plant, and microorganism species around the world. The climate crisis and biodiversity crisis are interconnected. In the Anthropocene, humans are in what historians Claire Bond Potter and Renee Romano call a "zone of imperfect visibility."[32] This imperfect visibility applies in two ways. First, the far-reaching and unfamiliar changes occurring in Earth's climate. Second, the intense reorientation society needs to undergo to reduce its impact on the climate and contend with environmental change.

MOBILITIES PARADIGM

The mobilities paradigm examines the importance of mobility and immobility to contemporary society, including movements of tangible things such as people, goods, and services, as well as intangibles including ideas, information, and policies. Sociologists John Urry and Mimi Sheller formalized the mobilities paradigm to explore the interaction of social and spatial dynamics, animating a sedentary social science that overlooked the role of mobility.[33] Or, as geographer Deborah Cowen describes it, the mobilities paradigm is about "interrogating the radically undervalorized role of movement and circulation in everyday life."[34] It lies at an interdisciplinary crossroads, incorporating social analysis of power, geographical analysis of space, cultural analysis of discourse, and technological analysis of materials.[35] Its focus ranges widely from the experience of cycling to school, to the dynamics of international migratory law, to interplanetary space tourism.

In their agenda-setting editorial introducing the mobilities paradigm, Kevin Hannam, Mimi Sheller, and John Urry refer to global heating, hurricanes, and oil wars as potential research trajectories.[36]

Certain events, such as the devastation wrought by Hurricane Katrina (2005) and the global aviation disruption caused by the Icelandic ash cloud (2010), attracted intense research. Overall, however, links between mobility, disruption, and climate change are undertheorized. In an editorial on the mobilities paradigm, Tim Schwanen, David Banister, and Jillian Anable call for greater engagement of the social sciences with the mobilities literature, including the non-linear and catastrophic dimensions of climate change.[37] The intersection of mobility and disaster is a small but growing field.

The mobilities paradigm focuses on speed and flow, as well as immobility and friction to understand how movement is experienced and represented in society, including related issues of power and inequity.[38] Sheller is careful to distinguish the mobilities paradigm from metaphors of flow such as, sociologist Zygmunt Bauman's work on liquid modernity where individuals experience and endure continually shifting economic, geographic, and personal conditions,[39] and sociologist Manuel Castells's approach to society as spaces of flow where social connectedness is permitted by technology rather than physical proximity.[40] Sheller avoids such totalizing narratives. She allows for both flow and turbulence as intrinsic to pervasive movement. Though philosopher Michel Foucault does not address mobility specifically, he applies the lens of circulation to a variety of phenomena, such as ideas, orders, and commerce. Foucault's theorization of circulation provides an alternative to the mobility/immobility dichotomy. Rather, circulations, as with pulsations of blood through veins, may be strong or weak.[41]

Urry elaborates on the co-dependence of flows and fixities, or what he terms mobilities and moorings.[42] Transatlantic air travel, for example, requires a fixed network of airports, air traffic controllers, and customs officials to enable the movement of millions of passengers. The concept of turbulence is also useful in capturing intertwining social and ecological movement.[43] Tim Cresswell and Craig Martin use the example of the MSC *Napoli* container ship, which broke open off the coast of England in 2007, to argue that turbulence is productive: it exposes the inner workings of seemingly effortless or unobserved processes, sparking creative reordering.

Mobilities scholars interrogate a grey area where mobility systems teeter between entrenchment and evolution, between smooth functioning and shutdown.[44] A hurricane can bring bustling mobilities to a halt in a matter of hours. The source of disruption, however, need not be large. A reported drone sighting shut down London's Gatwick airport for three days: one thousand flights cancelled, disrupting travel for more than 100,000 passengers.[45] The closer one looks the more order and disorder are co-present. Cresswell and Martin observe that the swirl of a hurricane appears to have its own order, while the impacts of a hurricane are characterized as chaotic and disorderly.[46] With climate change, the power of a hurricane is intensified by warmer ocean water resulting from human action. Both the storm and its impacts are increasingly disorderly. Following the breakup of the MSC *Napoli*, two assessment reports recognized "systemic failings [but] still promote a worldview premised on the potential for smooth laminar flow."[47] Under a changing climate, there is need for greater expectation and accommodation of turbulence in the movement of people, goods, and services. In the context of increased disruption, a paradigm shift is needed where smooth mobility is considered the exception and turbulence the rule.

Geographer Peter Adey theorizes the "inescapable pairs" of emergency and mobility.[48] He describes emergency mobilities: "whether in flight or in response, emergencies demand highly intensive forms of movement that radically transform one's life chances and quality of life."[49] Likewise, Sheller says, disasters

> demobilize and remobilize. They strike at mobility systems but also engender their own unique mobilities (and immobilities) as people seek to flee the onset of an impending catastrophe, to get resituated in its bewildering aftermath, or to locate their dispersed families, food, water and shelter. At the same time, emergency responders, relief workers ... and soldiers begin to move into the affected area and take control of infrastructures of mobilities, such as roads, airports, ports, and communications networks.[50]

The co-existence of mobility and immobility is intensified in the context of disaster given the threats to human life and safety. Geographer Lucy Budd questions societal "over-dependency" on mobility.[51] The mobilities paradigm illuminates the deep dependence on mobility in contemporary life. Disruptions related to climate change and other factors, such as technological glitches, infrastructure failure, and terrorism, prompt questions about how society could function with less movement. The global COVID-19 pandemic brought this issue to the fore, from governments limiting international air travel to individuals minimizing trips to the local grocery store. Reliance on mobility exacerbates emergency.

Sheller argues that the climate emergency requires attention to issues of power and justice.[52] Likewise, Cresswell describes a politics of mobility premised on movement, representation, and practice. Physical movement is the "raw material" of mobility.[53] All physical movement is experienced through identity categories such as class, gender, and race. This is central in Cresswell's analysis of "tourists, jet-setters, refugees, . . . immigrants, migrant labourers, academics."[54] Physical movement is represented by and attributed with meaning and worth. In some spheres the acts of driving and flying are associated with a kinetic elite; in others, they are a source of environmental shame. Some people have experienced both. Author Naomi Klein reflects:

> I denied climate change for a lot longer than I care to admit.
> I knew it was happening, sure. Not like Donald Trump and the
> Tea Partiers going on about how the existence of winter proves
> it's all a hoax. But I stayed pretty hazy on the details and only
> skimmed most of the news stories, especially the really scary
> ones. I told myself the science was too complicated and the envi-
> ronmentalists were dealing with it. And I continued to behave
> as if there was nothing wrong with the shiny card in my wallet
> attesting to my "elite" frequent flyer status.[55]

Klein was grappling with the paradox that contemporary society esteems and rewards hyper-mobility, while at the same time there is an increasing awareness of the environmental impacts of fossil-fuelled mobility.

Contrasting with the experience of Klein, David Chariandy, in his novel *Brother*, describes the experience of an immigrant mother living near Toronto, as imagined by her teenage son,

> He recognized her pride, but also the routes and tolls of her
> labours. He knew that for work as a cleaner, and sometimes a
> nanny, she has not only tough hours but long journeys, com-
> plicated rides along bus routes to faraway office buildings and
> malls and homes, long waits at odd hours at stops and stations,
> sometimes *in the rain or in the thick of heat of the afternoon,*

sometimes in the cold and dark of winter. He understood that
there is a specific moment during the trip back home from
work that a mother's body threatens to give out. A specific site
in the bus loop at Kennedy Station when exhaustion closes in
and the limbs feel like meat, and it takes every last strength
from a mother to make the two additional bus transfers home.
(Emphasis added.)[56]

This passage describes the reality of many low-income commuters. Emotional and physical frictions are palpable. The reference to
season and temperature are what I want to highlight. Imagine how
a severe snowstorm would impede this already marathon journey.
Imagine the lack of shade at bus stops, the radiant heat of a crowded
train, the cumulative mental and bodily exhaustion of such a wearying daily grind.

Immobility can also be problematic. Sociologist Eric Klinenberg
explores intersections of race, class, gender, and neighbourhood as
social determinants of health during the 1995 Chicago heat wave.
The disaster resulted in 739 deaths over a five-day period, disproportionately impacting the elderly and the isolated.[57] Klinenberg
describes the case of an elderly man who lived by himself: "Solitary
at the end of life, Laczko was joined by hundreds of other Chicago
residents who died alone during the heat wave and were assisted
by two potentially life-saving interventions – attention from state-
sponsored service providers and artificial cooling – only after their
bodies were delivered to the Cook County Morgue."[58] The intersection of time, air-conditioned space, and mobility was a matter of life
and death. Extreme weather, from heat waves to hurricanes, highlight the role one's body plays in determining experience of a disaster
and, at an extreme, one's life chances. Understanding diverse lived
experiences is important in creating equitable and ecologically sensitive mobilities, what Sheller calls mobility justice.[59] In a decarbonized
future, what mobilities will be prioritized? This question underlies the
following chapters and is explored in depth in chapter 8.

DISRUPTION, RISK, AND OPPORTUNITY

In addition to the mobilities paradigm, my focus on disaster incorporates an approach based on the risks and opportunities presented
by disruption. Anthropogenic or human-caused risks such as climate

change and mass biodiversity loss endanger the ecosystems of which humans are a part.[60] Risks are spatially and temporally diffuse. Their impacts may be felt far from their origins. Communities in the Canadian North, for example, are disproportionately impacted by climate change due to global atmospheric and oceanic circulations that amplify heating in polar regions far from the main sources of greenhouse gas emissions.[61]

Humans create many contemporary risks, such as the climate crisis. Sociologist Anthony Giddens describes this phenomenon as reflexive modernization.[62] In the case of the 2010 BP oil spill, environmental sociologists Robert Gramling and William Freudenburg trace a century of energy policy to illustrate that the Deepwater Horizon oil well blowout was not a one-off accident, but an artifact of cumulative government and industry policy decisions that resulted in the largest known marine oil spill.[63] Gramling and Freudenburg posit that the US government pursued two diversionary tactics that, in combination, perpetuated unjust and ineffective energy policies. The first diversion was that of public access to resources and related revenues by facilitating the transfer of offshore energy resources from the public to the private sector. The second was that of attention, by framing such a transfer as a way to foster domestic energy production and energy independence. Critically, while American energy independence has been advocated since the 1970s, oil imports increased from approximately 30 per cent to 60 per cent in the decades leading up to the spill.[64] Gramling and Freudenburg argue that energy independence was an appealing but artificial goal that diverted attention from the transfer of public assets to corporate coffers. The diversion of access needs to be paired with the diversion of attention to lend such wealth transfer the gloss of legitimacy and create a permissive environment for industrial practices, such as deep-water drilling and hydraulic fracturing that pose a high ecological risk.[65]

Freudenburg and colleagues found similar dynamics at work in the case of Hurricane Katrina. They detail how local leaders channelled significant public funds over several decades into creating canals to position Bulbancha/New Orleans as a significant port. Critically, during Hurricane Katrina, the canals channelled ocean water into the city, resulting in widespread flooding and loss of life.[66] In both the BP oil spill and Hurricane Katrina, as well as many other disasters, risks to communities as well as the broader environment "involved a three-part pattern, supported by the political system – spreading the costs, concentrating the economic benefits and hiding the real risks."[67] Such disasters are both "deadly and avoidable" events manufactured by humans.[68] The climate emergency is such an event.

Anthropogenic climate change reveals the fallacy of inside/outside dichotomies, as demonstrated by canals in New Orleans. Giddens observes that most contemporary issues are transboundary.[69] Likewise, Beck uses the term *manufactured risk* to describe hazards that endanger all life and future generations, adding a temporal dimension.[70] From an ecosystem perspective, and consequently from social, health, and economic perspectives, global and local, present and future are enmeshed. Manufactured risks are insidious: no aspect of global ecology is unaffected, from cellular integrity to the outer reaches of the atmosphere. These rebound effects of modernization are often invisible.[71] This is particularly the case with climate change, where there is a lag between greenhouse gas emissions and the resulting heating. Decades of greenhouse gas emissions have not yet reached their warming potential, making runaway climate change a possibility.[72] Runaway climate change refers to permanent and catastrophic shifts in global climate because of multiple positive feedback effects that accelerate global heating. For example, permafrost loss releases methane, a potent greenhouse gas, hastening more permafrost loss.[73] Ironically, Beck observes, sciences such as climatology are paradoxically necessary and insufficient to the meet the challenge.[74]

Beck raises the possibility of emancipatory catastrophism – what disaster sociologists refer to as windows of opportunity – where negative disaster impacts can be leveraged to create positive societal change.[75] Emancipatory catastrophism describes and constitutes an *in situ* experimental navigation of complex and unfolding situations. Beck calls on civil society to critically reflect on risk, questioning acceptable thresholds identified by government, industry, and even science.[76] Storms disturb, causing the everyday to rupture. These disturbances, range in scale from minor to catastrophic. Much is lost, from family photos to a sense of security, from neighbourhoods to lives. Time, energy, and resources are expended in profusion. Disruption caused by disaster can, however, also create positive social change, like the renewal of community ties and the introduction of backup plans. Anthropologist Anna Lowenhaupt Tsing studies matsutake mushrooms that flourish in forests damaged by industrial practices. These fungi show how communities can work within and move beyond states of ruination. Disturbance, argues Tsing, is an opportunity with transformative potential.[77] In ecology, disturbance refers to disruptions that shift ecosystem dynamics. Hurricanes and forest fires, for example, create room for new growth, revitalizing biodiversity.

The same is true of mobility: in response to the destruction of roads and fuel scarcity in the aftermath of Hurricanes Juan and Igor, alternate mobilities emerged, including helicopters, boats, and buses. Unused infrastructure was activated, such as old cabin roads and logging bridges. When dominant mobilities were disrupted, alternate mobilities emerged. However, as I describe in the next chapter, these mobilities are not limited to human transport and include ecological mobilities of wind, water, and carbon. Much like a forest after a fire or a storm, disruption can spur greater mobility diversity. Such moments of precarity can be emancipatory, offering first-hand experience of different ways of being and practising mobility. However, precarity is also dangerous. For instance, in 2016 residents of Fort McMurray, Alberta, had access to only one escape route, a main road, in the face of a fast-approaching forest fire.[78]

In this chapter, I discussed the link between human mobility and climate change, with a focus on hurricane activity. I described the mobilities paradigm and its value in understanding movement as a pervasive facet of contemporary society, and then reflected on the risks and opportunities created by disruption. Philosopher and anthropologist Bruno Latour says that if politics is the art of the possible, then the role of sociologists is to expand the range of possibilities. There is a need now – potentially weeks, months, or years before the next disaster in a given region – to prepare for how disruption might be leveraged to benefit communities. This needs to be the focus of robust public input and debate that I argue ought to centre on an ecological approach to mobilities, that is, a paradigm shift where the social and ecological are considered in lockstep.

2

Ecological Mobilities

This is when the ocean began appearing
in our dreams, often disguised as our mothers or hooded strangers

with something important to say, but when they opened their mouth
to speak, fish would swim out. The era of uncertainty had begun.

Our plan was to stand before the ocean with the small hook
of our intent, but when we did come face to face with it,

we found ourselves leaning in, having no choice
but to listen.

Sue Goyette, "Thirty-One," *Ocean*

ECOLOGICAL MOBILITIES

Earth is on the move with continuous ecological mobilities. The polar jet stream and ocean conveyor belt circulate to shape the global climate.[1] Carbon travels through the geosphere, biosphere, and atmosphere, combining with water, nitrogen, and sunlight to support life. Sedimentary substances formed over millions of years through compressed ancient wetlands are the source of fossil fuels that power much of today's human mobility. Glacial retreat carved the current landscape, and annually icebergs cleave off the Greenland ice sheet and migrate south of the island of Ktaqmkuk/Newfoundland.

Through complex interactions of wind, ocean currents, and temperature, Hurricanes Juan and Igor originated off the coast of Cape Verde in Africa, travelled across the Atlantic Ocean, and up Canada's east coast. Such storms often sweep tropical birds and fish along with them. Through wind and rain, hurricanes erode land and transport massive amounts of sediment to the ocean where it is circulated by global currents. Hurricanes transfer huge volumes of heat from warmer to cooler regions, as well as water from ocean to land. Storm surges leave salt in soil, creating habitat for salt-tolerant plants and related insects, birds, and animals, fostering biodiversity. Hurricanes create a temporary geomorphic signature characterized by slope erosion, fluvial outwash deposits, and stream bank erosion.[2] They leave a permanent signature in the form of tree rings, as precipitation from hurricanes has a different chemical composition than other types of precipitation. Researchers use this ecological database to identify hurricane patterns before the existence of modern weather records, giving insight into the impacts of climate change on hurricane frequency and intensity.[3]

Mobility is contingent on and inseparable from the environment. It involves a complex intersection of the social, ecological, and political.[4] The mobilities of wind, rain, and carbon are *ecological mobilities*, movements of biotic and abiotic entities from the gentle lap of waves to the rush of flood waters.[5] Biologist Jakob von Uexküll examined the unique social and physical environments that species create.[6] By looking at how ticks, sea urchins, and jellyfish interact with and shape their surroundings, he decentres dominant human perspectives and understandings. Likewise, anthropologist Anna Lowenhaupt Tsing declares that landscapes are "sites for more-than-human dramas" and "radical tools for decentering human hubris."[7] An ecological approach to mobilities decentres the human, placing people, carbon emissions, storms, and cars on a level playing field.

Historically, mariners took advantage of trade winds, dominant easterly winds that cross the Atlantic, which facilitated European exploration and exploitation of the Americas. Hurricanes also align with the trade winds.[8] Today mariners use technology to optimize navigation, reduce fuel use, and minimize travel time, but such technologies impact the environments through which goods and people travel. For example, seismic testing used in oil exploration to tap ancient reservoirs disrupts the communication and migration patterns of marine mammals. Heating of the ocean surface mixes into deeper layers causing species to move to different regions at different rates for survival, disrupting ecosystems.[9] Schedules of global tourists intersect with the migration patterns of whales and seabirds. Icebergs are tugged out of the path of fixed platform oil rigs, while shipping channels are adjusted to avoid North Atlantic right whale populations. Workers are flown by helicopter to platforms where oil is extracted from the seabed, carried in fossil-fuelled ships for refining, and then shipped to new destinations to fuel automobility. Hurricanes disrupt movements of people, goods, and services, including global supply chains and vital mobilities, like local ambulance services and global medical supply chains.

Geographer Tim Cresswell, in his poem called "The Two Magicians," explores the metamorphoses of male and female energy, illustrating the interconnectedness of the social and ecological where plankton transforms into hydrocarbons, powering cars, changing the climate, and impacting non-human populations:

> and he became phytoplankton and zooplankton …
> and he became kerogen   shales   gaseous
> hydrocarbons …
> and he became   anthrocite   dirty lignite   bitumous
> coal …
> and he became paraffin   aromatic hydrocarbons …
> he became internal combustion …
> he became one part carbon   two parts oxygen …
> and he became   auk   clyde   fulmar   shearwater …
> and he became   argyle   duncan   elgin-franklin …
> he became   Athabasca …
> he became night shifts   fly-ins from St John's …
> he became five-mile tailbacks on the interstate …
> he became   GMC Sierras   Chevy Silverados …
> he became   rock fractured by high pressure liquid

Ω

> then she became earth tremors in the kitchen in Norman
> Oklahoma   coffee   Patsy on the radio   snowdrops in January
> in Kew   *crazy*   iguanas   frozen   falling from trees   boiled
> bats in Sydney   Harvey howling like a freight   *crazy for*
> *trying*   and *crazy for crying*   iceberg twice the size of
> Luxembourg   *worry*   thirty-five   thousand
> Walruses   hauled out in Point Ley Alaska   *why do I*
> *let myself worry*   Irma   manatees swimming round a
> drowned Winnebago   ninety nine percent of green
> turtles born female   *wondering what in the world did I do*[10]

In Cresswell's writing the human and ecological are integrated, geoecologies and ecological mobilities are intertwined and, moreover, inextricable. Political theorist Jane Bennett elaborates on this human-ecological relationship: "Admit that humans have crawled or secreted themselves into every corner of the environment; admit that the environment is actually inside human bodies and minds, and then proceed politically, technologically, scientifically, in everyday life, with careful forbearance."[11] An ecological mobilities approach attempts to not just tolerate but instead embrace ecosystems in human mobility.

In this wide-ranging chapter, I introduce the concept of an ecological approach to mobilities, building the case step by step. First, I discuss how social scientists engage with the ecological, focusing on the contrasting cases of flood management in New Orleans and the Netherlands, as well as efforts to mitigate flooding in New York. Then, I define the concept and position it as a tool for thinking about mobility amid the climate crisis that considers the environment – such as bodies of water, urban and rural forests, and seasonal storms – in relation to human movement. Next, I describe how the negative ecological impacts of fossil-fuelled mobility strike back at global society in the form of climate change, most impacting those who have contributed least to global emissions. I then explore the interconnected nature of humanity's relationship with the non-human environment, focusing on two extreme events: the North American ice storm and the Icelandic ash cloud. Finally, I trace an evolution in transport from car-centred planning to sustainable transport to an ecological approach to mobilities. Traditional traffic planning operates on the scale of the private car, identifying how to move traffic efficiently. In recent decades, sustainable transport with its focus on environmental sustainability and social justice to some extent supplanted traffic planning, focusing on the movement of people rather than cars. I introduce an ecological approach to mobilities as the next step in acknowledging and learning to work with the integrated ecological, social, and physical dimensions of movement.

EMBRACING THE ECOLOGICAL

Philosopher Michel Foucault was interested in the "naturalisation of the urban," that is, circulations of people, resources, and waste.[12] He characterizes discipline as efforts to "concentrate, contain and

control" nature, while security embraces the "reality of natural processes, respects their autonomy and seeks to identify, optimise and
work through nature's discernible laws rather than stifle them."[13] In
relation to water flow, discipline is akin, literally and metaphorically,
to a concrete wall, while security is akin to a flood plain. Geographer
Mark Usher draws on Foucault's work to analyze the circulation of
water in Singapore. Water self-sufficiency is an ongoing issue in the
densely populated island city-state. Usher traces a shift from historical attempts to discipline water through canals to a contemporary focus on water security. This means working with, rather than
trying to control, ecological dynamics to meet human needs. Poet
Sue Goyette's description of a "master class of listening" is apt.[14]

Coastal communities embrace different approaches to living with
water and the threat of flooding. Two contrasting examples are New
Orleans and the Netherlands, both of which are characterized by
significant proportions of land mass below sea level. New Orleans,
Louisiana, is located two to six metres below sea level within the
Gulf of Mexico. For more than a century, New Orleans invested
in canals and dams to discipline water and grow its shipping economy. Journalist Elizabeth Kolbert writes, "Thousands of miles of
levees, flood walls, and revetments have been erected to manage the
Mississippi [River]. As the Army Corps of Engineers once boasted,
'We harnessed it, straightened it, regularized it, shackled it.' This
vast system, built to keep southern Louisiana dry, is the very reason
the region is disintegrating."[15] William Freudenburg and colleagues
study the relationship between New Orleans and its canals. Their
findings reveal that efforts to position New Orleans as a significant
port were, at best, only modestly successful. The cost of maintaining
such success was high as the canals needed to be regularly dredged
to combat continually accumulating silt. In addition, the canals
aggravate acute events; during Hurricane Katrina, canals channelled
flood waters inland, exacerbating flooding.[16] Such efforts epitomize
traditional attempts to control water.

By contrast, the Dutch exemplify a newer approach that
accommodates water dynamics. Over the past century, annual precipitation increased by a quarter in the Netherlands and is projected
to grow further.[17] The Room for the River initiative engineered links
between existing rivers and water flows. One of the project goals
was to improve safety of the 4 million residents who live in the
watershed. Interventions at thirty locations deepened flood plains

and riverbeds, strengthened and relocated dikes, built high-water and bypass channels, and removed obstacles, such as bridges.[18] To accommodate these changes, homes and farms were relocated, not without contention. Completed in 2015, the project allows four rivers, including the Rhine, to flood seasonally but with overall flooding decreased by half a metre. The Room for the River project marks an ecological turn in flood control, where flood potential is accommodated rather than suppressed.[19] The idea is to "give back land to the river system," a radical notion centred on recognizing the needs of the non-human environment.[20]

Though not as exposed to the sea as New Orleans and the Netherlands, New York City flooded during Hurricane Sandy. Subways and car tunnels were inundated. Approximately 8,000 street trees and 650 trees in Central Park were lost, in addition to losses in private property, parks, and woodlands. In response, the city implemented projects to enhance security as conceived by Foucault through robust ecosystems, including an initiative to plant 1 million trees and another to cultivate 1 billion oysters. By increasing the urban forest by 20 per cent, the Million Trees Initiative, which other cities are also undertaking, realizes a variety of environmental benefits, such as retaining stormwater, improving air quality, and creating habitat. Trees provide shade that cools streets and buildings, and by extension, reduces use of carbon-intensive air conditioning units.[21] Trees, while alive, also store carbon. Started in 2007, New York planted its millionth tree in 2015 with trees in every New York zip code. Today, New York has more than 5 million trees and 168 tree species.[22]

Historically, a large oyster reef, known as Half Moon, existed in New York Harbour. In the early 1600s, the reef was approximately 220,000 acres. Two hundred years later, "New Yorkers had eaten every last oyster, reefs were dredged up or covered in silt, and the water quality was too poor for regeneration of oysters or anything else."[23] The 1972 Clean Water Act resulted in improved water quality. In 2014, two years after Hurricane Sandy hit, the eponymous Billion Oyster Project was launched. By 2035, the project aims to create one hundred acres of living breakwater. "Oyster-tecture" is a field that restores historic coastal oyster reefs.[24] Oysters not only provide habitat and filter polluted water, but also the reefs act as a breakwater dissipating wave height and speed during storms.[25] As of 2019, 28 million oysters on nine reefs, a total of seven acres, were restored. This initiative reconnects New Yorkers to the surrounding ocean, what sustainable community professor Timothy Beatley calls *blue urbanism*.[26] Describing a similar education project focused on agriculture in Boriken/Puerto Rico, author Naomi Klein notes, "When students watch plants grow that they planted from seeds, it's a reminder that despite all the damage inflicted by the storm, 'You are part of something that is always protecting you.' The apparent rupture between themselves and the land – or water ... – begins to heal."[27] Protecting the climate is at the heart of an ecological mobilities approach, and an awareness of the relationship between human movement and the larger environment is central.

There is a sobering sidebar to the oyster initiative: ocean acidification. Due to excess atmospheric carbon dioxide, in part from fossil-fuelled mobility, the ocean is absorbing carbon at unprecedented rates.[28] As a result, ocean chemistry is changing, and oceans are 30 per cent more acidic since the start of the Industrial Revolution. The corrosive water compromises the shells of young oysters, causing mortality rates to soar.[29] Climate change complicates already challenging efforts, such as the Billion Oyster Project, illustrating complex feedbacks entailed in ecological mobilities.

AN ECOLOGICAL APPROACH TO MOBILITIES

Communities rewrite landscapes to suit their mobility needs. For example, to simplify the iconic London tube map at one point, designers removed the stylized pale-blue strip that flowed near the bottom of the image.[30] On paper, the River Thames disappeared. The ecological was omitted conceptually, even though it remained physically. In contrast, New York City was under water for a time. With Hurricane Sandy (2012) came a storm surge that flooded subway tunnels. The transit map was revised with flooded routes greyed out.[31] The ecological inundated the human. In the first scenario, the human is privileged. In the second, the environment dominates.

Ecological mobilities are multi-faceted webs with human, animal, material, informational, and energetic components. An ecological approach to mobilities frames the environment as an intrinsic consideration in human mobility: passengers, vehicles, schedules, fuel, and the atmosphere itself. Where a transport network focuses on physical and coordinated movement of buses, for example, an ecological mobilities approach takes a larger view that asks how the environment supports human movement, such as via fossil fuel extraction, and in turn, ways the environment is impacted by such movement, such as global heating. Ecological mobilities and an ecological approach to mobilities are interscalar concepts that can be applied to communities, regions, and the planet, encapsulated by sociologist Bronislaw Szerszynski as "birds and aeroplanes, fish and submarines."[32]

In this vein, geographer David Bissell describes an ecological approach to commuting:

Rather than imagining individual commuters as atom-like particles that mechanistically move from one point to another according to unchanged law, we need to develop an appreciation for the richer suite of forces at play ... [O]ur everyday journeys to and from work are entangled in complex webs of relations with other people, places, times, ideas, and materials ... these webs of relations are kaleidoscopic. They are shape-shifting rather than static ... [T]his ecological approach provides us with a richer appreciation of multiple sites of enablement and constraint.[33]

To this end, Bissell elaborates on six components of commuting ecologies: skills, dispositions, time, spaces, voices, and infrastructures that provide rich and complex insights into the experience of human movement. For example, related to space, Bissell describes the heat experienced by commuters in Australia, but he does not address climate change specifically. In contrast, with an ecological approach to mobilities a central focus is the fact that human mobility impacts the larger environment and, in turn, is impacted by the environment.

Mobility exists within and shapes the global environment, including the climate, water, and air. Just as ecosystems refer to "all the plants, animals, and people living in an area considered together with their environment as a system of relationships," ecological mobilities include human interactions with the environment. This relationship is indissoluble.[34] Other authors touch on such entanglements and feedbacks between mobility and the larger environment. Sociologist Mimi Sheller reflects on mobility justice in the context of global energy cultures:

The mobility regimes underlying modern infrastructure require constant high amounts of energy to be consumed in producing

round-the-clock transport of people, just-in-time delivery of
goods, and energizing communications and logistics networks.
Human mobilities are performed with and through deep geoecologies that are assembled with components that are
underground, under the sea, in the air, in space, as well as on
land. There is a global scale at which such infrastructure spaces
work, consisting of the entire vertical geography of planetary
urbanization, from deep mines to outer space, from micro to
macro, including the extraction of minerals and metals, and the
production, consumption, and circulation of energy and waste.[35]

My conception of an ecological approach to mobilities is
related but grounded in my research on experiences of managing disruption at the local level in Mi'kma'ki/Nova Scotia and
Newfoundland. Sheller engages with this scale in her work on climate impacts in Ayiti/Haiti, where she uses traditional knowledge,
such as water spirits and water power, to challenge and reframe
colonial approaches to climate change adaptation.[36] In a similar
way, Indigenous and environmental philosophers Kyle Whyte,
Jared Talley, and Julia Gibson observe in their work on Indigenous
mobilities and colonialism that the climate crisis is forcing some to
consider for the first time their relationship not just with territory
but with the "very earth system itself."[37]

Also related to an ecological approach to mobilities, Cresswell
analyzes animal mobilities in the context of food and public health –
an issue that emerged in 2020 when a wildlife market in Wuhan,
China, was linked with early COVID-19 cases.[38] Sociologist John
Urry examines the relationship between climate change and peak
oil, considering how to restructure life in a world where oil is not
an option.[39] Geographer Andrew Baldwin and peace and conflict
researchers Christiane Fröhlich and Delf Rothe challenge the idea
of a "climate refugee," noting both the complex circumstances that
shape a person's decision to migrate, of which climate is one of
many factors, and the varied forms such migration can take, such as
temporary internal displacement and seasonal international migration.[40] My goal is to demonstrate and elaborate upon an ecologically
inclusive approach to the mobilities paradigm that emphasizes the
contingent relations between human and non-human mobilities.[41]

I focus on contemporary mainstream North American mobility:
cars and buses, ships and planes, and walking and cycling. But there

is an example from Nova Scotia that illustrates the interface of human and non-human mobilities in even greater relief. Mi'kma'ki, in Atlantic Canada, which encompasses present-day Nova Scotia, is the ancestral home of the Mi'kmaq First Nations. Traditionally, the Mi'kmaq made canoes with birchbark and spruce root to travel along rivers and across lakes.[42] While all transport modes are derived from natural resources, such as aluminum and rubber, few but the canoe involve such minimal processing and ecological impact from point of origin to point of use.[43] Traditionally, the time to harvest summer birchbark was when the fireflies appear in June, but now there are fewer fireflies, and the bark is dry, not wet with sap.[44] In the case of Nova Scotia, traditional canoe building needs to adapt to a changing climate.

This case demonstrates my approach to ecological mobilities. Often in research, an ecosystem is framed as a techno-scientific entity that is to be managed, treated as complex inputs and outputs of energy and resources that benefit humans. Ecologist C.S. (Buzz) Holling, for example, advocates the use of models and statistics to describe the variable dynamics of complex ecological systems and to guide adaptive resource management.[45] Likewise, a key focus of sustainable transport initiatives is decarbonization. Although such approaches are valuable, through an ecological approach to mobilities, I suggest a higher level and broader ethos of environmental and climate care, where humans and human mobility are not prioritized over the ecology that sustains them. This orientation is captured in a poem I wrote on a ski trip when I was in Kazakhstan, not long after Hurricane Juan hit home:

rattle hum of chairlift
offering us to radiant
sky hanging over jagged
wafer-edge mountains

humans huddle
round rickety table
gripping plastic cups of vodka
biting frozen chocolate
perched on a mountain
half-way to frostbite
considering a glacier

However, the power dynamic in this human/environment relationship was blurred further on another chairlift ride up the mountain:

snow and
cloud
envelop

no horizon

only gravity
points down
and even that

begins to sway

In effect, the isolated human is subsumed by the environment not
just in a fleeting moment but also in all of life, from food to energy.
In this way it is possible to justify an ecological approach to health,
energy, and even disaster mobilities specifically.

BOOMERANG

In any given community along the North Atlantic, rain, snow, wind,
fog, cold, and heat are routine considerations for operators and
travellers alike. Heavy snowfalls and fog paralyze airports. Extreme
heat expands and kinks rail tracks. High winds restrict truck travel.
Intense rainfalls wash out bridges and roads. Heat waves and cold
snaps challenge pedestrians and cyclists. At the operational level,
such weather considerations are routine. There is, however, greater
need for consideration of the interface of mobility with a changing climate. The concept of an ecological approach to mobilities
acknowledges and embraces the broader environment in the context
of human movement.

Mobility results in a plethora of environmental impacts: generating air, water, and noise pollution; paving over soil; introducing
invasive species; and, of central interest in the present discussion,
contributing to the climate emergency. Humans burn fossil fuels,
which release greenhouse gases that cause climate change. The
Earth is a closed ecosystem and so, sociologist Ulrich Beck observes,
actions "boomerang" to their origins.[46] Sociologist Bruno Latour

observes that in the context of climate change, humans are engaged in a real-time climate experiment "happening on us, with us, through the action of each of us, on all of us, with all the oceans, the high atmosphere, and even the Gulf Stream." [47] It spurs Western society to reflect on its collective resistance to acknowledging and acting on the fact that humans are dependent on Earth for survival. Mobility is enabled by more-than-human assemblages, what Latour refers to as "imbroglios of people and things."[48] With climate change, the co-constructed networks of people and the larger environment "come out of hiding."[49] Understanding this relationship is predicated on recognizing that humans are not separate from ecosystems but rather are an interdependent component.[50]

Dichotomies such as society/nature simplify the degree of interconnectedness between the human and the non-human. Overcoming such dichotomies empowers an "ethics of care" because it blurs the boundary between other and us.[51] Bennett erases this boundary further. She notes that even the human body is not "exclusively human." The crook of the elbow – nonetheless the gastrointestinal tract – is an ecosystem "home to no fewer than six tribes of bacteria. The human body is not *a* body, but an 'array of bodies.'"[52] Bennett argues for a vital materiality that recognizes the capacity of things, such as carbon dioxide, flood waters, and windstorms, to support and thwart human efforts.

Mobility is enacted in coordination with extensive networks of people and things. This is what Latour refers to as actor-network theory, an ecological theory used to identify, describe, and analyze how "relations and entities come into being together."[53] It treats humans and non-human entities, such as trees, technology, and books, as constituting society.[54] With its emphasis on co-construction, it is useful in describing and challenging the way people relate to the environment. This theory drops habitual dichotomies in favour of examining actual, rather than predefined, relationships.[55] This idea of moving forward together as interconnected and embroiled ecologies can restructure society.[56] The ethos that the environment is impacted by, and impacts, fossil-fuelled mobility needs to be central in decision-making that relates to transport, at all levels, from individuals to corporations to governments.

Extreme events lay bare the tenacious and turbulent nature of humanity's relationship with the environment, revealing the necessity of conceptually unifying the human and non-human environment.

Human actions rebound. Given that excessive carbon emissions desta-bilize communities, communities need to reduce the environmental impact of mobility as well as prepare for the impacts of climate change. This includes both acute events, such as hurricanes, and chronic shifts like sea level rise, as well as interactions between the two.[57] It is pos-sible to imagine a carbon boomerang thrown by society that returns in the form of climate change. In the face of disruption, the instinctive reflex in Nova Scotia and Newfoundland, and communities across Canada, is to get things back to normal. While entirely understand-able, the efficacy of this strategy is limited as it reinstates vulnerabilities that contributed to disruption in the first place, namely, fossil-fuelled mobility is susceptible to a changing climate.

The damage left by Hurricane Juan (chapter 3) and Hurricane Igor (chapter 5) in Atlantic Canada can be understood as an ecolog-ical message. Road washouts and fallen trees rewrote the landscape. They are indications of the strain on an atmosphere and ocean over-loaded with carbon. Goyette writes, "we found ourselves leaning in, having no choice / but to listen."[58] If the global climate had a persona, I imagine it as overworked and under the weather. Just as humans can have nervous breakdowns, so too can the global climate break down. While such anthropomorphism is frowned upon in the natural sciences, interpreting the non-human environment as an actor that shapes society is apt, given that the climate shapes human communities. "The ocean," Goyette writes, "nibbles hungrily at the shoreline of our understanding, refusing to explain its moods and winning every staring contest."[59] In plain language, this might be framed as the mood or will of Mother Nature. Mobility disruptions are cause for consideration about the human relationship with the broader environment. Disruption, like emotion, is information, sig-nalling the need for reflection, reconsideration, and recalibration.

Attempts to treat movement as an isolated feat of design and engi-neering acting on a passive, peripheral environment do not fare well. Sociologists Anthony Elliott and John Urry observe that "non-human nature easily exposes the fallibility of such claims." [60] The first and final voyage of the *Titanic* offers a quintessential example: pressure to cross the Atlantic Ocean in record time resulted in a catastrophic course through an iceberg field. The remains of the *Titanic* now rest on the ocean floor off the coast of Newfoundland and victims are buried in Nova Scotia. Nature exerts power, says sociologist Barry Barnes, such as strong ocean currents that dictate the course of a ship and tree roots that destabilize building foundations.[61] Hurricanes, as a form of intense, albeit unintentional, movement through space and time, underscore the power of non-human nature and the frailty of human aspirations for control.

ICE AND ASH

In the face of disruption, mobilities are reconfigured temporarily and sometimes permanently. Disaster casts in a new light the unequal, but often tolerated, access to mobility within and between communities. Disruption may cause a return to old ways of doing things, like using boats and land lines, or it may offer an opportunity to experiment with new approaches, like using drones to survey damage and Twitter to contact victims in real time.

Two events, an ice storm and an ash cloud, illustrate different facets of an ecological approach to mobilities. These events disrupted human activity across huge geographic areas, illustrating the interconnectivity of human mobility and environmental forces. The North American ice storm and the Icelandic ash cloud are examples of two environmental events with far-reaching mobility implications. Cold immobile ice and hot mobile ash offer productive juxtapositions in terms of precipitating conditions and environmental effects, demonstrating diverse ecological mobilities.

Ice Storm

In January 1998, a freezing rain system stalled over eastern North America for eighty hours. The ice storm affected the Canadian provinces of New Brunswick, Nova Scotia, Ontario, and Quebec, as well as the American states of Maine, New York, New Hampshire, and Vermont. It is a quintessential example of an ecological approach to mobilities. Sociologist Raymond Murphy, who researched the storm and its impacts, draws on the metaphor of dance to describe the co-constructed relationship between humans and non-humans. Humans "dance with the moves of nature" to form hybrid constructions. The dance can be "adroit or inept" and, in the case of the ice storm, catastrophic.[62]

During the storm, ice covered trees and electrical poles. As the surface area increased, more ice formed adding additional weight: a positive feedback loop meant that freezing rain weighed down anything it touched. Trees snapped. Power poles cracked. Transmission lines crumpled. A state of emergency was declared. Homes were without electricity for weeks. In total, thirty-five people died, many from efforts to stay warm, such as carbon monoxide poisoning from burning fuel indoors and house fires caused by candles. Approximately 300,000 farm animals died due to a lack of backup generators for heating barns.[63] Residents navigated treacherous roads and sidewalks overhung by ice-encrusted trees and power lines. Patients with broken bones inundated emergency rooms.

Experiences in Montreal highlight the scale of disruption throughout the region. The bridges connecting the island of Montreal to the rest of Quebec were closed due to falling ice, raising questions about possible courses of action in the face of mass evacuation. Due to power outages, a municipal water plant in Montreal could not filter sediment. Residents were advised to ration and boil water to avoid depleting water supplies for drinking and fighting fires. The possibility of evacuation was considered. Montreal mayor, Pierre Bourque, stated that beyond asking residents to stockpile water by filling bathtubs and buying bottled water, "The top managers ... told me the only solution that they foresaw – and I was completely shocked – [was to] evacuate a million people ... I listened to their strategies and I thought about sicknesses, epidemics, water, the health of the people. I thought about the bridges and the people who would flee. I imagined the panic. I saw Montreal upside down."[64] In one city, water, sediment, electricity, and humans were enmeshed. The event illustrates how social and ecological spheres comprise complex, interconnected mobilities.

In this scenario, time, space, and mobility intersect: hours before water runs out; distribution of water and population; housebound residents and the potential full-scale evacuation of an urban population. This wait-and-see approach to evacuation contrasts with the immediate mass evacuations required in recent years in Alberta and British Columbia, where fast-approaching forest fires left residents with mere minutes to locate loved ones, collect belongings, and evacuate. Fortunately, in the case of Montreal an evacuation was averted as power was restored to the water filtration plant; however, the prospect of evacuation was daunting for officials.[65] Sociologist Anthony Giddens observes that in the management of unknown, non-linear risks, "we cannot know beforehand when we are actually scaremongering and when we are not."[66] Manufactured risk poses specific governance challenges.

Murphy contrasts the catastrophic impacts in Montreal with the relative lack of impact in Amish communities. The Amish live without electricity, using wood stoves for heat, and horse and buggies for transport.[67] While mainstream society struggled with impassable roads and gasoline shortages, the Amish relied on literal horsepower. For outsiders to this insular community, it appeared that the lives of the Amish continued much as before. Murphy concludes that vulnerability to disaster, rather than being inevitable, is socially constructed.[68] The everyday practices of the Amish yield, if not a specific model for mainstream society, the bold possibility of doing things differently, of transporting people and goods without reliance on fossil fuels.

In line with the work of environmental sociologist William Freudenburg and colleagues on the social construction of disaster (chapter 1), Murphy argues that disaster sociology can teach society about "errors of expectations concerning nature's dynamics, about the material consequence of such errors, and about the social barriers to learning from the prompts of nature."[69] During extreme weather, such as ice storms and hurricanes, the normally hidden co-constructed relationship between the human and non-human environment is exposed. A *New York Times* editorialist reflected on the ice storm: "A storm like this reveals the shallowness of technological civilization – how swiftly the grid collapses. But it also reveals its depth – into how many reaches of ordinary life electricity has penetrated and how high above the fundamental concerns that allows us to float ... *The wonder is not that cold is so powerful, but that we are so seldom aware of its power.*"[70] The impacts of winter weather on walking, driving, and flying are regular occurrences. The main differences between such everyday events and the ice storm are duration and extent. Disruption reveals that transport and electricity intensify links between the social and the ecological. After the ice storm, the electrical grid was strengthened through engineering measures, such as "pouring a larger foundation for each tower, using thicker transmission wires and making every 10th tower along a transmission line a so-called 'anticascading tower.'"[71] Such investments build resilience while also reinforcing reliance on the power grid.

Ash Cloud

In April 2010, an Icelandic volcano, Eyjafjallajökull erupted over several days. The resulting ash cloud reached heights of nine kilometres and spread over Europe. Near the plume, ash hindered pilot visibility, and far beyond the plume, atmospheric ash threatened to damage airplane engines. European airspace closed for six days, resulting in the cancellation of more than 100,000 flights, impacting more than 10 million passengers, and costing the airline industry almost $2 billion in lost revenue.[72] In this case, global air travel was vulnerable to environmental risk and was slow to adapt and recover. Geographer Michael O'Regan observes, "Just as the 2008 financial crisis shook the global economy, exposing the fragility of the foundations of global banking and finance, the eruption exposed the weaknesses of European institutions and the governance framework that regulates the free flow of people, labor and cargo by air."[73] It is disconcerting to realize and, even more so to experience, the vulnerability of massive systems, such as money and movement, which are central to contemporary society. The COVID-19 pandemic, through its global rupture of mobility, highlights such vulnerabilities even more starkly.

Mobilities scholars, many of whom were travelling to an annual international academic conference in the United States at the time of the volcanic eruption, used their personal experience of disrupted mobility to reflect on the Icelandic ash cloud event.[74] Urban theorist Ole B. Jensen describes his experience as he tried to return to Europe from the United States: "I felt drawn into a collective emotional rollercoaster of humour and laughter at the absurdity of the event on one hand; and on the other hand, I felt deep concern about how my family back home would cope."[75] He focuses on his emotional navigation of disruption ranging from the anxiety of uncertainty to the comfort of arriving home, and what the experience of "being stuck" means in contemporary society. Such experiences are even more stressful for anyone travelling under added pressures, such as attending a wedding or funeral, or status limitations, such as travelling on a visa or seeking asylum. In Europe, linguistics professor David Barton describes his overland journey by bus from Norway to Britain.[76] He observed that fellow travellers with strong literacy skills, that is, fluent in more than one language and skilled social media users, formed the centre of informal information networks, highlighting the role of context-dependent skill sets in the face of mobility disruption.[77]

International airspace in several European countries was closed on 14 April and reopened on 23 April, after the ash cloud shifted and regulations about acceptable levels of ash density were introduced and revised.[78] The event led Lucy Budd and colleagues to question the push to "get Europe moving" and reinstate the mobility status quo.[79] A focus on the short-term political and administrative impacts of the ash cloud diverted attention away from discussions about public safety, the aviation sector's contribution to climate change, and society's over-dependency on aviation.[80]

The reach of both the ice storm and ash cloud was massive. The ice storm impacted a broad swathe of North America and the ash cloud, while primarily impacting Europe, disrupted flights globally. The ice storm itself occurred over three days, but the impacts dragged on for weeks, and for some, months. The ash cloud disrupted flights for six days, resolving more quickly. Whereas the ice storm resulted in death and injury, the ash cloud resulted in delays and discomfort. The ice storm is the type of extreme weather event that is expected to occur more often as the climate continues to change. The ash cloud was caused by a volcanic eruption, activity in the Earth's crust that is unrelated to human-caused climate change.[81] However, the aviation industry is a "top-ten global emitter" contributing to 5 per cent of overall global heating.[82] Further, Lucy Budd speaks to the increasing awareness of the risks associated with air travel, from terrorism to infectious disease.[83]

The ice storm impacted all forms of transportation, from walking and cycling, driving, and transit within and between communities to domestic and international flights, but was more regional than the ash cloud. Residents were confined to unheated homes and hazardous streets. The consequences of the ash cloud were less dire for those travellers impacted: sleeping in airports and on buses, scrambling to book hotel rooms, and finding connections to reach destinations. As mentioned, the Amish, who live without modern technology, experienced the ice storm differently, with less disruption than most residents, illustrating the social construction of disaster and the potential for ecological approaches to mobility to buffer disruption. Next, I shift from air to ground to discuss another facet of mainstream mobility: urban transport planning.

FROM TRAFFIC PLANNING
TO ECOLOGICAL MOBILITIES

In the twentieth century, most transport planning focused on roads and cars, on engineering and economics. More recently, a shift toward sustainable mobility is gaining traction. Sustainable mobility expands traditional approaches to transport planning, incorporating social dimensions of transport decisions, in particular livability. In traditional transport planning, a street is viewed one dimensionally as a road for car use. Through a sustainable mobility lens, a street is a space with potential to be livable and vibrant, potentially used by pedestrians, cyclists, drivers of cars, buses, and more.[84] Through an ecological approach to mobilities, streets and roads, as well as homes and buildings, communication networks and utility grids are considered in relation to the environment, such as trees, wind, and waves.

In terms of speed, to focus on one dimension, traffic planning facilitates flows of car traffic. The machine is central. Sustainable mobility focuses on facilitating the movement of diverse transport users, including pedestrians, cyclists, and transit users. An ecological approach to mobilities accommodates human mobility within the context of both slow and fast ecological processes, from sea level rise to storm surges. Understandings of mobility, particularly urban mobility, are continually changing. Drawing on the work of urban designer Stephen Marshall and transport geographer David Banister, I trace an evolution from traditional traffic planning and engineering to sustainable mobility to an ecological approach to mobilities.[85] In the following sections I expand on each method before delving further into the latter.

Conventional Traffic Planning

Traditional traffic planning and engineering operate on the scale of the private motorized car. Together, they focus on how to move cars safely and efficiently. Conventional transport planning accommodates rather than manages demand for travel. Minimizing travel time and cost are priorities.[86] Traffic engineering tools include forecasting, modelling, and road design. Expansive highways and bumper-to-bumper traffic dominate the quintessential car city. People and traffic are segregated. While this is intended in part to ensure the

Table 2.1 Comparison of transport planning, sustainable mobility, and an ecological approach to mobilities*

Conventional transport planning & engineering	Sustainable mobility	Ecological approach to mobilities
Physical dimensions	Social dimensions	Ecological, social, and physical dimensions
Mobility	Accessibility	Human accessibility and non-human mobility
Traffic/car focus	People focus	People as part of larger ecosystem
Large scale	Local scale	Interscalar
Street as road	Street as space	Street as ecological, but also international shipping and aviation corridors, etc.
Motorized transport	All transport modes in carbon-intensity hierarchy	Local and global ecological flows considered in human mobility
Forecasting traffic	Visioning cities	Transforming social-ecological relationships
Modelling	Developing scenarios and models	(Re)imagining futures (e.g., utopian, dystopian)
Evaluating economic criteria	Analyzing multiple criteria, including environmental and social	Analyzing multiple criteria, including environmental, social, safety, humanitarian, economic, infrastructure, future generations, etc.
Travelling as derived demand	Mobility as valued activity	Mobility and immobility as valued activities and environmentally contingent
Demand-based	Management-based	Ecologically constrained
Speeding up traffic	Slowing down movement	Accommodating fast and slow social, ecological, and technical movements (e.g., tipping points, turbulence)
Minimizing travel time	Aiming for reasonable travel times and travel time reliability	Recognizing timeless time including "longue durée" and "glacial time"
Segregating people and traffic	Integrating people and traffic	Incorporating ecological flows and turbulences with human mobilities

* Adapted from D. Banister, "The Sustainable Mobility Paradigm"; and S. Marshall, "The Challenge of Sustainable Transport."

safety of pedestrians and other road users, in effect, the needs of other non-car road users are marginalized.

Under this system, as Sheller describes it, the average traveller is a white, cis-gendered, able-bodied, heterosexual, middle-class, nine–to-five commuter and a car owner.[87] So many people are left out. Sociologist Beverley Skaggs writes, "Mobility and control over mobility both reflect and reinforce power. Mobility is a resource to which not everyone has equal relationship."[88] There are a plethora of examples, from racial profiling of drivers (i.e., "driving while Black") to street harassment (e.g., unwanted sexual comments) to lack of wheelchair access, where race, gender, ability, age, and class shape an individual's experience of mobility.[89]

Traditional traffic planning and engineering were the norm in North America from the 1950s to the 1990s, and still dominate in many regions. However, there were early analyses and critiques of this car-centric model. In the 1960s, urban theorist and designer Donald Appleyard undertook mapping exercises in San Francisco.[90] Working with residents, he illustrated how traffic patterns impacted livability. He studied three comparable streets, one with low traffic volume (2,000 vehicles per day), one with medium traffic (8,000 vehicles per day), and one with high traffic volume (16,000 vehicles per day). Appleyard found that on the street with high traffic the number of social interactions between neighbours was much lower and residents described a much smaller home territory (the space where residents felt they could undertake daily living). On the high-volume street, some residents felt that parts of their own houses did not constitute home territory given the level of traffic noise. On low-volume streets, home territory might include both sides of the street or an entire block. It looked like neighbours chatting on front stoops and children playing on the sidewalk and in the street. Appleyard found that people living on the low-volume street had, on average, three more friends and twice as many acquaintances as people living on the busier street.[91]

In short, social interaction and cohesion were much greater on streets with light traffic volume. Appleyard's research contributed to a shift away from car-oriented traffic planning and engineering. It questioned the benefits of the status quo, asking what was gained and lost in different communities. Such research on the lived experience of different approaches to mobility is imperative in developing, navigating, and sustaining post-carbon mobility suited to increasing climate disruption.

Sustainable Mobility

Sustainable mobility marks a shift away from car-oriented traffic planning and engineering. In recent decades, sustainable mobility supplanted traffic planning in many cities and communities. Sustainable transport focuses on the movement of people rather than cars. It addresses issues of environmental sustainability and social justice, viewing the street as a space, rather than simply a corridor for cars. This space can be used for moving people under their own power, like walking and cycling, or using vehicles, such as buses and cars. The various ways of moving are integrated and prioritized according to carbon intensity and user vulnerability, giving preference to pedestrians and cyclists. Movement is viewed not just as a mundane task to get from origin to destination as quickly as possible but as a valued, even joyful, activity in and of itself.

Advocates of sustainable mobility view the street as a social place for local living, such as enjoying community parks and connecting with neighbours. The street is accessible for all. For example, crosswalk lights are long enough for slower moving residents to make it to the far curb in time, and storefronts are accessible for wheelchairs and strollers. Working with community members, sustainable mobility advocates engage in visioning exercises and develop future scenarios that address environmental and social concerns. They work to create policies, designs, and related investments that encourage sustainable mobility over hegemonic car use. There is a well-established suite of common sustainable transportation initiatives such as promoting compact, mixed-use development that reduces the need for cars, creating spaces conducive to cycling and walking, and discouraging car use through congestion charges and parking fees. These initiatives are promoted through infrastructure investments, zoning by-laws, financial measures like carbon taxes and insurance rates, education, and regulation.

There are a variety of comprehensive approaches to mobility design. Just three examples are: Complete Streets, Transit-Oriented Development, and Naked Streets, all of which combine elements of sustainability and equity. Complete Streets focuses on the inclusion of all street users, ensuring safe and continuous mobility regardless of transport mode. Transit-Oriented Development focuses on compact, mixed-use development that makes transit convenient and appealing to use, giving it a competitive edge over driving. Naked Streets is the most radical approach, but not as sensational as it sounds. It refers to removing all street markings – traffic lights, pavement markings, and even sidewalks – forcing traffic users to slow down and make eye contact to navigate the street. These approaches are being trialled around the world. Two other approaches are Open Streets, which close streets to car traffic and open them to human interaction and play, and critical mass bike rides, where cyclists take over urban streets. Both are temporary measures that let people experience an "alternate reality," where city officials prioritize streets for people and communities, rather than vehicles.[92] Like the scrambled mobilities that follow a hurricane (chapters 3 and 5), they provide experiences of and insights into other ways of being, doing, and moving.

Three emerging factors are shaping the ever-changing field of sustainable mobility: the introduction of zero-emission vehicles including cars, buses, and bicycles; the introduction of driverless vehicles; and ride sharing apps like Uber and Lyft. New expressions of automobility can complement or compete with sustainable mobility. Depending on how these technologies are designed, they can support sustainable mobility by offering diverse, accessible, and lower-carbon ways of moving. They can also be viewed as a potential reassertion of automobility with its negative impacts, including energy-intensive mobility and social exclusion. Evidence suggests such technologies decrease car ownership but can increase car use unless solely used to bridge the first and last mile of a transit journey.[93] To support an ecological approach to mobility, shared mobility services and autonomous vehicles need to be introduced in an intentional way.[94] Further, electrifying existing passenger and freight vehicle fleets without managing demand is insufficient to meet the Paris Agreement targets, and certainly not the more stringent IPCC target of limiting global heating to 1.5°C.[95] To this end, in North America, despite the many efforts and successes of sustainable mobility advocates, distance travelled by cars and the size of car engines are increasing, illustrating the technological and cultural lock-in of car culture.

An Ecological Approach to Mobilities

Baldwin, Fröhlich, and Rothe observe that as humans enter the Anthropocene, a geological epoch defined by substantial human impacts on Earth's functioning, "we leave behind ... the fraught separation of Nature and Culture that has underpinned Euro-Western humanism from at least the fifteenth century."[96] To this end, in line with Sheller, geographers Nigel Clark and Kathryn Yusoff propose a "geosocial" approach where society is shaped by geological dynamics at the planetary scale, such as a changing climate.[97]

In a similar but more local way, an ecological approach to mobilities brings together the ecological, social, and physical dimensions of movement. Non-human movements of water, wind, tree roots, branches, carbon, and more are considered in lockstep with human movement. An ecological mobilities approach entails co-operating with, rather than dominating, the environment. Conventional transport engineering is anthropocentric, disregarding environmental considerations except for technical issues, such as road surface water runoff. Sustainable mobility embraces the ecological in terms of mitigating the impact of transport on the environment, including climate change as well as air, water, and noise pollution. An ecological approach to mobilities places human and non-human movements on equal footing. Just as the Room for the River Project in the Netherlands gave land back to the river, an ecological approach to mobilities acknowledges and incorporates local and global environmental needs. Human mobility is not excluded but conceived as part of the ecological. The street, for example, is not just for cars and traffic, as under conventional traffic planning and engineering. It is for even more than people, as with sustainable mobility. The street is a space and place for the more-than-human.

Both humans and non-humans move, with the latter including daily tides, seasonal flooding, annual hurricane seasons, and growth of urban forest canopies over decades. Though the street provides a concrete and relatable example, an ecological approach to mobilities is interscalar, including housing, communication networks, utility systems, and more. International waterways used for shipping and atmospheric airspace used for aviation are also more-than-human corridors that include air and water, carbon and pollution, as well as migrating wildlife like whales and birds. Such ecological flows are considered along with all modes of human mobility. An ecological approach to mobilities recognizes and acts on fast and slow ecological movements, from the atmospheric turbulence of a hurricane to climatic tipping points. The approach addresses daily mobility, but with an eye to the "*longue durée*" or "glacial time" of the climate.[98] Consequently, imagining potential futures, both utopian and dystopian are part of such an approach.

The goal is to transform social-ecological relationships such that the impacts of human mobility on the non-human environment are minimized – or even positive – and, conversely, that the impact of the non-human environment on humans is not destructive. Environmental sociologist Stewart Lockie asks, "What happens if we accept that despite the technological advances of the industrial age human society has never transcended its ecological roots? If we accept that social change today is as much about ecosystems and climate processes as it is about institutions and power?"[99] An ecological mobilities approach overcomes human/environment dichotomies, asserting that human and non-human environments are indivisible. Our ecological impacts rebound upon us. The impacts of climate change, including sea level rise and extreme weather, are human impacts channelled through the medium of the non-human environment.

An ecological approach to mobilities ask what counts as "appropriate movement" in a society that needs to both eliminate carbon pollution and grapple with the impacts of a changing climate.[100] Baldwin, Frölich, and Rothe describe Anthropocene mobilities in which the environment is viewed as the "very material substance through which mobility itself is mediated, experienced, and conceptualized."[101] Ecological flows and turbulences are incorporated into considerations of human mobility. Such mobile commons, writes Sheller, require protections in the form of decreasing speed, preventing excess mobility, and pricing the negative environmental and social externalities of mobility.[102] Human mobility is checked and constrained by recognizing and respecting ecological limits, making it slower but more sustainable. This ethic of slowing and decentring the human is captured in a poem I wrote about swimming in Nova Scotia:

perched erratic

you know you've arrived
made it to the top
a real high flyer
when you wear
mosquito bites and
scraped knees

sea creature i emerge
from the tea bag lake
summit mottled granite
and sprawl

endless dragonfly arrivals and
departures on my airstrip skin

catch my breath

In slowing down my brain and body, I become part of the landscape and a conspicuous site for non-human mobilities, namely dragonflies.

An ecological approach to mobilities illustrates the inseparability of the social and ecological. In this chapter, I described diverse mobilities from hurricanes to fossil fuels and detailed how social scientists are embracing the ecological in their thinking. I defined this approach as a conceptual tool for thinking about mobility during the climate crisis, including how negative impacts of fossil fuel usage boomerang back upon communities. Following from Uexküll, humans are a component, but not the centre, of a global ecosystem.[103] Through the examples of the North American ice storm and the Icelandic ash cloud event, I illustrated the vulnerability of human movement to the environment. Finally, I traced an evolution from car-centred traffic planning to sustainable mobility, to an ecologically inclusive mobilities approach. In the next chapter, I describe how Hurricane Juan impacted mobility in Nova Scotia and consequently informed climate policy.

3

Hurricane Juan

The barbers taught us how to trim the trees.
They'd say *careful of their ears*, proving something

we'd all suspected. A farmer came to show us how to use
the chainsaw. *Say your names*, he said above the banshee

of its teeth. *That's how long it takes.* This is now a steadfast
rule about a lot of things though at the time all we could imagine losing

was a limb.

Sue Goyette, "Twenty-Six," in *Ocean*

CANADA'S OCEAN PLAYGROUND

With 7,600 km of coastline, we are exceptionally vulnerable to rising
sea levels caused by climate change.
Nova Scotia Climate Change Action Plan[1]

The slogan on Nova Scotian licence plates is "Canada's Ocean Play-ground."[2] The province is renowned for its proximity to the Bay of Fundy, which features the world's highest tides; the *Bluenose*, once a fishing schooner; and a lobster fishery. It is the size of Ireland and has a population of about one million people. Migration and colonialism are evident it the area's name: Nova Scotia is Latin for New Scotland, while the Mi'kmaq First Nations know it as part of the larger region of Mi'kma'ki. English and French, including Acadian, are by far the most common languages, with Arabic and Mi'kmaq next most common. There are colonial legacies expressed in and beyond Mi'kmaw communities who never formally surrendered their lands to settlers,[3] as well as ongoing community tensions, such as environmental racism affecting African Nova Scotian communities.[4]

Nova Scotia's coastline measures 7,600 kilometres, rising to 13,300 kilometres when Cape Breton's Bras d'Or Lakes, an inland sea, are included. A provincial coastal report says,

> Nova Scotia is rich in coastline and nearly surrounded by the sea ... No wonder we are fishing people. We are boating people. We are beach and cottage people. We are swimmers, sailors, surfers, and divers. We love the sea. Our province is shaped by the sea. We have stories of sea adventures and sea tragedies. We have calm harbours, windswept bluffs, and shifting sands. We witness the wind and the waves and the tides constantly reshaping our coastline – and sometimes sweeping away what we build. Respect for the sea – and the power of the sea – is a lesson we continue to learn.[5]

In addition, there is an offshore oil and gas production moratorium on the rich fishing grounds of Georges Bank. Production is permitted in other regions, though activity has steadily dwindled, with 2020 the first year in twenty-five generating no provincial royalties.[6] In short, Nova Scotia is a place of and on the ocean, no stranger to hurricanes.

Ferries connect Nova Scotia to New Brunswick (home of the Wolastoqiyik, Mi'kmaq, and Peskotomuhkati peoples), Newfoundland and Labrador, and Epekwitk/Prince Edward Island, and seasonally to Maine.[7] The Trans-Canada Highway runs north to Cape Breton, east to Halifax, and west to New Brunswick connecting Nova Scotia with the rest of Canada. Nova Scotia's capital, Halifax, itself is a busy port with an international airport. Multiple types of roads crisscross the province, in fact there are so many rural roads that fragmentation of wildlife habitat is a concern, highlighting ecological mobilities.[8] In terms of rail, Via Rail offers a limited passenger service to Montreal, and there is a growing freight sector.[9] Compared to other Canadian cities, Halifax enjoys a relatively high-use of sustainable transport with 12 per cent of residents commuting via public transit and 10 per cent via walking and cycling.[10] Before COVID, the Halifax Port Authority expected about 200 cruise ships carrying more than 300,000 visitors.[11] In Nova Scotia, there are regional transit services and private van shuttle companies as well as one private coach service.[12]

In this chapter, I describe six facets of Hurricane Juan as they relate to mobility. First, I describe the efforts to batten down the hatches in anticipation of Hurricane Juan's arrival before discussing the storm's impacts during landfall and then in its aftermath. From there, I consider public transit, which emerged as a quiet but versatile hero in the push to get things back to normal. In the months and years that followed Hurricane Juan, the provincial government began developing an "all-hazards" skill set after it was inundated by multiple complex events. How climate action is informed by widespread recognition of a new normal form the closing points of this chapter.

HURRICANE JUAN

> The fishing industry, well aware of its need to take weather warnings seriously, battened down the hatches and was generally "very well prepared." And while there was extensive infrastructure damage to wharves and other facilities during the storm, the fact that there was no loss of life is significant.
>
> Provincial report[13]

Hurricane Juan formed off the coast of Africa on 14 September 2003. It travelled across the Atlantic Ocean, hitting Bermuda on 23 September, and then tracked up the eastern seaboard. It made landfall in Nova Scotia at 12:10 am on Monday, 29 September.[14] The Canadian Hurricane Centre issued its first statements about the severity of the storm on the preceding Thursday. The provincial Emergency Management Office (EMO) initiated preparations on Friday.[15] Starting on 25 September, the EMO "encouraged people to listen to weather advisories, choose an appropriate shelter inside their residences, and have an emergency kit ready at all times."[16] It also suggested that Nova Scotians reduce hazards on their properties by trimming dead or rotten tree branches and removing dead trees entirely.

Nova Scotians braced for Hurricane Juan. Due to the timing of the storm, arriving just after midnight, most people were home – a circumstance to which the provincial government attributed lower rates of fatality and injury.[17] Six people in Nova Scotia died during the storm: two directly and four indirectly. A paramedic died when a falling tree struck his parked ambulance and a motorist died when debris hit his vehicle. In the aftermath of the storm a mother and two children died in a house fire. The smoke detectors in their public housing unit ran on electricity and did not function during the power outage.[18] One man died while assisting with relief work.[19]

In response to weather warnings, residents stayed home, and transport services shut down. The normal rhythm of mobility was halted. An article in Nova Scotia's provincial newspaper, the *Chronicle Herald*, describes preparations:

> People on the Halifax waterfront were preparing for the storm Sunday morning. Leading Seaman T.J. Peric and Ordinary Seaman Alex Zaslavskiy, taking care of HMCS *Sackville*, had to call for help to slacken the vessel's moorings. Already stretched tight by the morning's high tide, they needed to be looser for the surge. Peter Murphy of Murphy's on the Water cancelled all harbour tours and had *Theodore Too* and the *Mar II* moved to more sheltered wharves ... By late Sunday afternoon, all flights in and out of Halifax International Airport had been grounded ... Workers with the airport and airlines were busy Sunday afternoon securing equipment to prevent items from flying around in the high winds that were on the way.[20]

From water to land to air, human mobility constricted.

The Halifax-Dartmouth Bridge Commission, responsible for two major urban bridges, followed the guidelines set out in its wind threshold policy. Bridge access was restricted when winds reached seventy-five kilometres per hour and shut down when winds reached one hundred kilometres per hour. The bridge closure prompted the transit authority to shut down its operations. Transit manager Chad recalls, "On Saturday night we began bringing our equipment back into the garage ... We pulled it all in, we had the equipment safely off the road, with the exception of our service staff. They were out there doing their thing in strategic areas. We were trying to stay out of the weather."[21] Trying to stay out of the weather is both laudable and, in the larger context of the climate emergency, impossible.

A port authority official details the options for responding to severe weather:

> Most vessels are capable of putting out extra lines, particularly heavy lines that are intended specifically to withstand these abnormal weather conditions, such as hurricane-force winds.

The real question for the master of the vessel to determine is: is it safer for that vessel to remain alongside? Or should it ride at anchor or in the outer harbour? Or should it proceed to sea and do a slow loop around? And taking advance time, before the extreme weather hits, to safely navigate the harbour and then ride out the storm. Again, professional mariners have to make judgments on this.[22]

Ships operate in close relationship with the environment.

Amending and cancelling service as noted in the above cases of the port, airport, and bridge commission, as well as preventing damage to infrastructure by mooring ships are all strategies for managing mobility in advance of severe weather. In the face of a coming storm, Nova Scotians took a precautionary approach. While there was a chance the approaching storm might bypass the province entirely or, if it did make landfall, yield minimal impacts, the approach at all scales – guided by advice from the provincial government – was to batten down the hatches. Given the impending possibility of significant damage, transport operators, residents, and business owners reasoned that the time and effort needed to prevent potential damage was less than addressing actual damage. Such proactive practices can be transferred to dealing with the threat of climate change at a larger scale and in different regions (chapter 8).

LANDFALL

Oh, it was by far worse than we ever imagined. I mean, I don't think anybody had planned for – we get a lot of heavy wind and everything here in Halifax and throughout Nova Scotia. But no one planned for that. No one knew that was coming. And it was absolutely astounding what damage it caused.

Provincial government representative[23]

Despite meteorological data, the exact track and force of a hurricane is unknown until the moment it makes landfall. The force of Hurricane Juan surprised officials, resulting in far greater impacts than anticipated. The storm tracked over the Halifax Regional Municipality on the eastern edge of Nova Scotia, travelled through the centre of the province and continued to the neighbouring province of Prince Edward Island. The storm ranked a Category 2 on the

Saffir-Simpson Hurricane Wind Scale with sustained wind speeds of 151 kilometres per hour and wind gusts reaching 176 kilometres per hour. The Saffir-Simpson scale was developed in 1971 by civil engineer Herbert Saffir and meteorologist Robert Simpson.[24] Like the Richter scale used to measure earthquakes, the Saffir-Simpson scale ranks hurricanes from Category 1 to 5, where five is catastrophic, based on potential damage to the built environment.

A meteorologist, Sean, recounts uncertainty with respect to the storm forecast: "Neither me, nor my colleagues, envisioned the full-strength Category 2 at landfall. We were thinking a pretty well intact hurricane at landfall with trees coming down. ... Power outages pretty much guaranteed. So, we predicted things quite definitively and were confident with that. Definitely some impacts, but we certainly [weren't] expecting the massive tree blow-down that occurred ... The extent of the tree damage ... we didn't expect."[25] Hurricane Juan resulted in approximately 100 million trees falling across the province.[26] Along with damage associated with high winds, Nova Scotia was hit by a record-breaking storm tide of almost 3 metres.[27] A storm tide is the combination of the usual tide and a storm surge, in this case 1.4 and 1.5 metres, respectively. Hurricane Juan hit when these forces aligned to produce high water levels. If the storm hit two hours earlier at high tide, the storm surge would have been as much as 1 metre greater, for a total storm tide of 3.9 metres.[28]

The electricity system experienced severe damage, including "27 main transmission lines, several 120-foot transmission towers, 117 distribution feeders, and 31 major ... substations."[29] One utility official observed that the hurricane tracked along the "backbone of the ... transmission system from Halifax to Truro." This is a populated one hundred–kilometre corridor. About 70 per cent of customers in the province experienced service disruptions.[30] The president of Nova Scotia Power at the time reflected that it was as if the storm was "designed to come straight up the harbour [and] attack the major populations and the transmission system in its entirety."[31] The impacts of the power loss were wide-ranging, from outages in homes to the inability to pump fuel at gas stations to difficulty milking dairy cattle.[32] Disruption in the power grid resulted in disrupted mobility elsewhere.

Due to fallen trees and power poles, in addition to the storm surge, the road network was blocked. More than one kilometre of rail tracks was washed out along Halifax Harbour. Ten train cars, including fuel tankers, were derailed.[33] Vessels moored in Halifax Harbour broke their lines, damaging both the vessels and nearby infrastructure. Several yachts were swept onto land, and one boat sank. The hurricane disrupted air travel both before and during the storm. A lack of infrastructure damage at the airport meant that service could quickly resume; however, accessing the airport was difficult due to road blockages. The impact on the road network complicated all mobility, including critical health-related transport. The provision of care to home-based patients, as well as access to hospital-based care, was interrupted (chapter 6). Disruption intensified when the roof of the Victoria General Hospital in central Halifax was damaged, spurring a partial evacuation during the storm.[34] Loss of power meant that generators were needed for the safe storage of vaccines and other medical supplies that required refrigeration.[35]

The provincial government reported that Hurricane Juan "left the entire health care system, in affected areas, with a backlog of hundreds of surgeries and clinic appointments," overextending a system already grappling with long wait times.[36] The impact of the hurricane on health services was a theme in subsequent legislative discussions. Then minister of health Angus MacIsaac conceded, "Weeks and months after the trees and bushes are picked off the streets, and after windows and roofs are fixed, the effect of Juan will still be felt on the health care system. This impact reminds us just how much our health care workers do every day. Yet, while their extraordinary efforts continue, for those patients and their families who are waiting, I know that this is not an easy time for them."[37] Though fallen trees and power poles made compelling images, the enduring impacts on health care were less visible.

In the short-term, community health was also impacted. The prolonged lack of electricity affected food storage. As social support cheques were issued just before the hurricane struck, many households lost recently purchased groceries. In some neighbourhoods, residents hosted community barbecues to quickly use up food that required freezing and refrigeration. Officials were concerned about the risk of food-borne illness.[38] This risk was prevented in part because of proactive measures, such as setting up a food safety hotline and providing food vouchers of about $800,000 to low-income households. The Red Cross, in coordination with Community Services Nova Scotia, managed four shelters and assisted 30,000 people by providing water and meals. The province provided

$100,000 in emergency home repair assistance to low-income households.[39] At the same time as community health efforts were under way, crews worked to disentangle downed power lines from fallen trees.

The impacts of Juan were far greater than expected. Efforts to prevent damage reduced potential destruction. However, existing vulnerabilities, such as patients awaiting procedures and households with low-incomes, deepened. Some potential risks, such as food-borne illness, did not materialize but illustrate the possible cascading impacts of severe weather. Climate change compounds existing social, political, economic, and environmental vulnerabilities, as well as introducing new ones.[40] In Nova Scotia, the co-existence of an urban tree canopy and above-ground power infrastructure were key sources of pre-existing vulnerabilities to which I now turn.

ENTANGLEMENT

Throughout the city Tuesday, the sputter of chainsaws rang over streets choked with fallen trees and tangles of dead power lines as people continued to marvel at the hurricane's ferocity.

Donald McLeod[41]

Trees cover three-quarters of Nova Scotia. The province is home to Acadian forest, including northern white cedar, Jack pine, and eastern white pine. Some original old-growth forest remains in just nine pockets around the province, but most is new growth.[42] Forests, old and new, are home to black bears, red foxes, and snowshoe hares – just some examples of local wildlife.[43] Hurricane-force winds brought down trees and electrical power poles, entangling the human and non-human in a much more literal manner than usual, and thus hindering mobility. The storm rendered the everyday chaotic.

Hurricane Juan hit early enough in the fall that trees still had leaves that were buffeted by the hurricane-force winds. One property owner says, "We've had some great storms in the past, but the trees were full of leaves and were like big sails ... The gusts did the damage. The devastation is incredible."[44] A municipal planner observes that if the storm occurred later in the fall when there were fewer leaves "there wouldn't have been near that amount of damage."[45] Trees fell on vehicles and across roads. Power polls toppled resulting in widespread outages. Emergency manager

Figure 3.1 Fallen trees and power lines, Halifax, 2003

Mark states that the scale of treefall was "almost unimaginable ...
We're dealing with loss of critical infrastructure ... because the
trees were down you couldn't get fire trucks or police cars or
ambulances down certain streets."[46] Damage to the urban forest
canopy and provincial forestlands was extensive: trees toppled
and torn branches became projectiles. Mobile trees rendered residents immobile.

The resulting mix of leaves, branches, tree trunks, electrical wires,
and poles constituted major disorder. Meteorologist Susan states: "If
you've got trees and power lines together, that's a hell of a mess [and
that's] what happened with Hurricane Juan here. A big, big mess."[47]
Transit manager Chad recalls the sight: "Power lines, fallen trees, cables,
I mean it was just a mess ... It was just chaos all over the place."[48] A
transport manager recalls the changed landscape: "It just looked like a
bomb hit down there off the harbour. It was unbelievable. All those big
old trees down covering the whole road, and we had to detour around
another way."[49] The scale of damage was difficult to process.

In the aftermath, restoring electricity was the primary goal, followed
by clearing roads. The effort involved the Emergency Operations

Centre, Nova Scotia Power, police, and military, among others.[50] Three hundred power crews from Nova Scotia, New Brunswick, and Maine reconnected the electrical grid. Two thousand members of the Canadian Forces cleared roads.[51] An upside was the relatively warm weather that ensued. One power worker experienced both Hurricane Juan and the 1998 North American ice storm (chapter 2). He remarks of Juan: "The weather has been good – at least it's not forty-five below and people dying."[52] What transpired following Juan was a painstaking disentanglement of the ecological and technical, tree-by-tree and line-by-line, to reinstate the mobility status quo, despite its evident vulnerability to severe weather.

What officials viewed with equanimity as a difficult but necessary part of their jobs, community members met with grief. A powerful sense of loss surfaced as residents saw the damage to trees on their properties and in public green spaces. Such damage was starkly apparent in Amntu'kati/Point Pleasant Park, a popular recreational area for both humans and dogs in Halifax's South End. Founded in 1866 on unceded Mi'kma'ki territory, the park is protected from natural regeneration processes and was experiencing an insect epidemic. Municipal planner Katherine notes: "If you look at the urban forest and susceptibility – certainly, what you don't want is an even-aged stand with low biodiversity. What you want is something with a range of ages of trees, and also trees that are structurally sound ... a lot of the failures that we saw ... were the result of poor pruning practices."[53] The park was vulnerable not only because of its location in relation to the storm track but also due to other human factors.

A resident who lives near the park recalls the sound of the storm: "It sounded terrible ... like lumber cracking."[54] Author Donald McLeod describes the damage to the park. It "looks tattered and torn as if picked up by a giant and vigorously shaken."[55] In a *Chronicle Herald* article, city councillor Dawn Sloane shares her shock at the damage to the Public Gardens, a popular Victorian park in Halifax's centre: "It just seemed like all the greenery was gone."[56] The response to the loss of trees reveals the emotional connection between humans and the environment, particularly the appeal of parks and other green spaces. It is notable that older, higher-income neighbourhoods in Halifax, such as the South and West Ends, have far more trees than newer developments or lower-income communities. Therefore, while damage was significant, households and neighbourhoods of the former were able to clean up and recover more readily.

While damage to Point Pleasant Park was severe, damage to the nearby port was relatively minimal. A seawall and shed roof were damaged, though little else. Containers blown into the harbour were promptly recovered.[57] The port was functional within twenty-four hours of Hurricane Juan hitting. By contrast, Point Pleasant Park was closed to the public for eight months. The juxtaposition of the damage to the park and the relative lack of impact to the hardened coastal port infrastructure is notable. The experience of damage was highly variable and disproportionate to respective contributions to climate change in the sense that the port generates greenhouse gas emissions through marine shipping, while the trees in the park absorb carbon dioxide, mitigating climate impacts. Sources of ecological resilience, such as healthy urban forests and coastal buffers, need to be strengthened (chapter 8).

Influenced in part by the experience of Hurricane Juan, the Halifax Regional Municipality developed an *Urban Forest Master Plan* to manage the more than 700,000 trees on public property and to fill 90,000 vacant spots with diverse native species to achieve an average 40 per cent forest canopy across the city.[58] Other goals within the plan relating to Hurricane Juan impacts include pruning street trees every seven years to avoid damage to electrical infrastructure, using trees to decrease stormwater runoff in areas with a lot of pavement, prioritizing tree planting in neighbourhoods with fewer trees, and encouraging residents to plant food-producing trees on their properties.[59] In the immediate aftermath of Juan, however, the focus was on clearing streets so that essential services like public transit could resume operation.

IN TRANSIT

Most people, I think, in an urban area, once the buses start coming back out again, people start saying, 'Ah, well, we can get out and around.' And I think that's something we were quite focused on at the time.

Transit manager[60]

In the aftermath of Hurricane Juan, as the trees were painstakingly disentangled from the electrical grid, there was a focus on restoring public transit as an essential service. Seen as symbolic of normalcy, public transit emerged as a source of innovation and adaptability. There was relatively little physical damage to buses and ferries. One terminal was damaged: "We sustained a lot of damage to our Halifax Ferry Terminal, which kind of took the brunt of it. The [ramp] to the ferry was smashed up quite badly, so we had a lot of repairs there."[61] The focus was clearing roads to enable movement of buses. Transit manager Chad says, "The priority was to try to get things rolling, get the city operational."[62] Basic repairs were made just to get things up and running. "We had established, through some of our situation reports, that getting transit on the road was a priority because people would have some feeling of normalcy … 'Oh, well transit is running again, we're good. We're going to start coming back, right?'"[63] For transit users and non-transit users alike, seeing buses on the streets indicated that the city was once again on the move, that disrupted mobility was being restored. Alec observes that the return of buses serves to "bring commerce back, to bring people back to their sense of comfort, and also be an indication that if transit is running, then the primary roads are clear, which means public safety vehicles can get down them."[64] The movement and circulation of buses and ferries are part of the practical and visual rhythm of city life.[65]

In the face of confusion, transit was versatile. During and after the storm, buses were used for evacuation and temporary shelters. Two hundred and fifty residents of one apartment building found themselves homeless the night of the storm when the roof of their building was torn away. Buses were used as temporary shelter.[66] Alec, an emergency manager, recalls, "We went out in the storm to evacuate these people … hiding behind fire trucks because there was no safe place to be because the wind was that strong. It was blowing leaves off the trees, and the leaves they were actually wadding up like little mini bullets. There were garbage cans flying everywhere … Bus drivers came out and put them in buses … the buses backed up the road because there was no place to turn around."[67] Such work requires presence of mind, skill, and organization.

Buses were also used to transport cleanup crews: "The main component was to clear the roads and try to restore power at the same time. So, we had crews that were going around with [Nova Scotia] Power to try to get the trees and branches off the road … We did that quite effectively."[68] Transit buses and drivers emerged as a versatile and central component of the hurricane response and recovery efforts, shifting from moving the public to sheltering the public and transporting workers to restore normal mobility.[69]

The mobilization of the existing robust and versatile public transit system was a key practical and symbolic element in post-Juan recovery. Investments in public transit infrastructure and staff can be framed, in part, as investments in disaster response generally and climate change mitigation and adaptation specifically. In everyday contexts, buses as a form of mass transit are crucial to reducing carbon pollution. During Hurricane Juan, buses sheltered residents and transported work crews. In more extreme circumstances, buses and trained drivers provided a means to evacuate communities – a pronounced shift in purpose and scale from the normal operation of public transit.

A limited holiday service schedule was restored on main routes within approximately twenty-four hours of Juan hitting. Full transit service was restored four days later on 4 October. Provincially, all major roads were cleared and passable by 3 October, with a goal of clearing minor roads by 31 October, one month after Juan.[70] Clearing roads and restoring electricity occurred in tandem, with 95 per cent of utility customers reconnected by 3 October, and the remainder restored by 12 October.[71] At the same time as Nova Scotia was getting back to normal, it was also in a process of coming to terms with a new normal defined by disruptive events, such as extreme weather.

NEW NORMAL

We were involved in Swissair for months. We were involved in Hurricane Juan. We were involved in White Juan. We have one, I always say, every eighteen months.

Provincial risk manager[72]

In the years leading up to and following Hurricane Juan, Nova Scotia experienced diverse extreme events, ranging from environmental to technical to intentional.[73] The experiences highlighted Nova Scotia's exposure to risk, many of which are associated with what sociologist Anthony Giddens calls reflexive modernization in that they are human-made (chapter 1).[74] Further, many risks are transboundary, facilitated by global ecological mobilities. Hurricane Juan highlighted the risk of transport disruption – static infrastructure like roads, rail, and ferry terminals were particularly vulnerable to mobilities of wind and storm surges.

Table 3.1 Disruptive events impacting Nova Scotia, 1996–2004

Year	Event
2004	White Juan blizzard
2003	Hurricane Juan
2003	Bovine Spongiform Encephalopathy (BSE or mad cow disease)
2003	Spring floods
2002	Severe acute respiratory syndrome (SARS)
2001	9/11 flight diversions
2000	Brown spruce longhorn beetle epidemic
1999	Kosovo refugee arrival
1998	Swissair crash
1996	Hurricane Hortense

One of Canada's national newspapers, the *Globe and Mail*, dubbed 2003 as Canada's "year of affliction," referencing events such as the British Columbia forest fires, the North American blackout, mad cow disease, the SARS respiratory infection, and Hurricane Juan.[75] Nova Scotia's provincial paper, the *Chronicle Herald*, remarked on the number of events that Nova Scotians managed in recent years and the competency they were developing for "coolly coping in the face of adversity," from plane crashes to floods.[76]

On 2 September 1998, Swissair Flight 111 out of New York crashed eight kilometres off the coast of Nova Scotia, near the fishing village of Peggys Cove. All 229 passengers and crew were lost. The crash was attributed to a technical failure. In 1999, another form of movement under duress, facilitated by planes, occurred as refugees fleeing war-torn Kosovo landed in provinces across Canada, including Nova Scotia. On 11 September 2001, passenger planes were hijacked and used as weapons in the United States, eliciting ripple effects that impacted the world. North American airspace was closed, and 225 planes bound for the United States were diverted to Canadian airports. A large-scale response was mobilized to provide food and shelter for passengers. Paula, a non-governmental organization representative, exclaims,

Who would think 8,000 people from 44 planes [would arrive]
in Halifax because of 9/11? ... Who would even think that
Canada would say we would agree to receive 5,000 refugees,
and that Nova Scotia would take 2,500? And then after these
events saying, "Well, that's once in a lifetime. That's never going
to happen again." And then you see events like Superstorm
Sandy and then you see events like the tsunami in Japan ...
So what it says is this is more and more possible, and that
Superstorm Sandy could have been easily Halifax instead of
New York and New Jersey.[77]

Due to the succession of diverse disruptions, the sense of such events
being unique or "one-offs" eroded, shaping disaster response culture
in Nova Scotia.

During the same period of disruptive events, the transmission
of disease was a pressing concern. In 2000, there was an outbreak
of the brown spruce longhorn beetle, an insect that attacks healthy
trees by preventing the transport of food to tree roots. It is suspected that the invasive species was unintentionally introduced to
Nova Scotia through wooden packing crates offloaded in Halifax.
Provincial forestry lands as well as Point Pleasant Park, which
is adjacent to the port, were quarantined. Among humans, there
was an outbreak of SARS, severe acute respiratory syndrome, in
2002/03. The outbreak originated in China, spreading to thir-
ty-seven countries. In Canada, there were 438 suspected cases and
44 deaths.[78] The outbreak was a source of concern for the general population, as well as frontline health-care workers. In 2003,
an outbreak of bovine spongiform encephalopathy (BSE), also
known as mad cow disease, threatened human health and the beef
industry.[79] The Canadian epicentre of the crisis was Alberta, and
ramifications were felt across the country, including Nova Scotia
where beef exports declined.

In addition to transport, refugee, and disease-related events,
weather events posed challenges. Hurricane Hortense (1996) and
spring floods (2003) incurred $3 million and $10 million in damages, respectively.[80] In winter 2004, just six months after Hurricane
Juan, a record-breaking blizzard dubbed White Juan hit Nova Scotia.
While municipalities declared states of emergency due to Hurricane
Juan, it was White Juan that prompted the Nova Scotia government
to declare its first ever province-wide state of emergency.[81]

Mobility figures differently in each of these events. The Swissair crash relates most directly to conventional notions of mobility as human transport, while in the case of 9/11 airplanes were a tool of terrorism. For refugees from Kosovo, movement was a welcome escape from adversity combined with the stress of forced migration. In terms of BSE and SARS, spread of disease from animal-to-animal, human-to-human, or from animal-to-human was a concern. In the case of the beetle epidemic, the focus was on containing its spread through the enforcement of quarantines, while in the case of the spring floods water was the focus of containment.

The overall effect of the frequency of disruptive events and managing the unexpected is both a heightened awareness of the province's vulnerability to a range of disasters and an increased familiarity with, and competence in, dealing with disaster. An RCMP superintendent observes, "We've dealt with multiple tragedies, so it's fortunate and unfortunate that it's second nature now to kick into emergency mode ... It's fortunate that we have that ability, it's unfortunate the way we acquired it."[82] Nova Scotians are developing a necessary, albeit undesired, skill set. The need for disaster preparedness will increase as climate emergency escalates in tandem with the growth of global mobility.

Looking Back

There is a historical dimension to Nova Scotia's disaster experience. In 1917, Halifax was the site of one of the largest, and certainly most destructive, human-made explosions prior to the development of nuclear weapons. Two vessels, a French ammunition ship, the *Mont-Blanc*, and a Norwegian relief ship, the *Imo*, collided in Halifax Harbour. Approximately 2,000 people died and 9,000 were injured. Much of the city was destroyed. Following from sociologist Ulrich Beck's work on emancipatory catastrophism, the Halifax Explosion was "emancipatory" in three ways. First, it led to the creation of domestic, as compared to wartime, disaster prevention, preparedness, response, and recovery efforts. Second, in an era before socialized medicine, the Massachusetts-Halifax Relief Committee set up public health clinics from 1918 to 1924 to improve community health.[83] Third, due to the death of tramline operators, women were hired for the first time in this role. Though after World War I, women were required to give up their jobs, illustrating that emancipatory change is not necessarily enduring or linear.[84]

Figure 3.2 Damage to containers, Halifax Port Authority, 2003

A report on the provincial government's response to Juan states that it "mounted the greatest emergency response effort in Nova Scotia since the Halifax Explosion of 1917."[85] Political scientists Malcolm Grieve and Lori Turnbull note that officials continue to look to the Halifax Explosion for "lessons in the challenges of sound emergency preparation. In particular, the city must prepare for the hazards associated with port, rail and road transport."[86] A municipal staff person likens the damage to trees caused by Hurricane Juan to that experienced a century earlier: "This is quite possibly the worst damage to our urban canopy since the Halifax Explosion. It's that significant and that order of magnitude."[87] Knowledge and memory of disaster, even in the absence of direct experience, leave an impression. The climate crisis brings new heightened complexity to the spectre of disaster.

The experience of storms shifted because of Hurricane Juan. Goyette writes of a before time, where "all we could imagine losing was a limb."[88] Health geographer Ashlee Cunsolo and environmental social scientist Neville Ellis say that such "grief and mourning illuminate our relational ties and fundamental dependency upon complex ecological communities and, in turn, our ethical and political responsibilities to these systems."[89] Now officials and residents were confronted with a whole new scale of damage and an inkling of the experience of grief that the climate crisis portends if significant and rapid mitigation and adaptation measures are not taken (chapters 8 and 9).

Government Response

The cumulative impact of such diverse disasters was a theme in the provincial legislative assembly in the year following Hurricane Juan. The Progressive Conservative Party was in power, with the left-wing New Democratic Party in official Opposition. John MacDonell, member of the Opposition for Hants East, spoke to the cumulative effects of BSE, spring floods, and Hurricane Juan on agriculture, calling for sectoral support.[90] Likewise, Howard Epstein, member of the Opposition for Halifax Chebucto, addressed the risks identified by the EMO: "more forest fires, more flooding, more tidal surges, and severe winter weather thanks to climate change. EMO has also predicted that Nova Scotia will experience a flu pandemic in the next few years. The agency is also concerned over security issues."[91] This statement, which with the benefit of hindsight reads like a checklist, indicates the increasingly complex and compound nature of disaster management.

In response to successive disruptive events, the physical and economic security of residents became a governance concern. Key sources of resilience include cultural awareness of the need to prepare for severe weather events, that is, to batten down the hatches; the creative use of public transit as both emergency transport and shelter as well as a symbol of a reinstatement of mobility; and the coordinated and collaborative approach to disaster management in Nova Scotia facilitated by both formal and informal relationships.

A key source of vulnerability is the precarious co-presence of urban and rural forest canopies with the electrical grid. Given the damage to the electrical grid during Hurricane Juan, it is notable that discussion of burying power lines was not prevalent in legislative debates or media coverage. Nova Scotia Power notes that burying power lines costs ten times more than above-ground infrastructure and requires disruption to streets for installation, an issue noted by other

Figure 3.3 Washed-out train tracks with fuel tankers, 2003

Canadian municipalities.[92] With more frequent disasters cost-benefit calculations will change; tipping points will shift. Safety concerns surrounding service provision, such as ensuring an aging population need not evacuate their homes, may instigate regulatory requirements for underground power lines.[93] Other sources of vulnerability include static infrastructure, such as roads and railways; reliance on finite and carbon-intensive energy sources for fuel; and reliance on electricity to access fuel and the lack of generators given this reliance (chapter 6). Mobility disruptions exacerbate pre-existing vulnerabilities, such as the movement of community members with physical challenges and lengthy hospital wait times.

Longer-term planning was also influenced by these disruptive events. Given their diversity, an adaptable all-hazards approach is now employed by emergency management officials. This means that the same protocols are used regardless of the nature of the incident: "emergency managers regard terrorist emergencies as they do any other hazard, yielding the same demands for shelter, food, and communications as weather or accident-related emergencies."[94] Reflecting on Hurricane Juan, an emergency manager states, "It reinforced how we do things ... The process hasn't changed. The actual how we get information, how we make decisions, and how we catalogue that – that hasn't changed because it was sound to begin with."[95] Rather, through iteration, emergency response procedures are updated and fine-tuned with each event.[96]

One aspect of the emergency planning system in Nova Scotia that is credited with its efficacy is the location of federal, provincial, and municipal emergency officials in one building.[97] Physical proximity facilitates informal connections and swift consultations, increasing the efficiency of decision-making, as it is easier to confer with counterparts.[98] Another emergency manager attributes success to autonomy in decision-making: "We have full empowerment to make decisions and create activities to move a disaster, a remediation of a disaster, forward. That's really the big thing that we have."[99] Officials were satisfied with available disaster response processes and mechanisms.

A review of EMO responses conducted after Juan identified three broad lessons. First, improve the use of staff and resources. For example, justice department employees are licensed to operate large vehicles and could transport residents in case of disaster. Second, improve operational protocols. For instance, identify backup sites for emergency operation centres. Third, improve communications by providing callers to emergency hotlines with hold time estimates.[100] Additionally, since 2001, the Canadian government has directed attention toward border issues and international security, delegating responsibility for extreme weather-related events to provinces and municipalities.[101] This includes responding to the ever-increasing threat posed by climate change.

CLIMATE CHANGE

Only a fool would act on the supposition that it would not happen again.

Canada Department of National Defence official[102]

Many people who attended a post-storm debriefing session suggested that "Hurricane Juan was a 'hundred-year storm' in name only – that with a changing global climate and warming ocean currents, a repeat was possible, if not likely."[103] The influence of Hurricane

Juan on future policies and responses was immediately apparent. In the legislature, member of the Opposition for Dartmouth East, Joan Massey, drew links between Hurricane Juan and climate change, challenging the government's response:

> Mr. Speaker, we have been told that climate change could lead to an increasing severity in these storms. In expectation, we should be working with Nova Scotia Power to safeguard our infrastructure. In response to 1998's massive ice storm, both Quebec and Manitoba developed environmental targets. Manitoba took steps to upgrade its transmission systems. Mr. Minister, has your department assessed how we can be better environmentally protected in case of another storm?[104]

The minister of environment responded by stating the government's intentions to work with Nova Scotia Power. Although improvements were made, examples of which include retiring aging equipment and replacing older power poles, issues of vulnerability and reliability persist.[105]

Climate Plan 2009

Hurricane Juan is referenced on the first page of the provincial *Climate Change Action Plan* (2009), released six years after the event:

> When it comes to climate change, Nova Scotia faces a triple threat:
>
> · Because most of the energy we use comes from fossil fuels, we have an unusually long way to go in curbing the emissions that cause climate change.
> · We're at the northern end of the Atlantic hurricane track, where more storms similar to Hurricane Juan could hit us as the planet warms.
> · With 7600 km of coastline, we are exceptionally vulnerable to rising sea levels caused by climate change.[106]

The plan addresses the transport sector, focusing on increasing vehicle efficiency, promoting sustainable modes of transport such as public transit, and designing more compact communities to reduce the need for transport. It asks fundamental questions that strike at the heart of societal reliance on mobility: "Are Nova Scotians willing to move closer to work or public transportation? ... How can we redesign communities to minimize the need for transportation? Can more efficient urban layouts for our towns and cities be encouraged by rezoning?"[107] These are bold questions given the reliance on fossil-fuelled automobility.

However, such transformative questions are not reflected in action items listed in the plan. Six actions pertain to vehicle efficiency, such as implementing maximum speeds for semi-trailers, and three actions pertain to the expansion of sustainable transportation projects. None of the actions focus on land-use planning. Translating intention to practice is challenging, especially in the context of goals that involve several provincial departments and municipalities.

One of the actions resulting from the plan was to develop a *Sustainable Transportation Strategy*. Released in 2013, the strategy does not reference Hurricane Juan specifically but takes an integrated approach that addresses climate change, energy, and health. The strategy focuses on increasing vehicle efficiency, as well as more transformative mobility shifts, such as a small infrastructure grant program based on a "vision that all trips under two kilometres in Nova Scotia communities can be made using sustainable transport modes."[108] Seventy-five projects received a few million dollars over five years – a figure dwarfed by investment in road infrastructure, which runs into the hundreds of millions annually.[109] Furthermore, freight transport and air travel are not addressed by the *Sustainable Transportation Strategy*, illustrating significant strategic gaps in terms of decarbonizing transport and promoting transport resilience in the context of disaster.

Climate Change Reduction Act 2021

In 2021, the government of Nova Scotia released an *Environmental Goals and Climate Change Reduction Act* with a new climate plan to be released in 2022. Since Nova Scotia met its 2020 target of reducing emissions by 10 per cent below 1990 levels, the act commits the province to reducing emissions 53 per cent below 2005 levels by 2030 and to achieve net zero-carbon by 2050. Related to an ecological approach to mobilities, measures include developing an active transportation network "accessible for all ages and all abilities in 65% of the Province's communities" and conserving a minimum of 20 per cent of land and water by 2030.[110]

These goals need to be reconciled with parallel efforts to improve transport infrastructure and expand trade to bolster the economy: "free trade with Europe and expanding markets in Asia offer exciting opportunities to leverage our advantages as a global trader if we can shift to higher value products and build stronger trade linkages."[111] Nova Scotia's trade is positioned to grow both within and beyond provincial borders. Given how ships are currently fuelled, there is an uncomfortable contradiction between economic goals of expanding market share and environmental goals of reducing greenhouse gas emissions. This separation works to maintain the idea that increasing mobility is unproblematic in relation to discourses about climate change.[112]

Of note, the act refers to Mi'kmaw intellectual traditions demonstrating a new approach to governance that bridges Indigenous and settler perspectives. For example, Netukulimk refers to the "physical, emotional, cognitional, social and spiritual relationships a person has with everything, including the physical features of the land, the rhythms and cycles and patterns of Wskitqamu (Mother Earth), and all her living beings and nonliving things."[113] Engaging with this tradition would allow me as a researcher to deepen my conceptualization of an ecological approach to mobilities and generate new approaches to climate routing (chapter 8).

In sum, Hurricane Juan brought mobility to the fore in multiple ways, from the mobility of the storm itself to the immobilities caused by ensuing destruction. At the local scale, public transit was an important means and measure of mobility. The inundation of numerous large-scale disruptive events led to officials and residents of Nova Scotia developing capacity in disaster response. The next chapter details how, for some, an approaching storm and the resulting damage are charismatic, for others, catastrophic.

4

Charismatic Mobilities

We unearthed fear that day, our first act of real
archeology. Understand, at that point, maps charted roads

and the humble footpaths between rumours crooked
with love. The ocean took up the most room

with its tidal pull and tentacled beasts inventing
their own recipes. Some days we knew we were nothing

but ingredients, other days we felt like honoured guests.

Sue Goyette, "Four," in *Ocean*

WHALES AND OWLS

Max Weber described charisma as a gift of grace. In the political
upheaval that followed World War I, Weber was concerned with
the ethics of responsible governance.[1] He developed a theory that
human charisma, what he calls charismatic authority, is one of three
conditions, along with traditional and legal authority, that allows
the leader of a country to use force in the name of the greater good.[2]
Charisma, in this case, refers to traits like intelligence and skills like
rhetoric that make an individual exceptional and influential in the
eyes of peers.

A century later, climate change poses an ethical governance challenge on a global scale. Geographer Jamie Lorimer observes that
flagship species in the United Kingdom have non-human charisma.
Certain animals, birds, and insects are popular and act as boundary

objects that broaden human ethical considerations when addressing issues such as biodiversity and climate change.[3] The ecological term *charismatic megafauna* refers to large and recognizable species that humans find compelling, such as the iconic panda used in the World Wildlife Fund logo. In Atlantic Canada whales are such a species. They evoke an emotional response in humans that some environmental organizations leverage for conservation purposes to benefit entire ecosystems, including less charismatic species.[4]

Lorimer quotes one British birder's encounter with a flagship bird species, a short-eared owl. Naturalist and author Mark Cocker recalls his first-hand experience in detail. The owl had an

> indefinable quality of beauty and strangeness. It floated away across the moor and then suddenly wheeled around and turned towards us, its silent and loosely bowed wings knitting a course through the up draughts in long exaggerated beats ... A short-eared owl had entered my life and for those moments, as it swallowed me up with its piercing eyes, I had entered the life of an owl.[5]

Lorimer describes how such "interspecies epiphanies" leave viewers "reterritorialized."[6] Such encounters shape and shift what it means to be human.

Guided by an ecological approach to mobilities that emphasizes the contingent relations between human and non-human mobilities, in this chapter I introduce the concepts of charismatic and catastrophic mobilities. If the flight of an owl is an expression of charismatic mobility for some, then the invisible movements of the COVID-19 virus are a catastrophic mobility for many others. Likewise, the sight of a mother and pup walrus resting on an ice floe in the Arctic Ocean is an expression of charismatic mobility, while a dozen walruses fighting for space on increasingly scarce ice sheets is catastrophic.

The concepts of charismatic and catastrophic mobilities are useful in describing and thinking through the experience of extreme weather and, by extension, an ecological approach to mobilities. Charisma and catastrophe are not dichotomies but rather different experiences and interpretations of a given event. Just as a polar bear is charismatic at a distance, it is dangerous in proximity. Similarly, Goyette describes "tidal pull and tentacled beasts," two contrasting experiences of the ocean – on one hand allure, appeal, and magnetism, on the other hand risk, threat, and calamity.[7] Charisma is compelling, catastrophe is concerning. These encounters shape and reshape humans and their movement.

This chapter has four sections. First, I describe charismatic mobility focusing on the case of Hurricane Juan. Next, I describe how K'jipuktuk/Halifax residents governed their own mobility to navigate a transformed mobility landscape. Then, I describe catastrophic mobility, including the experiences of hurricane evacuees in Bulbancha/New Orleans and Puerto Rico. Finally, I discuss climate mobilities within and beyond national borders.

CHARISMATIC MOBILITY

In the cases of Hurricanes Juan and Igor, people were drawn to watch and feel the approaching storms, as well as to explore the aftermath. The charismatic pull that some people feel is an expression of what biologist E.O. Wilson called biophilia, the love of life.[8] The wind and waves were, for some, a siren call. Anthropologist Tim Ingold reflects on the nature of wind: "Almost always, it is in a state of flux. Sometimes these fluxes are barely perceptible; at other times they are so strong they can uproot trees and bring down buildings. They can power mills and send ships around the world."[9] The capacity of hurricanes to generate strong winds that make it difficult, if not impossible, to move in controlled ways is central to their charisma. Likewise, Goyette writes of craving the ocean,

We'd drive for miles to get a glimpse
of it because, let's face it, it revitalized the part of us
we kept rooting for, that apple seed of energy that defied
multiple choice career options.[10]

The vastness of the ocean, a source of its charisma, puts human concerns in perspective.

Such novelty is even more resonant in the context of the Anthropocene characterized by climate instability. While carbon dioxide molecules released through fossil-fuelled mobility constitute imperceptible and mundane mobilities, their cumulative effects result in catastrophic mobility, such as more intense hurricanes, floods, and heat waves, as well as thawing Arctic permafrost and melting ice caps. The chronic use and disposal of single-use plastics like straws and cutlery that then result in massive garbage gyres in remote ocean locations are another example of mundane mobility culminating in catastrophic mobility.

Reflecting on the interface of humans and weather, Ingold observes: "To feel the wind is not to make external, tactile contact with our surroundings but to *mingle with* them."[11] Goyette describes a similar but more imbalanced relationship,

> Imagine, the ocean *basting* us. But how often
> had we walked into its salted air then licked our arms
> to taste it later? We were being seasoned. Lightly.[12]

Humans shift from actor to object, aware of our mortality and, in many instances, powerlessness. According to Goyette, in relationship with the ocean, depending on the circumstances, one might feel like an "ingredient" or an "honoured guest."[13] Leading up to Juan, people reported being able to taste salt in the air.[14] Salt in the air mingles with taste buds, exemplifying political theorist Jane Bennett's call for blurred boundaries between the external environment and the internal body.[15]

The phenomenon of charismatic mobility can also be thought of as a charismatic mingling. Humans navigate a world continuously "in formation."[16] For some, such as urban dwellers, the opportunity to feel the power of the weather – in contrast to static office environments and ubiquitous screens – holds novel appeal. Disruption might be welcomed. One *Telegram* editorialist describes how being in Hurricane Igor, "without phone and electricity meant enjoying the uncharacteristic quiet, giving us even more excuse to have romantic candlelight dinners, and seeing the brightness of the stars, undiminished by light pollution. How, sometimes, it's in the midst of swirling confusion that we can see things most clearly."[17] For some, disruption offers a reprieve from the routines and pressures of everyday life.

Watching storms illustrates how humans are both drawn to observe unusual and charismatic mobility and to undertake mobility to achieve this end. Hurricane Juan brought mobility to the fore, from the charismatic mobility of the storm itself to the immobilities caused by entangled trees and power lines. For one person a hurricane is humbling, for another it is a playground. Surfers in Mi'kma'ki/Nova Scotia anticipate big storms and the waves and adrenaline rush that they promise. In terms of moving both for transport and recreation, there is a fine line to negotiate between safety and precarity, exhilaration and hazard.[18]

Charismatic mobility centres on the appeal of ecological mobilities. On the night of Hurricane Juan, the EMO issued an advisory to stay indoors. For some, the charismatic experience of the storm prevailed, and a small but visible number of people were drawn to coastal areas like the Halifax waterfront to experience the force of the storm. The atmosphere was like a "carnival."[19] As the hurricane approached, there was "almost a celebratory mood ... even as Juan was picking up speed over the Atlantic on a collision course with the Nova Scotia capital. People flocked to the beaches to watch the huge waves pushed ashore by the pressure of the approaching storm."[20] Environmental scientist Karl Benediktsson and colleagues describe the appeal of feeling "mortal danger with a certainty of being safe."[21] The approaching hurricane provided an opportunity for people to feel the power of the ecological, while at the time feeling sheltered, albeit misleadingly, by an urban environment.

A Nova Scotia transport manager recalls the precarious movement of residents: "We all saw the images of ... young adults down on the waterfront with their shirts flapping open and the water breaking over them. That's not safe to do. We shake our heads; at the same time, we see people standing near the waves down at Peggys Cove. People die that way."[22] Peggys Cove is a scenic coastal area in Nova Scotia known for impressive waves that, on occasion, sweep people, often tourists unfamiliar with the unexpected power of the ocean, into the water. In Ktaqmkuk/Newfoundland, the equivalent is Cape Spear, a headland which is the easternmost point in Canada, where the urge to explore lures people past warning signs (chapter 5).

In Halifax, one person describes leaving a pub and his subsequent precarious navigation of a downtown street in the hours before Juan made landfall: "Out on Barrington [Street], the top of a streetlamp rattles down the street. Venus Envy's sign breaks free from its chains and crashes onto the pavement ... the wind rips my glasses off my face. Passers-by stop to help me search for them. Suddenly there's an awful noise and a hail of debris. As we dive into an ATM [Automated Teller Machine] for cover, fragments of the Green Lantern building's roof slam into the Plexiglas."[23] Just as the storm's force exceeded the expectations of transport and emergency professionals, so too were the expectations of this pedestrian surpassed. The experience of the storm shifted from novelty to hazard. "Ocean Playground," the slogan on Nova Scotian vehicle licence plates, takes on a more worrying tenor in the context of climate change as seen in Halifax's pre- and post-storm landscape (chapter 3).

CHARISMATIC IMMOBILITY

Wind, waves, and rain are charismatic mobilities, which become charismatic immobilities when they reach a scale that disrupts human mobility. Charismatic immobility is a counterpart to charismatic mobility and refers to blockages caused by, in this case, hurricane impacts such as fallen trees and flooded rivers. It includes damage wrought by a fast-moving hurricane as well as a slow-moving iceberg that blocks the entrance to a Newfoundland harbour, hindering marine transport.

Just as hurricanes constitute charismatic mobility, the after-effects – impassable roads, blocked sidewalks, displaced boats – can for some constitute charismatic immobility. The transformed landscape is a source of obstacle and spectacle. A *Chronicle Herald* reporter observed, "Halifax was made up of two main groups Monday: those who walked the streets to see what they could see, and those who stayed at home to see what they could [chain]saw. In the heavily treed west and south ends, camera-toting gawkers exchanged tips on where to take in the most spectacular damage. 'Have you seen Vernon Street?' asked one. 'You've got to go over there.'"[24] The landscape was both a spectacle and a work site.

This is a form of disaster tourism or sightseeing. Disaster tourism ranges from visiting the ancient ruins of Pompeii in Italy to touring the impacts of Hurricane Katrina in New Orleans. Such disaster tourism is motivated by novelty, personal bonds, intellectual and cultural interest, and desire to connect to history or history-in-the-making.[25] Some Nova Scotia residents travelled by foot and by car to observe and assess the damage in their neighbourhoods and, where possible, travelled to even harder hit neighbourhoods. Hundreds of residents gathered outside Halifax's historic Public Gardens to witness the damage.[26] The response to the loss of trees – awe, disbelief, grief – illustrates the emotional connection between humans and the environment, as does the clarion call of the charismatic mobility of storms. There is an element of wonder at the

power of the environment and the vulnerability of human infrastructure and systems, as well as of the landscape itself.

In the case of Nova Scotia, as mentioned, winds brought down
trees and power poles blocking roads in an arboreal and electrical
entanglement. With the blockage of streets, many forms of mobility –
bus and ferry, car and ambulance, walking and cycling – proved
challenging. Despite requests from emergency services to stay clear
of the roads to prevent injury and allow cleanup crews to carry out
their work, what occurred was a persistent, albeit more localized
and limited human mobility. Emergency officials contended with
blocked streets that prevented the movement of emergency vehicles,
as well as the mobility of residents, whose purpose ranged from
surveying property damage, consulting with neighbours, accessing
goods and services, helping out, and exploring.

For some the storm was charismatic, at least initially. Between
the scale and duration of storm impacts, others grew weary of disrupted mobility within a few days – an experience echoed later on by
pandemic lockdowns. Experiences varied based on diverse factors,
including access to mobility and electricity. Donald McLeod writes
of how, in the hours after Juan, one woman who used a wheelchair
required the assistance of two strangers to carry her up six floors to
her apartment, as the elevator was not functioning.[27] While McLeod
does not speak to the quality of this particular experience – it may
have resulted in a sense of community – it is easy to imagine that
multiple such experiences could be wearying.

GOVERNMOBILITY

Preceding Hurricane Juan, at 9:25 pm then mayor of the Halifax
Regional Municipality Peter Kelly declared a state of emergency.[28]
The main directive centred on immobility, that is, to stay at home
and keep off the roads. A state of emergency has several practical implications for human mobility, including curfews and travel
bans. Provincial risk manager Alec comments, "The powers that the
declaration gives you are fairly extensive ... You don't enter into it
lightly."[29] Declaring a state of emergency allows a municipality or
province to order an evacuation of a given area, control or prohibit
travel to an area during certain hours, go on land without a warrant,
recruit qualified workers, and implement controls to prevent price

gouging. Financially, declaring a state of emergency is a necessary step in the process of claiming federal disaster relief funds through the *Disaster Financial Assistance Agreement.*[30] A state of emergency aims to ensure the safety of residents by creating time and space to reconnect transport and electrical networks.

In the case of Hurricane Juan, officials opted to issue voluntary warnings rather than compulsory curfews and mobility restrictions. In advance of the storm, targeted evacuations were ordered for residents living in coastal areas from urban Halifax to the rural communities of Clam Harbour and Sambro.[31] As well, residents of an apartment building and hospital damaged during the storm were evacuated. One non-governmental organization representative, Susan, reflects on the need for adequate shelters: "One of the learned lessons ... was to ensure that in the future the pre-positioned, pre-designated shelters would be on generated power. Because how can you even feed people if they're in the dark, and you've got ... volunteers with flashlights?"[32] The trauma of being forced to evacuate your home only to land in an uncomfortable, dark, and stressful shelter, for many, extinguishes any charisma attached to the storm.

In Halifax, in the days following Hurricane Juan, many residents countered official efforts to curb mobility, navigating disrupted mobility to meet a range of needs. Judging by the low injury and mortality rates, residents were successful. A post-storm debriefing attributed the limited injuries and fatalities to "good luck, good timing, and the good sense of Nova Scotians."[33] A *Chronicle Herald* reporter describes with pride how community members governed their own mobility:

> At times like this, we find what we are made of ... We find that people will drive carefully and patiently through intersections that don't have [functioning] traffic lights. We find that young [people] will clear tangled brush in the rain without being asked ... We find that people will put up warning signs and hang reflector tape from dangerous wires ... We find that we are made of something good.[34]

Official calls for immobility or limited mobility did not reflect the needs and compulsions of the population, though they may have set an appropriate tenor of caution that residents incorporated into their movements.

Governmobility means deciding for oneself if, and how, to move. Geographer Jørgen Ole Bærenholdt introduced the term to explore how mobility is governed.[35] Understanding the interaction of governance, self-regulation, and mobility is useful in analyzing states of disruption and emergency, as seen in geographer Peter Adey's work on emergency mobility.[36] In Nova Scotia, governmobility occurred with residents treating states of emergency as suggestions tempered by their own needs and contexts. In Newfoundland, the scramble by residents and officials alike to improvise and repurpose mobility was an expression of governmobility (chapter 5). Governmobility was shaped in both regions by the declaration of a state of emergency, allowing officials, to impose exceptional restrictions, if needed, on the movement of residents, such as curfews and evacuations. Two spheres overlapped: relying on the common sense of residents and enacting extraordinary regulatory measures. In the middle ground, a form of disaster governmobility was negotiated, highlighting how residents navigate disrupted mobility. While everyday mobility also involves ongoing negotiation between common sense and regulations, risks are heightened in the context of disaster governmobility.

Governmobility is an adaptation of Michel Foucault's *governmentality*. Governmentality refers to how a state safeguards the population and manages the behaviour of its citizens. Foucault likens it to the governance of a ship, including taking care of the ship, its sailors, and its cargo.[37] Unlike a ship, perhaps, governmentality focuses on persuasive rather than coercive means of governing.[38] Through governmentality the population internalizes rules of ideal behaviour, managing their own conduct: "human practices have been institutionalized with certain understandings and routines, whereby the population governs itself."[39] The population shifts from being passive recipients of protection to active participants, "defending society" against threats such as disease transmission.[40] Climate change poses just such a threat. For Foucault, political representatives are responsible for the management of the environment, that is, the entanglement of the geographical, climatic, and physical dynamics upon which the population relies.[41] Governmentality, with its focus on the regulation of mobile subjects, is useful in the analysis of liminal states of disruption and emergency that characterize acute events, such as hurricanes or chronic climate-related migration.[42]

In everyday contexts there is a negotiation between self-regulation and state regulation of mobility, such as deciding what speed to drive, whether to use a crosswalk or jaywalk, and whether to cycle on the road or sidewalk. In the face of extreme events, such negotiation or governmobility also occurs but may be more visible or consequential. Declaring a state of emergency, as was done in the cases of Hurricanes Juan and Igor, allows the state to impose coercively exceptional restrictions on the movement of residents, such as enforcing curfews. Community members negotiated their own mobility. The governmobility of residents and the mobility limitations imposed by a state of emergency are a source of both resilience and vulnerability. Generally, Halifax residents, enticed by charismatic mobility of the storm and charismatic immobility of storm impacts, and also motivated to meet basic daily needs and assist with recovery, successfully navigated the disrupted post-storm mobility landscape.[43]

Emergency officials endeavoured to manage not only the movement caused by the storm, such as fallen trees and electrical lines but also the mobility of humans drawn to experience the approaching storm and observe its aftermath. A further complication was the risk of electrocution that fallen power poles presented. A police officer expresses frustration at having to assist people who put themselves at risk by venturing into unsafe conditions: "Despite the many warnings we put out through the media to stay home, stay off the streets unless absolutely necessary ... You're still going to get those that are going to challenge that and come out."[44] Isabelle, a resident, recalls the tension between the messages conveyed by emergency officials to stay off the roads to permit clearing and the behaviour of residents: "There were so many downed trees, and ... power wires. Whether ... the streets were passable or not, definitely the message from the provincial authorities and EMO was 'People stay home so we can clear this,' and urging people not to walk around and not to bike around, so as not to run into live wires. *No one really listened to that*" (emphasis added).[45] Many people were compelled to assess, explore, connect, and access goods and services. Isabelle recalls regularly trekking to a friend's house to get a hot shower, travel deemed vital at an individual level if not by officials.

The owner of a taxi company, Tom, reflects on subjective distinctions between essential and nonessential mobility. A key component of the taxi business is transporting health workers to hospitals and care workers to private homes. The company endeavoured to carry on this work in the storm aftermath. Tom contrasts this with the demand for inessential mobility: "How many people all of a sudden decide they want to go out shopping [chuckles] ... It's unbelievable ... They figure [the mall] won't be very busy ... But a lot of people that take cabs, they don't own their own vehicles ... they don't know what it's like to be out there driving during that kind of stuff."[46] The impacts of Hurricane Juan induced human movement at the same time it repressed it, streets blocked by fallen trees and power poles worked in opposition to an instinct to explore the changed landscape. There is a balance to target in selecting the appropriate mix of persuasive and coercive measures within a state of emergency.

This involves permitting governmobility where possible, while also ensuring the safety of residents. Sociologist Mimi Sheller addresses the need for a finer-grained approach to mobility justice, as the specific context or policy is experienced differently by different groups. It is important to ask: "Who moves? Who is displaced? Who benefits?"[47] In addition, there are questions of timing: who moves first? last? most? Although research is under way on the intersection of gender, race, class, age, ability, and citizenship status with disrupted mobility, more is needed. For example, in Canada, researchers affiliated with the Centre for Community Disaster Research at Mount Royal University study emergency evacuation protocols for women escaping male violence and the links between traditional masculinity, resource dependence, and disaster recovery.[48]

A mass evacuation was not considered in the case of Halifax.[49] Evacuation is an extreme measure officials use sparingly. Whereas voluntary mobility motivated by a desire to observe the storm and its damage is charismatic, forced mobility or immobility is stressful.[50] Given the peninsular geography of both Halifax and Nova Scotia, large-scale evacuation poses a major logistical challenge.[51] Further, the isthmus that connects Nova Scotia to the neighbouring province of New Brunswick is a significant transport and trade corridor that is narrow, subsiding, and susceptible to flooding.[52] Along with permanent retreat from coastal areas, skill in organizing temporary evacuations will be necessary as extreme weather increases.

CATASTROPHIC MOBILITY

Here I shift from charismatic to catastrophic mobilities. These are examples of where the impacts of severe weather tip into traumatic and permanently changed ecological and social states. Catastrophic mobilities are intense disruptions that "shatter" the familiar.[53] I profile two cases: Hurricane Katrina in New Orleans and Hurricane Maria in Puerto Rico. This is not to say that there were not traumatic and catastrophic dimensions of Hurricane Juan and Igor: lives, homes, and jobs were lost. However, the storms discussed in this section are Category 5 Atlantic Ocean hurricanes, as compared to Hurricanes Igor and Juan, which rated Category 1 and 2 respectively, providing insight into the scale of devastation wrought by the most severe hurricanes. Category 5, as currently measured, is defined by sustained winds over 252 kilometres per hour. The US National Hurricane Center describes the impact of such storms: "Catastrophic damage will occur. A high percentage of framed homes will be destroyed, with total roof failure and wall collapse. Fallen trees and power poles will isolate residential areas. Power outages will last for *weeks to possibly months*. Most of the area will be uninhabitable for *weeks or months*."[54] This scenario contrasts with Hurricanes Juan and Igor where, in most cases, recovery efforts were measured in days and weeks. By learning from the diverse lived experiences of severe weather, communities can prepare and respond in ways that reduce social and ecological vulnerability, resulting in more charismatic or mundane rather than catastrophic experiences of extreme weather of all types.[55]

New Orleans

Sociologists Alice Fothergill and Lori Peek conducted a seven-year study into the lives of children aged four to fifteen at the time Category 5 Hurricane Katrina hit New Orleans in August 2005.[56] Seven children, selected from a larger sample of 650 children, represented three "well-being" trajectories found in young people who experienced Katrina. These trajectories were defined as declining, finding equilibrium, and fluctuating. The well-being of all children declined after Hurricane Katrina hit. However, depending on the availability of resources such as family, housing, and school, overall life trajectories could worsen, improve, or oscillate compared to before the storm.

Fothergill and Peek tell the story of Cierra, an African American girl who was eleven years old when Katrina hit. She is part of the finding-equilibrium cohort. Cierra endured the brunt of the storm in the New Orleans hospital where her mother worked. For

Cierra, Hurricane Katrina is the "sound of people screaming."[57] The experience of awaiting evacuation was a form of catastrophic immobility that resulted in psychological trauma for Cierra. She and others were rescued by boat four days after Katrina made landfall, and they stayed at a temporary shelter in Lafayette for three months.

> Debra and Cierra had never been outside New Orleans. They had no family or friends in Lafayette, and as they would learn over the coming weeks, the rest of their loved ones were scattered across several states: Cierra's dad and his family evacuated to Texas, while her favorite aunt, her uncle, and her grandmother were separated and relocated by the government to other parts of Texas, Louisiana, and Georgia. For the first time, Debra and Cierra were truly on their own. Their rental home in New Orleans was damaged beyond repair. All of their belongings and keepsakes, including photos and Cierra's childhood artwork, achievement ribbons, and trophies, were gone. Nothing could be salvaged. Cierra's school was not scheduled to reopen until January 2006, at the earliest, and Debra had no job to return to because the hospital where she had worked was closed indefinitely.[58]

They moved into a Federal Emergency Management Agency (FEMA) trailer for two years before securing a Habitat for Humanity home in Lafayette where they would permanently settle.

During this time, after having lost so much, Cierra wanted to stay at the school she attended before Hurricane Katrina hit. Evidence indicates that a positive school environment is a key contributor to the success of children who experienced Hurricane Katrina. While the school remained open and welcomed Cierra despite her living in a different community, transportation was an issue. A small group of community members volunteered to drive Cierra to school each day. Eventually, Debra was given a car. She learned to drive, got insurance, and was able to drive Cierra to school. The goal of ensuring Cierra's education and well-being was underpinned by mobility. With significant personal determination and community support, Cierra and Debra were able to bridge this gap and create a new life.

This traumatic but ultimately successful experience contrasts with the catastrophic experience of twelve-year-old Daniel, an

African American boy who was in a precarious situation before
Hurricane Katrina hit. Before the storm, Daniel lived with his
mother and baby sister. His mother suffers from untreated mental illness and finished only elementary school. Before Katrina,
the family lived in cheap rentals and homeless shelters. For seven
years after Katrina, they lived in "disaster shelters, hotel and motel
rooms, in government-subsidized single-family housing, in homeless shelters and on the streets."[59] Daniel missed a total of two
years of school and never caught up. He says, "I very seldom had a
stable place where we could stay. We were always [moving around]
and I was never in school. So that kind of threw me off math, when
I was goin' from this place to that place and should have been in
the classroom learning."[60] Daniel's experience is one of deepening
poverty where each move further weakened the family's prospects.

Daniel and Cierra's cases illustrate different types and impacts
of catastrophic (im)mobility.[61] Extreme weather events, such as
heat waves and hurricanes, highlight the roles age, class, social and
economic status, (dis)ability, gender, race, sexuality, geographic
location, and citizenship status play in determining the experience
of disaster and, at an extreme, one's life opportunities.[62] Mobility
capital and connectivity constitute empowerment. To use Sheller's
term, these individuals were socially "islanded."[63] Critically, as geographer Andrew Baldwin and peace and conflict researchers Christine
Frölich, and Delf Rothe point out, Daniel's case is "irreducible to
climate change" but entangled with systemic issues related to and
inseparable from gender, race, class, and more, and how these shape
social services.[64] The differential and uneven experiences of disaster,
both globally and within communities, prompts a call for mobility
and climate justice.

Puerto Rico

For smaller islands, hurricane impacts can be even more devastating as entire mobility systems are impacted. In September 2017,
Hurricane Irma hit Boriken/Puerto Rico, followed two weeks later
by Hurricane Maria, both Category 5 storms. Direct impacts killed
64 people, but over the course of following months more than 4,500
people died due to a lack of medical care and electricity. Residents
had no power for six months.[65] Further, there were intangible losses.

Disaster researcher Gemma Sou describes how "people's attachment to place; their sense of home and belonging; their identities; people's sense of community; as well as the social relations between family members" were all disrupted.[66]

In the absence of government action – FEMA representatives would not arrive until two months after the storm hit – residents relied upon family, neighbours, local charities, and international non-governmental organizations. Notably, one of the greatest sources of assistance came in the form of payments of US$1,500 issued to families in Puerto Rico. The funds were donated by a charitable organization led by entertainer Jennifer Lopez, who has family on the island, demonstrating a different facet of charisma in the form of celebrity.[67] The payment enabled residents to attend to their own specific needs in the absence of government assistance.

Due in part to the lack of timely and adequate emergency response and longer-term erosion of social services in years preceding the storm it is estimated that more than 200,000 residents – out of a population of 3 million – left the island. Initially framed as a temporary measure, there are concerns that the lack of investment in social services and recovery efforts are attempts to create a "blank canvas" upon which private investors can remake the island.[68] Author Naomi Klein describes disaster capitalism, where the shock of collective crisis is exploited to pursue profit and introduce often unpopular policies. Climate and mobility injustice make communities even more vulnerable to hazards, tipping events into the realm of catastrophe.[69] After Hurricane Maria, land and public assets were sold cheaply for resorts and private communities. Such plans beg the question: "who is Puerto Rico for?"[70] Klein notes residents were already worn down by a decade of deep public sector cuts; the resulting despair and distraction muted community activism in the months following Hurricane Maria.[71] Inadequate response to Hurricane Maria was a contributing factor that resulted in sustained mass protests forcing the resignation of Governor Ricardo Rosselló.[72] Further, after Hurricane Maria, there are continued efforts to decentralize the energy grid so that when the main grid is damaged communities can instead rely on renewable microgrids.[73] After the catastrophe of Hurricane Maria, local and green sources of electricity emerge as an expression of charismatic mobility. Though New Orleans and Puerto Rico are physically far-removed from Atlantic Canada, and the hurricanes far stronger, they are indicative of the vulnerabilities that the climate crisis exposes and the injustices it can intensify.

CLIMATE MOBILITIES

Climate change is a threat multiplier, exacerbating existing environmental, social, and economic challenges and disparities. In response to the mobilities arising from severe weather, the term *climate refugee* has emerged. Defining what circumstances constitute climate refugee status is complex. For example, in Syria a five-year drought from 2006 to 2010 contributed to crop failures resulting in high food prices and mass migration of rural families to urban centres.[74] This was one of many factors that contributed to the ongoing Syrian Civil War. As a result of the conflict, of the total pre-war population of 18 million, 7 million citizens are internally displaced and 6 million are in other countries, with 25,000 Syrian refugees accepted in Canada.[75] However, to describe a Syrian refugee as a climate refugee is an oversimplification of multiple complex factors.

Globally, the number of people who could be described as climate refugees is unknown, in part due to the lack of an international treaty that addresses the asylum needs of such a group. The *1951 Refugee Convention* does not address climate change. Looking forward, the International Organization for Migration (IOM) reports that there are "no reliable estimates" of climate-induced migration within or across national borders. However, 200 million is a widely cited estimate. The World Bank estimates that by 2050, in sub-Saharan Africa, South Asia, and Latin America, 140 million climate migrants are anticipated within national borders due to slow-onset climate impacts, including disease and desertification, suggesting the IOM figure of 200 million climate migrants is conservative.[76] Such figures suggest there will be significant shifts and reorderings of global settlement patterns as countries address internal displacement, as well as cross-border mobility.

Climate governance scholar Ingrid Boas and colleagues warn of how estimates of future climate migrants, such as those just presented, are used to justify exclusionary security agendas. Boas et al. describe, for example, how the United Nations Security Council warns of "mass climate migration and the subsequent risk of aggravating conflicts." Although the potential for climate change to disrupt livelihoods and threaten lives is real, such narratives reinforce the idea of large and disruptive waves of climate refugees.[77] In short, the movement of climate refugees has the potential to be framed as a form of catastrophic mobility and subject to punitive policies that aim to limit such movement.

Boas and colleagues contest the term *climate refugee* on multiple grounds. First, they argue that human mobility, including migration, has a long history and is just as prevalent in the contemporary world. Critically, it is actions taken "by home, host and transit states" that determine the quality of the experience.[78] Second, while climate change will instigate human mobility, little is known about the diverse ways that such mobility will be expressed. When faced with risks to personal safety, will people move temporarily, seasonally, or permanently? Near or far? Individually or as a family? Third, as climate change exacerbates existing societal issues, it is difficult to distinguish climate migrants from economic and political migrants. Philosopher Thomas Nail observes that a climate refugee is not just fleeing changing environmental conditions but structural issues such as violence and racism.[79] Likewise, Baldwin, Frölich, and Rothe describe "displacees of a globalised network of intersecting mobility regimes fuelled by fossil fuel extraction."[80] Boas's team argues the term *climate mobilities* is more accurate and less likely to reinforce prejudices that result in exclusionary border policies. Further, robust research is needed into different expressions of climate mobilities to counter the "self-perpetuating myth of climate change migration as a looming security crisis."[81] In this way, they warn that climate-related mobility need not necessarily be framed as catastrophic. A step further, Baldwin, Frölich, and Rothe propose *Anthropocene mobilities* to think through mobility in a geological era defined and threatened by human activity, including the climate crisis.

Sheller, in her work on mobility justice, advances the principle that people "displaced by climate change shall have a right to resettlement in other countries, and especially in countries that contributed most to climate change," that is, high-emitter countries such as Canada.[82] In this way, she frames the mobilities of individuals in high-income countries as an expression of catastrophic mobility, not the climate mobilities of individuals in lower-income countries. High-income countries are destructively dependent on fossil-fuelled mobility.[83] Sheller argues that people living in cultures centred on automobility and aeromobility "need to first stop living in disregard of our own involvement in producing these injustices. We must acknowledge our own responsibility as 'high emitters' of carbon dioxide. We must acknowledge our role in the splintered provision of unequal mobilities ... and the exposure of the mobility poor to greater climate risk and vulnerability."[84] Rather than focusing on maintaining carbon-intensive mobility, local and global impacts need to be understood and mitigated.

In 2019, Nova Scotia was hit by Hurricane Dorian. Category 2 winds once again toppled the power grid, incurring three times as much damage and impacting 100,000 more customers as Hurricane Juan. Without wanting to minimize the protracted experiences of some, the storm impacts were largely resolved within weeks and months. In contrast, Ichi-rougan-aim/Barbados was hit by Hurricane Dorian days earlier, when it was a Category 5 storm. Prime Minister Mia Mottley described the scale of damage as *generational* with infrastructure not just damaged but destroyed. Mottley, in keeping with Sheller, observed that the Barbados contributes minimally to the climate crisis but bears the brunt of its impacts: "We are on the front line of the consequences of climate change but we don't cause it."[85] In terms of total national carbon emissions, for example, Canada ranks 7th, whereas Barbados ranks 160th.[86]

Addressing the Caribbean context, Sheller critiques what she calls *climate coloniality* where the impacts of the climate crisis are the compound consequence of historical colonial practices, including the "transatlantic plantation economy and a five-century system of slavery in the Atlantic world," as well as contemporary neocolonial practices in the form of racialized capitalism, structural adjustment programs, and extractive foreign investment.[87] The climate crisis is a symptom of "slow disasters and impossible futures."[88] Likewise, Indigenous and environmental philosophers Kyle Whyte, Jared Talley, and Julia Gibson, describe settler colonialism as practised in North America in a way that aligns with catastrophic mobility. This was done via two broad, simultaneous efforts. First, settlers remade social-ecological dynamics to meet their needs through practices such as deforestation, agriculture, and resource extraction. Second, settlers contained or attempted to contain, the mobility of Indigenous communities through the violence of relocation, reserves, and residential schools. In short, "Settler societies impose preventable harms on Indigenous people to facilitate the former's process of homeland inscription," the catastrophic impacts of which are reproduced.[89]

Returning to the start of this chapter, Weber describes charisma in terms of leadership as the gift of grace.[90] As the world grapples with the climate crisis, which deepens myriad other societal inequities, including scarcity, disease, and conflict, there is a need for gracious or charismatic climate leadership that embraces an ethic of care for the climate and those surviving on the front lines of the climate crisis. However, even well-intentioned humanitarian initiatives led by higher-income countries to support lower-income countries in mitigating and adapting to the climate crisis, as well as recovery from severe weather events worsened by climate change, often miss the mark, exacerbating catastrophic impacts. Efforts intended to help often fail to empower. Instead, Sheller advocates for both physical and social infrastructures that are "self-governed, decentralized, resilient, community-led ... that can integrate water, energy, food, health, education, and social protection," resonating with an ecological approach to mobilities.[91] In this way, work on climate mobilities is integral to an ecological approach to mobilities.

5

Hurricane Igor

This is how we first learned of storms. The fish

in our cooking pots would swim hard then,
the lash of their home coming down for them

through our roofs.

Sue Goyette, "Five," in Ocean

THE ROCK

If the trend is that there's going to be more impact from weather or
we're going to see more severity in weather systems, I think ... we have
to expect that there's going to be an impact to supplying the island.

Marine operator[1]

Ktaqmkuk/Newfoundland, a rugged island in the North Atlantic,
is colloquially called The Rock.[2] It is part of Canada's easternmost
province, Newfoundland and Labrador. It is known for whales and
icebergs, fjords, and fish. The province is larger than Germany, but its
population hovers at just over half a million. The province consists
of the island, Newfoundland, in the North Atlantic, and a portion of
the continent that borders the province of Quebec, Labrador, for a
total coastline of almost 30,000 kilometres.[3] Both regions have limited transport options due to their remoteness. I focus on the island
portion as it experienced the brunt of Hurricane Igor's impact.

Newfoundland has Irish, English, and Scottish heritage. Settler
colonialism led to the cultural extinction of the Beothuk people
by 1829.[4] Today there are Mi'kmaw communities on the island of

Newfoundland and Innu, Inuit, and Southern Inuit of NunatuKavut communities in Labrador.[5] In terms of language, the place is known for its distinct dialects of English and is also the "most homogeneous province in Canada" with English as the sole language of most residents.[6] The province has an aging population and will have the highest proportion of seniors – defined as age sixty-five and over – in Canada by 2026, an important factor when considering mobility under a changing climate.[7] In the Eastern region, where Hurricane Igor hit, the landscape is made up of oceanic barrens and the Avalon Forest. Moose, lynx, black bear, red fox, and caribou are prevalent.[8]

Since the 1992 cod fishing moratorium, successive governments pursued two prominent strategies to diversify Newfoundland's economy: attractive development in the form of tourism and extractive development in the form of oil.[9] Geographer Tim Cresswell writes in a poem titled "Newfoundland":

The cod have long gone
but now there's oil.
There is dark rock, thick fog
and thin soil.[10]

Both sectors are embedded in fossil-fuelled mobility: the tourism sector is a global, fossil fuel-dependent mobility system that includes airplanes, cruise ships, ferries, and cars, while the province is bound to the oil sector through employment and royalties.[11] Both sectors are central to the provincial economy, and both were impacted by COVID.

Travellers reach Newfoundland by air or ferry. There are three hub airports: St. John's International Airport in the capital city on the east coast; Gander airport, in central Newfoundland, a former transatlantic aviation hub; and Deer Lake airport, near Gros Morne National Park, a UNESCO World Heritage Site serves the west coast. Marine Atlantic, a Crown corporation, operates two ferries. The first is a year-round ferry that travels between North Sydney, Mi'kma'ki/Nova Scotia, and Port aux Basques on the western side of the island, taking six hours under ideal conditions. There is also a seasonal ferry that runs between North Sydney, Nova Scotia, and Argentia on the eastern side of the island, taking twelve to fourteen hours. Marine Atlantic also transports freight, as do private sector companies.

On the island, the most common way to travel is by road. The Trans-Canada Highway, completed in 1965 and running between Port aux Basques on the west coast to St. John's on the east, is the only highway that crosses the province. A private bus company offers daily service, taking nine hours to travel the length of the highway. St. John's offers a modest public transit service, and taxis operate in both the province's capital and smaller communities. Several provincially operated ferries connect communities.

Vast spaces and limited options define Newfoundland's mobility system; it lacks redundancy. In the aftermath of Hurricane Igor, Phil, a road manager, observes: "One of the problems we faced was the fact that some places there was no other route. The Trans-Canada, for instance. There's ways that you just can't get around the Burin Peninsula Highway."[12] Redundancy means having more than one way to get to a destination. It also means being able to meet needs independent of mobility, such as local provisions of food, fuel, and medicine. Limited routes render Newfoundland more vulnerable to severe weather. A reliance on ferries and one highway means that disruptions are "reflected almost instantly in empty shelves" as the average five-day food supply dwindles.[13]

Most goods are shipped from outside the province. A marine operator speaks to the lack of self-sufficiency:

We're not self-sufficient. So, if it's a trend that weather conditions are going to be more severe in the future, I guess – and I hate to say that we've just got to live with it. We've done it for hundreds of years. We've made our life around the water all along the coast of Newfoundland. And we're so dependent on the ocean to maintain, I suppose, to develop the lifestyle that we have. But even now as things change, as the economy changes, look at the offshore oil, the oil industry. It's huge, and it keeps growing. But we've got to be able to supply their needs. So, there is a huge impact.[14]

This statement indicates an appreciation for the environmental exposure of the province of Newfoundland as a coastal region with communities reliant upon the ocean. It also reveals a tension between a lack of provincial self-sufficiency and the impetus to ensure that the oil industry is fully equipped. It reveals a larger disjuncture between the oil industry and climate change impacts.

In this chapter, I describe different facets of Hurricane Igor as they relate to mobility. First, I discuss the anticipation and impacts of this hurricane. Focusing on the destruction of the road network, I detail how, in its absence, improvised and repurposed – or scrambled – mobilities emerged alongside a simultaneous push to restore the road network as quickly as possible. I then analyze how officials praised Newfoundlanders for their resilience in the face of disruption, distracting critical attention from systemic issues, such as public safety and climate change. Finally, I reflect on how Newfoundlanders perceive climate change and steps the province is taking respond to the climate crisis.

HURRICANE IGOR

I'd never seen anything like it that severe ... I realized how forceful nature could be, but I'd never seen it. We've been through wind and rain ... but nothing like this ... We didn't anticipate the seriousness of it because we'd never seen anything like this before.

Town manager[15]

Like Hurricane Juan hitting Nova Scotia, Igor took two weeks to reach Newfoundland. It formed off the coast of Africa on 8 September 2010. It travelled across the Atlantic Ocean, reaching Bermuda on 20 September, and intensified as it tracked up the Eastern seaboard. Approaching Newfoundland, it combined with a moving storm front, Hurricane Julia, and a trough of low pressure. It made landfall on 21 September at midnight. The storm hit the eastern region of the province including the capital, St. John's. As with Hurricane Juan, Igor's arrival at night contributed to lower rates of injury and mortality. One life was lost on Random Island when an eighty-year-old man, ventured out to check on a neighbouring property and the road washed out.[16]

Fire and Emergency Services Newfoundland and Labrador, the provincial body responsible for emergency response, monitored the storm a week in advance of its arrival.[17] Minor shifts in trajectory could have meant the difference between the storm making landfall or heading into open ocean. Preliminary data indicated the storm would track over the Atlantic Ocean. The day before the storm hit, the Canadian Hurricane Centre revised its warnings: the storm might track over land. "Even during the day of the event," an Environment

Canada report states, "the position and track forecast had to be continually adjusted closer to land as the details of the upper-level trough influence were evolving."[18] Earlier the same month, storm warnings were issued for Hurricane Earl, which was forecast to track over land. Hurricane Earl received media coverage, but the impacts were mild compared to Hurricane Igor. By contrast, Hurricane Igor, which was projected to track offshore, received less media attention prior to landfall. Due to the "false alarm" of Hurricane Earl, the mobility of Hurricane Igor was not deemed as charismatic as it might otherwise have been.

Though the actual severity of Hurricane Igor was yet unknown, Newfoundlanders readied themselves. The Eastern District School Board closed schools, preventing the movement of dozens of school buses.[19] Oil companies evacuated 200 workers from offshore oil rigs.[20] Eastern Health set up shelters in case of evacuation.[21] A non-governmental organization stockpiled supplies because "if it's foggy we don't get flights in. If it's windy we don't get flights or boats in." The Canadian Forces assembled in Nova Scotia, ready if needed to make the crossing to Newfoundland.

Hurricane Igor ranked a Category 1 on the Saffir-Simpson Wind Scale,[22] but lower wind speeds are not necessarily cause for complacency. Due to their slower pace, they can produce significant damage as there is more time for rain to inundate a given region.[23] As Igor passed over Newfoundland it transitioned into an extratropical hurricane. Such transitions are typical in the North Atlantic and are characterized by a larger rain and wind field.[24]

Igor was a record breaker. Spanning 1,480 kilometres in diameter, it was the largest recorded storm in the Atlantic Basin, until Hurricane Sandy hit two years later.[25] Sustained winds reached 130 kilometres per hour, with gusts of 170 kilometres per hour. It was the third wettest hurricane in Canadian history. It deluged the Bonavista and Burin Peninsulas with up to 250 millimetres of rain: the equivalent of approximately 20 per cent of annual regional precipitation.[26] A resident of Garden Cove in the eastern region commented, "No one can get in or out of the community. The wind is just howling here now and the rain is just pouring, pouring down."[27] Oil barrels, picnic tables, and fishing sheds were among the objects seized by the wind.[28]

The intense precipitation saturated the province's thin soil.[29] Stream flow increased from an average of 10 to 600 cubic metres per second.[30] One community member describes the impact: "It sounded like a roar, like an airplane was going to land in the backyard, but it was the brook."[31] An owner of a general store says, "I went to secure the gasoline storage facility ... and by the time I got back to the store, I had to fight the current to get back inside ... You can't stop nature at that point."[32] Thirty communities declared states of emergency.[33] The storm devastated Newfoundland's mobility system. Damage to the road network was catastrophic, resulting in prolonged road and bridge washouts. More than 150 communities were isolated for up to ten days. Approximately 70,000 households lost power and countless boil water advisories were issued.[34] The damage disrupted the mobility of people, goods, and services, including utility crews reconnecting electrical services and health professionals transporting oxygen cylinders. The vital mobilities of goods, such as food, water, and fuel, as well as access to medical treatments, such as insulin, dialysis, and methadone, proved challenging.

Estimates for infrastructure and property damage range between $100 and $200 million. Outlays for Hurricanes Juan and Igor include insurable costs and costs recovered under the federal Disaster Financial Assistance Arrangements. Estimates do not include uninsured costs, indirect costs, neither do they include ecological and social costs, which are not reflected in the market. Critically, overland flooding was not insurable. At the time, an Insurance Bureau of Canada representative stated, "There's no policy available to homeowners in Canada that would cover that kind of damage." As of 2015, overland insurance is available, but this does not benefit property owners impacted by Hurricane Igor.[35] One Random Island resident whose home was flooded commented, "What I worked for all my life is gone."[36] Weeks and months after Hurricane Igor hit, homeowners were dealing with flooding and water damage. Due in part to structural damage caused by Igor, the Port Union fish processing plant, located at the northern tip of the Bonavista Peninsula, closed permanently. One hundred and seventy workers lost their jobs in a town of approximately 1,800 people.

MOBILE ROADS

We went down to Random Island and it hit us. Total destruction over
there ... [It] wasn't gaps – there were just roads just sort of gone, right?
My thoughts were, "My god, we're going to be years putting this place
back together."

Provincial politician[37]

The first step, once the storm passed, was assessing damage: determining what routes were intact and what routes had structural
failures. Roads were on the move; transformed from fixed to fluid.
Journalist Barb Dean-Simmons wrote,

I never imagined life without a highway, no connection between
communities ... Huge chunks of pavement had disintegrated,
leaving gaping holes and sheer drops. Streams and rivers had
changed their courses ... The thirty-five kilometre route that
I took every day to get to work was practically obliterated.
Guardrails hung like slack clotheslines across huge gaps. Asphalt
was ripped apart like paper.[38]

The orderliness of the road network was scrambled by flood water:
human mobility yielded as water took the right of way.

Society reoriented itself, navigating a transformed mobility
landscape. A road manager, Phil, recalls gathering information
via word of mouth: "We were getting calls coming in from everywhere, and our staff couldn't get out to check on a lot of it because
the roads were [gone]. Once they got to the first washout, that's as
far as they got."[39] Phil describes the process of piecing together the
mobility impacts of Hurricane Igor. Fire and Emergency Services
set up a

command centre and they had different government agencies at
that centre, and we would feed that centre with information ...
The first day, none of that was in place. It got better as a couple
days went ahead. But the first day ... you couldn't get a chopper
or fly because the winds were too high. And it was still raining,
so you couldn't get out and really assess the damage ... [But
after] that first day we had a pretty good idea. We might have

missed some smaller ones, like a side road in a community, that kind of thing, but we had a pretty good idea that all our major routes were compromised.[40]

Given the weather conditions and infrastructure damage, even conducting a basic situational assessment of the road network proved challenging. Some officials were able to get a bird's-eye view from helicopters, but most relied on first-hand experience and second-hand accounts. If a similar event occurred today, drones would be used when weather conditions permitted.

One road manager describes the stretch of highway for which he is responsible: "It runs ... pretty much the path that Igor took."[41] The hurricane traced the path of the road network, an unfortunate alignment of ecological and human mobility. The manager uses a war metaphor: "It looked like a war zone. It looked like strategically dropped bombs on bridges and crossings."[42] An editorialist for the provincial newspaper the *Telegram* recalls, "It's the closest I've ever felt to being involved in a battle, except the enemy was the weather and it had far more in its arsenal than we did."[43] Given that many regions in Newfoundland only have one primary road, Igor hit where it hurt. Fire and Emergency Services lamented the lack of "overland re-routing options."[44] The storm exposed the pre-existing vulnerability of a fragile mobility system that lacks redundancy. Stuart, the manager of a fuel distribution company, comments on the variable state of road maintenance across the province. While some sparsely populated areas attract less provincial road investment, they often experience relatively high drive-through traffic volumes. He observes that there were many roads in a "lot worse shape than those areas that got washed out, that probably didn't get as much wind and rain, so they were lucky."[45] If the storm track shifted, damage to Newfoundland's roads could have been even greater.

While roads were in shambles, other transport modes were comparatively unharmed. Air and marine routes are malleable. Air travel shut down during the hurricane, but a lack of infrastructure damage meant that service quickly resumed. Blizzards are far more disruptive to airports than hurricanes, given the time needed to remove snow and ice. Ferries were taken to sea to avoid damage to terminal infrastructure. Marine and air services are, however, integrated with the road network. An airport manager observes that the airport was accessible by air, but not by road. A marine shipper finds that while disruption on the shipping side of business was minimal, they were impacted by the road washouts: "We're not just a shipping company. We have about 500 trucks on the road every day."[46] Such connectivity is integral to mobility.

Marine Atlantic was similarly impacted, albeit by a different storm. Road washouts caused by Igor did not disrupt the Marine Atlantic ferry service. The seasonal ferry that serves the eastern side of the island was not in operation, and Igor did not impact the west coast, where the ferry runs year-round. In August 2007, Tropical Storm Chantal hit when the seasonal ferry was still in service. "We had to turn the vessel around, now, not because of the weather event. It was because of the damage to the road network that occurred overnight in Argentia. We wouldn't be able to get the passengers out ... because the roads were washed out."[47] As a result, 600 passengers were detoured. In the aftermath of Hurricane Igor, the mobility system reconfigured to cope with the sudden absence of road infrastructure.

SCRAMBLED MOBILITIES

Newfoundlanders are very diverse. Yeah, the bridge was washed out,
but they get down there with a quad to make it over to the other side.

Road manager[48]

Confronted with impassable roads, other ways of moving emerged. Phil states: "What I find with Newfoundland[ers] is that they're very diversified ... A lot of them have quads and Ski-Doos and boats and generators ... They coped very well."[49] Transport diversity within local mobility systems was a key component of community resilience. It was an expression of governmobility, that is, deciding at an individual and community level if, and how, to move (chapter 3).[50] Residents demonstrated resilience by leveraging alternate mobilities, such as quads and boats. This is a common feature in Newfoundland communities. Many residents are accustomed to navigating mobility in areas where there are no formal routes; therefore, they were well-prepared to circumvent damaged roads. Just as forest fires clear room for new growth, revitalizing biodiversity, Hurricane Igor disrupted the dominant mobility paradigm, creating space for alternative mobilities to shift to the forefront.

Cresswell writes that turbulence in mobility has the potential to produce a "positive and creative moment that can occur when that which is mostly taken-for-granted becomes suddenly visible."[51] Disruption allows improvised and repurposed mobilities to take centre stage, temporarily changing mobility. Sociologist Satya Savitzky calls these *scrambled mobilities* to indicate both the rush to restore disrupted mobilities, as well as the interconnected or scrambled nature of broader social, technical, and ecological systems.[52] This resonates with sociologist Mimi Sheller's observation that disasters "demobilize and remobilize."[53] Likewise, geographer Thomas Birtchnell and sociologist Monika Büscher observe that travellers "invent new and often inconvenient routes" activating different modes and social capital.[54] These alternative modes, routes, and skills are held intentionally and unintentionally in potential as a form of mobility redundancy. Just as governmobility describes how people govern their own mobility in the context of disaster, scrambled mobilities describe how disrupted mobilities are improvised and reconfigured. Scrambled can have negative connotations related to chaos and stress. Scrambles can also be productive, demonstrating different ways of being and doing, as well as accelerating innovation and transition.

Provincial and local governments demonstrated resilience, too, by improvising on and repurposing modes and routes. Politician Chris states: "People were cut off, but we started immediately to look at how can we get to them by sea. Could we use our provincial ferry system? Our helicopters?"[55] A government news release issued three days after Hurricane Igor illustrated the latent potential within the existing mobility system:

> The Department of Transportation and Works has established marine and air support for communities isolated as a result of Hurricane Igor. A ferry vessel stationed at Clarenville will be dedicated to moving supplies to isolated communities on the Bonavista Peninsula. A second ferry vessel is also positioned at Portugal Cove, awaiting shipments of gasoline to be taken to Marystown. As well, two helicopters are stationed at Clarenville to be dedicated exclusively to addressing any essential transportation requirements to and from isolated communities.[56]

In addition to substitute modes, different routes were used. Road manager Phil recalls, "We used some alternate routes that were, like old cabin roads. We got some fill on them, and we used gravel roads. We used some old bridges that hadn't been used in the last twenty or thirty years."[57] Hegemonic automobility was supplanted. Ferries, ships, helicopters, and off-highway vehicles filled the gap left by cars and trucks. Travel by air and water, and a peripheral automobility based on quads and side roads created a new, albeit temporary, mobility.[58] Almost all these modes are powered by fossil fuel.

After Hurricane Igor hit, one senior resident of Knights Cove at the northern tip of the Bonavista Peninsula relied on a kerosene lamp and limited food supplies. A provincial emergency helicopter rescued her four days later. When she learned that Prime Minister Stephen Harper had earlier surveyed the area via helicopter, she commented: "Well, I think that he should have pitched down and took me with him."[59] Her joke hints at the weariness and even trauma of immobility.[60] Her personal mobility was reduced to her home and her governmobility was limited to looking after herself within that space. She required the activation of a larger mobility system to get to safety. Such struggles played out across the region.

Geographer David Harvey observes that disruptions and changes in mobility are "challenging, exciting, stressful, and sometimes deeply troubling," triggering a multiplicity of social responses.[61] Following Igor, the provincial government took measures to improve redundancies. Before Igor, emergency bridges were stored on Newfoundland's west coast. Prefabricated Bailey bridges, first used in World War I to advance troops and equipment, are now used as temporary bridges. Given the scale of disruption caused by Hurricane Igor on the east coast, the bridges were difficult to access. Today emergency bridges are stored on both sides of the island. Given the necessary volume of fill (baseball-sized rocks used to create roadbeds) after Igor, the material is now readily available in case of emergency. Such low-cost measures increase Newfoundland's preparedness. Igor was a source of intense disruption that reconfigured Newfoundland's mobility. Dominant automobility is defined by autonomy, speed, and directness. After Igor, mobility was heterogeneous and collaborative. Communities experienced their "latent potential."[62] Mobility was slower and smaller scale, focused on achieving vital movements of people, food, water, and medical supplies. As scrambled mobilities emerged, there was a simultaneous push to restore roads.

TEN DAYS

We hauled contractors off the west coast, we hauled them off the east
coast. They all came together... but it went like clockwork: bang, bang,
bang. We knew all the gaps.

Provincial politician[63]

There was a push to get things back to normal as quickly as possible.
The impulse was to restore automobility – the system of vehicles
and related infrastructure that relies on fossil fuels. The government
excelled at this specific kind of response. Politician Chris recounts,
"Over the next few days, and it was ten days really, we had our goals
set. We wanted to make sure that we connected every community in
as short a possible time. And everybody stepped up. I mean we had
our workers working eighteen to twenty hours a day."[64] Chris provided ongoing updates to the media on the status of the roadwork.
He used a countdown approach, tracking completed and pending
repairs. He wanted to give the public the sense that "we were getting
ahead, not falling behind." Approximately 1,000 members of the
Canadian Forces assisted with recovery. Counting down, mobilizing
workers from across the province, and labouring long hours define
the frenetic rhythm of recovery.

Road manager Phil reflects the estimate was "weeks, if not
months, to put it all back together and we did it in ten days. Now,
I mean, let's face it, it's three years later before we got it all straightened out."[65] According to government officials, in the span of ten
days some form of physical connection was made with the more
than one hundred communities isolated by road and bridge washouts. Roads were reduced to one lane and weight restrictions were
imposed.[66] The Canadian Forces installed three temporary bridges
on the Bonavista and Burin Peninsulas near Marystown (Long
Pond), Rattling Brook, and Trouty, reconnecting communities to the
Trans-Canada Highway.[67] Over the course of the following years,
permanent measures replaced temporary repairs. One reason for the
slower pace of recovery was that asphalt and tar plants required for
road rebuilding are seasonal, shutting down operations in winter.[68]
Typically, demand for asphalt is lower in winter and operation costs
are higher due to the cold.[69]

There was pride in the collective experience and efforts of all levels
of government, the military, contractors, and communities to restore

the road network. Communities and employees who exceeded the call of duty were praised. One community chief administrative officer recalls, "Our fire department and our [public] works are excellent examples of this … They were out trying to save other people's properties when their own homes were getting flooded out. It was really amazing. I was proud to be associated with them."[70] Residents were able to pull together with an all-hands-on-deck mentality, uniting behind a common goal.[71]

While the road rebuilding effort was impressive, moving forward it raises concerns about the resilience of the road network, having proved catastrophically vulnerable. The merits of re-establishing it, while understandable, also raise questions about future resilience. One issue is rebuilding policies and practices. Phil reflects: "We have a very strict Public Tendering Act for our hiring contracts. All bets were off. I was told by my executive, do whatever you got to do."[72] This included waiving environmental assessments and hiring less experienced machine operators. Phil continues: "we had [contractors] digging holes in the side of the road and everything trying to get enough material to fill in a washout." Depending on how and where fill was removed, it could promote erosion. The use of heavy equipment near waterways compacts riverbanks, making such areas more conducive to flooding. Another issue that arose involved public perception of how best to prevent flooding. Debris, such as trees, blocked some culverts, impairing their flow and contributing to the road washout. Public sentiment was that "you go back in the country and clean all the brooks out so that the debris doesn't come down again."[73] Withdrawing biomass, however, could potentially disrupt natural flooding buffers.

While things were restored to normal, they were not the same. At the provincial level, officials gained a greater understanding of road construction standards given intense rainfall and peak stream flow and recommended combining flood maps with data on event intensity, duration, and frequency.[74] Based on continual learning from previous events, improvements were made such as installing larger culverts; using concrete abutments to keep culverts in place; monitoring weather more closely; getting work crews out in advance of storms to clear culverts and catch basins; improving coordination among organizations; and undertaking disaster simulation exercises.

Geographer Norm Catto and political scientist Stephen Tomblin observe that some people viewed the damage caused by Hurricane

Igor as preventable: "the difficulties were seen as the result of inadequate preparation (the failure to install larger culverts, lack of maintenance), and it was assumed that better pre-storm management would have resolved most issues."[75] In some places, such as Marystown, culverts were replaced rather than upgraded. These culverts washed out again the following year during post-tropical storm Ophelia.[76] Marystown mayor Sam Synard says: "I'm just stating the obvious. If a hurricane blows through and knocks out culverts that are some four feet in diameter, it might be a better idea to put them back six feet in diameter, or something [with] increased capacity."[77] Replacing, rather than upgrading culverts, was a form of climate maladaptation, that is, it maintains or increases vulnerability to climate change impacts.[78]

Others viewed the damage as unavoidable given the scale of the storm. Then minister of transportation Tom Hedderson responded, "When you get a significant flow as we've got, we do expect that there will be some damage, and hopefully damage that we can mitigate very quickly."[79] This exchange reflects a larger tension between upgrading infrastructure construction standards and incurring guaranteed upfront costs, versus allowing infrastructure to wash out – with related risks to public safety – and incur replacement costs if, and when, needed.

On the one hand, residents observe that they had never seen anything like Igor. On the other, there was a push to get things back to normal as quickly as possible – an urge to return to a normal that had proven vulnerable. This conceptual tension mirrors the literal gaps that emerged in the road network. An editorial in the Clarenville *Packet* suggests, "In this province, we're used to being at the mercy of the weather, but rarely has the weather been so merciless."[80] Town manager Gregor states, "I'd never seen anything like it that severe ... I realized how forceful nature could be, but I'd never seen it."[81] He continues: "we've been through wind and rain ... but nothing like this ... we didn't anticipate the seriousness of it because we'd never seen anything like this before." One resident captures the dissonance between expectation and reality: "Tied my barbecue down. Forgot to tie the house down."[82]

Igor was unique in Newfoundland's storm history. Its geographical extent meant that it impacted numerous communities at the same time, straining response and recovery resources.[83] The scale of Igor was beyond previous experience, giving Newfoundlanders

a new and discomfiting appreciation for the power of the environment. Just as infrastructure was under stress, so too were residents.
However, despite feeling overwhelmed by the scale of disruption,
there were many stories of residents pitching in to help themselves
and others.

RESILIENT NEWFOUNDLANDERS

> We turned this around because we're resilient, we're tough.
>
> Former premier Danny Williams[84]

The reputed resilient Newfoundlander has connotations of being
hearty, resourceful, and competent in dealing with hardship. The
label stems from a history of isolated, rural, and outport communities dealing with emergencies through informal means, independent of government.[85] The ascription of resilience is common
to remote places and colonial landscapes and can often be inter-
changed with endurance.[86] After Hurricane Igor, one RCMP officer
remarked, "The locals do what they've done for centuries ... They
look after what they can, and when they can get outside help for
the community, then we'll support the ongoing efforts that are currently in place."[87] One journalist recalled a man who "ferried us
across the raging river to Trouty, where a bridge had been two days
before ... when I asked him about the items he had lost – a pickup,
a boat and motor, most of his furniture and appliances – he shook
his head and smiled. 'No, my son, that's not important. We're all
OK. That fellow [who died] down Random Island way wasn't as
lucky. We're all OK. It's only stuff.'"[88] This comment is a reminder
of the value of life, but it can be viewed as relying on individual
toughness in lieu of policies needed to protect homes, communities,
and lives.

Political and public figures recognized the resilience of residents.
Then premier Danny Williams reflected on one scene:

> There were at least twenty people on their knees in the mud,
> cleaning up so these elderly people could get back in their
> home ... You know, we turned this around. We turned this
> around because we're resilient, we're tough." He continued:
> "It was a truly humbling experience to see people, faced by
> their own hardship, putting others before themselves and going

above and beyond to assist in any way humanly possible ...
Newfoundlanders and Labradorians have a reputation for being
some of the kindest and most resilient people in the world, and
this past week was certainly a testament to this claim.[89]

Then prime minister Stephen Harper said that Newfoundlanders are facing the aftermath of the storm with their "characteris-
tic resilience and determination."[90] The minister of defence stated,
"Newfoundland-Labradorians have great resilience. They're getting
on with sorting themselves out and helping their own situation."[91]
What emerges is a normalization of the resilient Newfoundlander.
The compliment celebrates the response of individuals and communities and, at the same time, diverts attention from government
responsibility.[92] The capability of individuals and communities to
cope is highlighted, while larger issues that require government
deliberation and action are absent. Climate change mitigation and
adaptation are prime examples.

The first sitting of the provincial House of Assembly, governed at
the time by the right-wing Progressive Conservatives with the centrist
Liberals in official Opposition, took place more than two months after
Hurricane Igor. The storm was mentioned in half of the House sit-
tings the following year. Volunteers were acknowledged. The closure
of Port Union fish processing plant was discussed. In contrast, Nova
Scotia's legislature, governed by Progressive Conservatives with the
New Democratic Party in Opposition, met two days after Hurricane
Juan hit. The storm was mentioned in three-quarters of sessions in
the following year and discussions were substantive, including links
with climate change, impacts on workers and landowners, and the
status of emergency preparedness (chapter 3).

Yvonne Jones, Liberal Member of the House of Assembly, questions the lack of financial support for community members who lost
work due to Igor. She references the oil economy, focusing on the
distribution of revenue but she does not make links between the oil
sector, climate change, and Hurricane Igor:

These are the people who pay in their hard-earned money to
the government every day ... that you are using to drill holes
in the ground for oil, that you are using to buy shares in oil
companies ... That is their money, and today a lot of them down
in the Port Union and Bonavista area are out of a job, have

damages to their homes, and are not getting any help from the
government [following Hurricane Igor]. Mr. Speaker, you can
understand why people would be frustrated. There is a complete
dependency as well in that area around the fishery.[93]

She implies that the resilient Newfoundlander is worn down by compound challenges, such as Hurricane Igor and the fisheries' decline.

In the case of Newfoundland, praise is a form of persuasion. Such
admiration is deserved and genuine. A journalist commented that
in all the communities he visited following Igor there was a strong
sense of "OK this is over now, we now have to pick up and move on,
and who needs help first? ... We've got to solve this problem because
we're left to our own devices."[94] At the governmental level there was
a similar urgency to put things back together, but there is a concomitant lack of discussion, whether intentionally or unintentionally,
about larger issues such as safety, resulting in a naturalization of the
status quo.

Environmental sociologists William Freudenburg and Margarita
Alario identify that blame is used by high-level figures to divert
attention from the allocation of resources to the private sector.[95] The
act of blaming shifts attention from concerns about legitimacy and
competency from one social actor to others. Rather than responding
to questions about an organization's own practices, representatives
divert attention to a real or constructed opponent. In Newfoundland
praise, not blame, operates as such a diversionary tactic. Admiration
and approval divert attention away from questions about infrastructure resilience, disaster preparedness, and climate change. The
combination of praise and an absence of critical questions from the
official opposition party and media legitimize the status quo.[96]

CIMATE CHANGE PERCEPTION

> Climate change is here, for sure.
>
> Road manager[97]

The phrase "hundred-year storm" describes the expected frequency
of severe weather, meaning that a severe hurricane, such as Hurricane Igor, has a 1 per cent chance of occurring each year. Such
expressions are out of date, no longer reflecting reality. A marine
operator quips, "It feels like we're having a one-hundred-year storm

every two months."[98] Phil, a road manager, observes that "some people are saying it's the storm of the century. We'll never have another one. But all you've got to do is watch the news in other parts of the world. Climate change is here, for sure. So that was one opportunity, I guess. But we haven't [taken advantage of it]."[99] There is a pervasive sense that the climate is changing.[100]

Climate change brings more frequent extreme weather events. Newfoundlanders know harsh weather. They are exposed to the many moods of the North Atlantic through living near and working on the ocean, including oil and gas extraction, fishing, and tourism. As such, they are well positioned to observe changes. Transport operators, given their first-hand experience of monitoring and managing weather, offer specialized insights. Gregor, a road manager, comments on increases in storm frequency: "I've been here twenty-six years now. I've got to say, it seems like it's more frequent. And that certainly impacts what we do because one of these storms certainly sets you back a long ways [in terms of damage to infrastructure and cost of recovery]."[101] A marine operator describes shifts in storm intensity:

Bad storms are worse than they used to be, it seems. Like we had a period one time last year … one of our ships was in the Corner Brook area, and for six hours straight it had, I think it was 180 kilometres plus [winds]. It was totally unheard of, right? I mean, I never! The periods of bad weather are definitely different. They're more extreme. So obviously over time that will degrade everything at some stage. Is that going to continue? Well, who knows? I mean they had 380 kilometres [per hour winds] in Asia recently, so maybe it could come here too.[102]

As observed in Nova Scotia, in Newfoundland, too, there is an uneasy consciousness that events occurring elsewhere could hit home next time. Another marine operator speaks to the impacts on service delivery: "Last year we had in the vicinity of thirty days that we actually had to cancel … There were probably more impacts, but they wouldn't have necessarily meant cancellations [but] delays probably arriving in port because of wind conditions."[103] The interface of the environment and mobility is inextricable and intensifying. Goyette imagines how "we first learned of storms."[104] Now there is a sense that Newfoundland is relearning what storms can entail and how to prepare.

Another expression of severe weather is flooding. Flooding has occurred in Newfoundland almost every year since 2000, from tropical storms like Gabrielle and Chantal in 2001 and 2007 to the Stephenville floods in 2005, and the Northern Peninsula storm surge in 2007. To manage the flooding impacts, some homes in Stephenville were permanently relocated after the 2005 floods. Catto and Tomblin observe "a plethora of meteorological and geological events since 2000 has necessitated intense activity by first responders and government agencies."[105] Costs incurred, measured in terms of the amount of federal Disaster Assistance funding provided, range from a low of $1 million for the Burin flood to a high of $28 million for the Stephenville floods. This casts the $95 million cost of disaster recovery for Hurricane Igor in sharper perspective.

Despite the frequency of floods, they do not form part of a collective cultural story about weather or climate change. Instead, they tend to be viewed as isolated events. Catto and Tomblin suggest that such floods are "perceived by residents as a feature of the local environment to be endured, rather than a hazard to be combatted."[106] Severe weather events are treated as unrelated incidents rather than as components of a larger integrated narrative about severe weather. This echoes a wider disconnection in Newfoundland between the oil industry, carbon emissions, and climate change. In Nova Scotia following Hurricane Juan, references were made to historical and contemporary disasters, such as the 1917 Halifax Explosion and 9/11. By contrast, despite a history of environmental disasters including the 1914 sealing disaster, the 1929 Burin tsunami, the 1982 Ocean Ranger oil platform disaster, the 1992 cod moratorium, and the 2009 Cougar helicopter crash – all of which related to the ocean, including fisheries and oil and gas extraction – these events were not referenced in the aftermath of Hurricane Igor.

While flood management is moving in a promising direction, it is important to note that significant attention is also paid to circulations of oil. Former premier of Newfoundland Labrador Paul Davis states, "Based on the work that has been done and what we know about potential oil reserves off our shores, we know that there is a long-term future for oil and gas business in Newfoundland and Labrador ... We'll have markets for many years to come; the reserves are significant."[107] Efforts to facilitate circulations of oil

Table 5.1 Newfoundland and Labrador weather events that triggered federal
Disaster Financial Assistance Arrangements program, 2000–10

Year	Event	Federal Assistance (M)
2010	Hurricane Igor	95
2008	Northeast Coast Flood	2
2007	Tropical Storm Chantal	24
2007	Daniel's Harbour Landslides	3
2007	Northern Peninsula Storm Surge	3
2006	Burin Flood	1
2006	Northeast Coast Flood	5
2005	Stephenville Flood	28
2003	West Coast Flood	10
2003	Badger Flood	8
2001	Tropical Storm Gabrielle	6
	Total	$185 million

to markets and to manage circulations of water, particularly storm
and flood waters, illustrates a disjuncture between the production of
greenhouse gas emissions and adaptation to the impacts of climate
change. At the time of Hurricane Igor, the oil sector contributed
about one-third of total provincial GDP though only about 5,000
jobs.[108] Such carbon-intensive development was at odds with the
provincial emission reduction target, which the provincial government did not plan to meet due to growth in the industrial sector.[109]

A few, however, unconvinced that the climate is changing due to
human action. A town manager wonders: "Everybody keeps blaming
all the stuff we're putting into the atmosphere. I wonder if that's true
or not. I just wonder, like we've had climate change throughout our
history, ice ages, and receding. I just wonder if we're not part of that
bigger cycle. I don't know. I'm convinced that there is a change, but I
don't know if we're part of the bigger million-year transition or it is
something that we're doing."[110] Similarly, a marine operator reflects:

"I read an interesting article a few weeks ago about sunspots, and some guy made a lot of sense that it's really tied to sunspots, and in actual fact the Earth is going to start cooling down. It's not getting warmer at all. And that's not hard to understand. I just came back from Florida, and a couple of mornings I got up it was warmer here than there."[111] While climate change is related but peripheral to the work of both professionals, it is interesting to note their engagement with the issue and efforts to reconcile their experience and with the misinformation to which they are exposed [112]

In Newfoundland, post-Igor discussion about mobility was limited to infrastructure maintenance and economic development. Kelvin Parsons, Liberal Member of the House of Assembly, expressed concern about the outsourcing of highway maintenance jobs:

> We have a tremendous amount of highway maintenance and repair work needed in communities, particularly in the aftermath of Igor. Government has surpluses, major maintenance work is required, they are laying off these [highway] depot workers when, at the same time – in my District of Burgeo, for example, on the Burgeo Road – we are seeing government contract out work to put signs up. Can the Minister of Transportation and Works explain the logic of us closing down depots, laying off workers, and contracting the work out to others?[113]

The budget speech was delivered later the same month. Finance Minister Tom Marshall described how offshore oil and gas revenue would be invested in repairing damage incurred by Hurricane Igor. Through a "multi-year infrastructure strategy currently valued in excess of $5 billion, we have reinvested those [oil] revenues in communities ... laying a solid foundation for investment attraction and new economic growth ... Initiatives will include: Funding to repair roads damaged by Hurricane Igor, a portion of which is recoverable from the Federal Disaster Financial Assistance Program."[114] Connections were not made between the contribution of the oil and gas sector to climate change and, by extension, severe weather events such as Hurricane Igor.

The lack of discussion in the House of Assembly about systemic issues, including the integrity of road infrastructure, disaster preparedness, and climate change, suggests that the status quo is perceived as unproblematic. The security of the population was framed narrowly as reconnecting the road network. Broader considerations were not addressed, such as how to mitigate future road washouts by maintaining infrastructure; distributing generators for pumping fuel (chapter 6); diversifying mobility; addressing potential shortages of vital goods like food, water, and medicine; and supporting senior citizens who live on their own. A focus on small-scale and short-term questions related to engineering diverted attention from critical issues, such as climate change mitigation and adaptation. Focusing on the experience of residents during the ten days it took reconnect the road network, and not the months and even years of recovery, erases rather than acknowledges links between human well-being, climate change, and disaster.

There is tension between the perception of climate change and the response to it. Officials are uncertain of how to proceed. Storm events are challenging and surpassing the upper edges of infrastructure design limits. Maintaining current infrastructure, nonetheless building to higher standards to withstand stronger storms, incurs significant costs. A road manager describes this struggle:

> One of the things that we've noticed – and we've discussed this a lot since Igor – is that when it comes to storm systems, we don't design for hurricanes. We design for fifty to maybe one hundred year [storm] maximums. To design for a hurricane is financially unfeasible. But what we're finding is that extreme weather events seem to be happening more often, and when they do they're more severe. So, it looks to me there may have to be some work done in that area, but I certainly can't see … I mean, we just can't afford to design and build for something that's going to happen for 200 millimetres of rain. We just can't.[115]

There is a sense of being stuck between a rock and hard place, as the apt idiom goes: on one hand, the experience of changing weather conditions, on the other hand, limited resources to act. Phil suggests the creation of a "provincial think tank on this or some kind of committee" to determine a practical direction forward.[116] Hurricane Igor sparked a conversation that now needs more formal means, whether in the form of a working group, committee, review, or other process, to flesh out the issues. A stronger connection needs to be made between extreme weather, climate action, and Newfoundland's contribution to climate change.

8 CLIMATE ACTION

2011 *Climate Plan*

The Government of Newfoundland and Labrador's 2011 *Climate Change Action Plan* released one year after Hurricane Igor, references the impact of severe storms such as Igor, particularly on infrastructure:

> Climate change is an important issue for Newfoundland and Labrador. As a large coastal province with over 90 per cent of the population living near the sea, Newfoundland and Labrador is exposed to many long-term impacts of climate change including sea-level rise, more storm surges, greater coastal erosion and volatile changes in seasonal weather patterns. These have important social and economic implications:
>
> • Storm surges and flooding can affect infrastructure, services, and business activity, as seen with Hurricane Igor.
> • Coastal erosion and sea-level rise can impact community development and place homes, businesses and coastal infrastructure at risk, such as wharves and causeways.[117]

The plan addresses the transport sector, which it identifies as a limited source of greenhouse gas emission reductions:

> There are unique challenges in Newfoundland and Labrador with respect to the transportation sector. Newfoundland and Labrador is the most rural province in Canada, with 50 per cent of the population living in rural locations. Its largest centres do not have large enough population to support mass transit options such as rail and the provincial population is too small to support unique vehicle efficiency standards. In addition, biofuels are not readily available in sufficiently large quantities to power the province's vehicles. As a result, GHG [greenhouse gas] savings in the transportation sector will largely depend on individual decisions concerning means of transportation, vehicle purchases, driving habits and distance traveled, for the foreseeable future.[118]

The 2011 climate plan frames constraining transport emissions as narrow. This is confirmed by the fact that, in contrast to Nova

Scotia and other provinces, the Government of Newfoundland and Labrador does not have a sustainable transportation strategy. In 2006, the government developed a discussion paper pertaining to Labrador; however, it focuses solely on transportation infrastructure investment and economic development.[119] The document does not reference climate change, which is notable given the impact of extreme weather and melting permafrost in northern regions.[120]

Static road infrastructure is vulnerable to wind and storm surges. A sense of a new and disconcerting normal materializes, both in terms of climate and of expectations of mobility disruption. Due to the rural profile of the province, where more than three-quarters of the population lives outside the capital city, combined with pervasive automobility, minimal consideration is given to emissions mitigation in a growing transport sector. According to Catto and Tomblin, "Effecting change requires a sense of problem (or crisis), a new vision that reflects core values and objectives, a coalition in support of new reforms, and institutions capable of getting the problem onto the radar screen and implemented."[121] The impacts of Hurricane Igor were insufficient to spark a sense of transformative crisis. This may, in part, be due to the combination of praise officials employed and a genuine sense of pride in managing the crisis and restoring the road network. Hurricane Igor, while a major event, was viewed in isolation from numerous other flooding events, and was insufficient to instigate a societal shift on climate action, indicating limits to Ulrich Beck's concept of emancipatory catastrophism (chapter 1).

2019 Climate Plan

In contrast to its 2011 counterpart, the updated 2019 climate plan is more optimistic in tone and content. It states that hurricanes and tropical storms are now twice as frequent compared to last century.[122] It focuses on greening personal and freight road transport and the fishing fleet. Spurred by federal initiatives, including carbon pricing in the form of a modest carbon tax, vehicle fuel efficiency requirements, and public transit investments, the province aims to increase the share of zero-emission vehicles.[123] Proposed actions include developing a long-term strategy to increase the market share of electric vehicles and electrifying "marine ports, truck stops and public transit."[124] More recently, the Canada-Newfoundland and Labrador Offshore Petroleum Board was rebranded as an Offshore Energy Board with a mandate to diversify into renewable energy, a notable shift from a long-standing commitment to oil and gas investment.[125]

This tight coupling of electricity and mobility requires robust power grids, as well addressing ongoing vulnerabilities, such as static road infrastructure susceptible to washouts and reliance on global supply chains (chapter 6). A key area for future attention is the mobility of senior citizens who will make up a quarter of the population in coming years, as well as the caregivers, paid and unpaid, and health professionals upon whom they rely. The strategy states that "with at least 85 per cent of older Newfoundland and Labrador adults living with at least one chronic disease/condition, ease of access to support systems becomes even more critical."[126] The provincial aging strategy describes transportation pilot projects and "aging in place" strategies. A key question is how to make more age-friendly mobility and living arrangements that can withstand severe weather impacts.

In sum, because of Hurricane Igor, Newfoundland experienced extensive road washouts. Government, military, private contractors, volunteer firefighters, and community members co-operated to create scrambled mobilities based on formal and informal use of quads, boats, ferries, and helicopters, as well as to reconnect the road network. The community spirit and resourcefulness embodied by the so-called resilient Newfoundlander are critical but need to be paired with larger policy conversations in the House of Assembly. The absence of discussion regarding climate change and public safety resilience is a notable source of vulnerability. There was also a dearth of discussion about the lack of fuel availability, which is the basis of the next chapter.

6

Running on Fumes

They'd built a fire, burning everything we had ever

taught them. They had no choice, they explained,
it was the only way they could imagine keeping us warm.

Sue Goyette, "Thirty-Two," in *Ocean*

MOTIVE FORCE

When can you get us gas? When can you get us gas?

Gas station manager[1]

Mobility systems organized around fossil fuels, like gas and diesel, are both precarious and enduring. When there are road blockages and power outages, as was the case with both Hurricanes Juan and Igor, fuel fails to flow. In both provinces when electricity was lost so too was the capacity to pump fuel. Sociologist John Urry describes a system of "steel-and-petroleum" automobility that is locked in both in terms of infrastructure and culture.[2] *Automobility* refers to the system of vehicles and related infrastructure, such as streets and highways, that rely on fossil fuels and support supply chains, manufacturing, commuting, and more. Within the climate crisis, there are dual pressures to transition to a post-carbon or net-zero paradigm while at the same time adapting to a post-normal climate (chapter 8).

Motive force is what makes a thing move. It may refer to the ecological mobilities of wind, rain, and waves tracing a line from Cape Verde, where hurricanes originate, to the North Atlantic (chapter 2). Curiosity may also be a motive force, as with charismatic mobilities (chapter 4). Motive force for vehicles is most often provided by fossil fuels. The prominence of fossil fuels as the means of movement is striking not only because of the climatic implications but also due to the pervasive societal reliance across contexts, as seen in Ktaqmkuk/ Newfoundland, Mi'kma'ki/Nova Scotia, New York (Lanape Territory), and Boriken/Puerto Rico. Mobility contributes to climate change and, in turn, is impacted by climate change in a way that is cyclical and dynamic, posing an increasing source of societal disruption. This raises questions about how to mitigate reciprocal impacts and how to reimagine social-ecological relationships generally, and the human relationship with mobility specifically. There are three sections in this chapter. First, I look at the impacts of fuel immobility in the aftermath of Hurricanes Juan and Igor, as well as surprising parallels with the aftermath of Hurricane Sandy, which hit New York in 2012, and Hurricane Maria, which hit Puerto Rico in 2017. Next, I describe a fuel shortage that impacted Nova Scotia in 2015, which illustrates the precarious supply chains upon which communities rely. I conclude with a discussion juxtaposing fuel, health, and climate emergencies.

IMMOBILE FUEL

During Hurricanes Juan and Igor, moored ribbons of infrastructure, such as roads, electrical poles, power lines, and substations, were susceptible to storm impacts. By contrast, transport modes – quads, cars, boats, ships, ferries, and airplanes – were often sheltered, diverted, or repositioned to avoid them. Despite the diversity of ways to move, most transport energy is derived from fossil fuels. Automobility requires fixed roads, while travel by water and air require only fixed nodes in the form of ferry terminals and airports. While such modes were flexible, their fuel sources were not. The mobility of fuel – from supplier to market and from holding tanks to fuel tanks – was an issue. Concerns about accessing fuel were paramount for car owners, transport managers, and emergency services.

During both Hurricanes Juan and Igor, the normal order of mobility was flipped. Roads were mobile, in that they were literally moved by the hurricanes. Fuel, by contrast, was stationary: available but either quickly depleted or, because there was no electricity to operate pumps, immobile in its tanks. Electricity is needed to produce and pump liquid fuel; fuel is needed to generate electricity. Fuel and electricity are an example of a tightly coupled system. The provision of one relies on the other and, by extension, the absence of one prevents the provision of the other.[3] Energy must be available in the "right places at the right times" to enable other activities.[4] Critically, this includes mobility. What comes to light is a fragile energy system subject to cascading collapse. With the failure of electricity after both storms, even available fuel stores became stranded assets. Tightly coupled systems are vulnerable.

Newfoundland

In Newfoundland, the average gas station carries about 15,000 litres of fuel: enough to last two to three days. Hurricane Igor disrupted the mundane task of obtaining fuel, critical for automobility.[5] One regional fuel provider, Stuart, recalls his interactions with gas retailers in the aftermath of Igor. The public was asking about availability of gas:

> And we're like, "Guys, the road is washed out. It's not like we can just go and drive down through that big hole and get a tractor-trailer over to the other side." So they understood, but everybody was kind of really anxious, I guess, to have that taken care of ASAP ... The road was cut off, the residents down there panicked and started buying gas like it was going to be made no more. [Gas stations were] selling everything they've got in one day. And then some of them even actually rationed gas. When they realized they were going to run out, they would stop letting people take whatever they wanted. Some sites actually stopped it and said, "If I sell out everything I've got, then how is the ambulance and the fire truck going to move if there's an emergency?" ... They're going to sell the litres anyway, so it's just as well that they make sure a lot of people get some instead of only a few people.[6]

Fuel scarcity prompted feelings of anxiety at the prospect of immobility.

In the short term, ferries delivered fuel. Ferry operations around the province were reconfigured, with boats loading fuel trucks and diverting to where they were needed.[7] Newfoundland worked quickly to adapt and respond, but at the same time reinforced fossil fuel dependence.[8] In the longer term, the experience of fuel scarcity left a mark. Even long after the storm, residents were sensitive – on "high alert" – to the possibility of fuel shortages.[9] Phil, a road manager, recalls a storm that occurred a couple of years after Igor: "The eye went right through and we didn't have hardly any damage – twenty millimetres of rain, no high winds – but people were ... lined up at the gas station."[10] Movement of fuel, usually taken for granted, akin to the expectation that water will flow when a tap is turned on, was a lingering concern.

Stuart notes that the vulnerability of the fuel/power coupling is an ongoing concern: "It happens a lot, even now, when we had the power outage ... Some small places do carry generators where they can get a [gas] pump running, a single pump. This is very uncommon though. It should be more common, given our climate."[11] The lack of a backup system for gas pump failures is striking, given the reliance on fossil fuels for day-to-day functioning of mobility in Newfoundland. Fossil fuels are required even for equipment used in recovery efforts, such as generators and chain saws. Stuart concedes, "I think if there was another Igor ... maybe we'd have the same thing happen again and we'd just have to suffer through it like we did last time. Hopefully, the road holds up this time."[12] Hope is a precarious strategy, especially in the context of Newfoundland's reliance on automobility.[13] The issue of fuel shortages was not raised in Newfoundland's House of Assembly (chapter 5). Such an absence of debate is worrying given the public safety implications.

Nova Scotia also experienced fuel immobility in the aftermath of Hurricane Juan. Post-storm, efforts to get transit up and running were top of mind. Transit manager Chad recalls, "The priority was to try to get things rolling, get the city operational. And so we were trying to open up all the priority routes ... I mean you're making remedial, just basic repairs to what you need to get you going again. And of course, one of the main focuses was getting transit re-established, so that we could actually have people start moving around again ... But we were dealing with power outages."[14] While Hurricane Juan did not damage buses, problems arose due to a lack of electricity. Gas pumps located in the main bus terminal were inoperable. Public transit is directly reliant on fuel and indirectly reliant on electricity, though with the transition to an electric fleet this relationship is increasingly direct raising critical questions about the resilience of the power grid. Chad recalls, "If we didn't have the ability to refuel our buses, we wouldn't be able to put our service out ... I was being pushed to find areas to fuel the buses, because our fuelling stations weren't working."[15] Chad relied on contingency plans set up prior to the storm to source fuel. Fortunately, power at the bus terminal was restored and the crisis was short-lived.

In K'jipuktuk/Halifax at large, access to gas was also an issue. At one point, only one gas station was open in the Halifax Regional Municipality, an area the size of Epekwitk/Prince Edward Island. The station in Lower Sackville was inundated with customers. Sales tripled. Police managed extensive traffic backups and tensions rose as customers jostled for position in line.[16] In short, fuel immobility threatened the viability of human mobility leading to stress.

New York

Further down the Atlantic coast, such frictions also developed in New York after Category 5 Hurricane Sandy hit in 2012. Though the scale of Hurricane Sandy was much greater than that of Hurricanes Juan and Igor, lack of fuel access was an issue common to all three, from rural Newfoundland to central Manhattan. Hurricane Sandy damaged the refineries, ports, and terminals that enables gas to get to the pumps.[17] The situation was unprecedented: "Hurricane Sandy unleashed a record storm surge that exposed the surprising fragility of New York Harbor's fuel supply chain – the largest, most varied trading and distribution hub in the world – serving America's most populous urban area."[18] While fuel was on-site at New York terminals, it was not accessible in part due to flooding. A smaller storm that followed Hurricane Sandy prevented repair of the terminals and delayed fuel barges en route to New York.[19] Many gas stations closed as they either ran out of product or were unable to pump due to a lack of electricity. Of 800 stations, only 200 were open at a given time. Police officers were posted to open stations, managing line-ups that lasted for hours.

New Jersey governor Chris Christie and New York City mayor Michael Bloomberg imposed gas rationing for the first time since the 1970s oil crisis. Following Hurricane Sandy, rationing was based on licence plate numbers "restricting sales to cars with even-numbered license plates on even days, and odd-numbered on odd days."[20] It applied to private vehicles, not taxis, buses, or emergency vehicles. New York State governor Andrew Cuomo required gas stations on major routes to install backup generators.[21] A fund (US$12 million) was created to assist gas stations in buying backup generators and installing transfer switches at a cost of approximately US$12,000 per station.[22]

Puerto Rico

Even further down the Atlantic coast, Puerto Rico experienced devastating and enduring damage to its energy system when Category 5 Hurricane Maria hit in 2017. Puerto Rico relies upon imports to function; the American territory imports 98 per cent of its energy and 85 per cent of its food. Its grid relies upon fossil fuels – oil, gas, and coal – which are all imported. The fuel is then transported by truck and pipeline to power plants. Above-ground power lines and an underwater cable transmit power to households. The cumbersome system results in Puerto Ricans, who earn far less than the national median wage, paying electricity rates more than twice the American average.[23]

The electrical grid was already physically and financially precarious before Hurricane Maria made landfall. The storm destroyed this expansive and expensive energy system. Above-ground power lines were toppled, and the underwater cable was damaged. Imported supplies were stuck at the docks due to failures in the road network and a lack of available fuel, "with diesel in short supply across the island, some just couldn't find the fuel to drive. The lines at gas stations stretched out by the mile. Half of the island's stations were out of commission." Imported food was stuck at port, and grocery store shelves were empty. Author Naomi Klein writes, "Maria caused devastating ruptures within every tentacle of Puerto Rico's energy system."[24] As a result, one resident comments, "We didn't have food, we didn't have water, we didn't have electricity, we didn't have anything."[25] Hurricane Maria exposed the island's reliance on fossil-fuelled electricity.

This devastation is viewed by some as a window of opportunity to transition to renewable and decentralized energy to increase self-sufficiency and prepare for future climate change impacts. "Though poor in fossil fuels," Klein notes, Puerto Rico is "drenched in sun, lashed by wind, and surrounded by waves."[26] Spurred on by storm impacts, community groups are developing small-scale solar and wind projects that can ensure the lights stay on in local communities, even when the larger grid is down.[27] In addition, community groups are

growing crops like yucca, taro, and sweet potato that grow underground or near to the ground. Unlike high-hanging bananas, these
crops are less susceptible to high winds. By taking control of energy
and food production, Puerto Ricans are increasing their capacity for
controlling the mobility of the resources upon which they rely.

Puerto Rico's re-evaluation of its energy system and New York's
program subsidizing generators contrast with the more hands-off
approach taken in the aftermath of Hurricanes Juan and Igor in
Nova Scotia and Newfoundland and Labrador, where electrical and
fuel systems remain intertwined. The storms, while destructive, did
not disrupt the fuel system enough to instigate change.

Fuel Circulations

Urry refers to the precarious state of capitalism as a phenomenon,
much like the climate, that is within human influence but beyond
human control.[28] Just as climate change disrupts movement of people, goods, and services, it disrupts, challenges, and troubles circulations that rely on speed and flow. Circulation is central to mobility.
Take as an example, the global circulation of oil and gas via networks
of pipelines, ships, refineries, and gas pumps, and the concomitant
flow of greenhouse gas emissions from the wellhead to tail pipe to
atmosphere. These flows are entrenched and precarious, technologically, economically, and ecologically.[29] In 2005, Hurricane Katrina
disrupted oil processing plants with continent-wide ramifications
for fuel distribution and pricing, affecting nearly 10 per cent of US
supply.[30] With an international logistics supply chain, delays in one
region can cause backups on a global scale.[31] Just-in-time delivery
means that regions do not store goods but bring them in as needed.
In the context of disruption, just-in-time is just too late.

Geographer Deborah Cowen observes that "efforts to protect
supply chains invest logistical systems with biological imperatives
to flow and prescribe 'resilience' as a means of sustaining not only
human life but the system itself."[32] This is perhaps no more the case
than with oil. Sociologist Mimi Sheller observes how the mobilities
paradigm draws attention to the "geoecological underpinnings ...
including the global political economies of oil" that support infrastructure like roads, vehicles, and even the internet.[33] Sheller describes
how urbanization generally, and even efforts to green cities such
as increasing residential density and expanding public transport,

draw on global resources, from underground mines to satellites in orbit: urbanization is a "deeply cultural project organized around discourses of modernization, acceleration, lightness, and speed, ... founded on environmental destruction and toxic pollution of hinterlands, peripheries, and remote wilderness areas."[34] In effect, cities and in fact most communities regardless of size, extend far beyond their geographical borders. On the one hand, movement, growth, and overcoming distance are lauded, with concessions reluctantly made for what are perceived as extenuating circumstances such as weather. On the other hand, such patterns destabilize the global climate; they are unsustainable.

FUEL SHORTAGE IN NOVA SCOTIA

It is normally so reliable that we take it for granted but it is such a long and complex chain that it does not require an intentional act to interrupt it.

Provincial fuel shortage report[35]

In 2015, Nova Scotia experienced a fuel shortage. The cause was not dramatic, such as a hurricane, epidemic, or terrorist attack. Rather the seventy-three-hour shortage was caused by a series of unlikely but mundane events related to delivery and product quality. In this section, I describe inward-facing supply chain disruption followed by outward-facing disruption affecting the public sphere. Sociologist Charles Perrow observes, "Tightly coupled systems predictably fail ... in unpredictable ways."[36] A lean fuel supply chain amplifies impacts. The shortage, though not related to Hurricanes Juan and Igor, brings the broader implications of fuel immobility into focus. Communities that rely upon just-in-time delivery, including fuel, food, and medical supplies are vulnerable to mobility disruption and introduce vulnerability throughout social systems.

Supply Chain Disruption

In 2015, there was one main fuel storage terminal on mainland Nova Scotia in Dartmouth, across the harbour from the capital of Halifax. This meant that all gasoline, diesel, and, in winter, heating oil was obtained from one source: Imperial Oil. The terminal receives, on average, one shipment per week. Bill Simpkins of the Canadian Fuels

Association says, "Just like any business, just like stocking shelves in a grocery store, it's a just-in-time operation."[37] Atlantic Canada is not a large fuel market: it accounts for less than 8 per cent of Canadian fuel demand. Despite its market size, Nova Scotia is just as reliant on fuel as larger markets due to its lack of energy diversity. Former Royal Canadian Mounted Police officer Alphonse MacNeil and former Nova Scotia deputy minister of justice Douglas Keefe led an independent review following the fuel shortage. The resulting report observes that Nova Scotia's fuel supply is precarious, with many potential points of failure. This also characterizes a wide range of supply chains, as highlighted by the 2021 Suez Canal, where one ship running aground blocked a route that permits 12 per cent of global trade.[38]

Typical of global supply chains, Atlantic Canada both exports and imports fuel products. From 2000 until 2019, Nova Scotia produced offshore natural gas for domestic use and for export to the American northeast. Natural gas is not, however, commonly used to fuel vehicles.[39] The Irving Oil refinery in Saint John, New Brunswick, imports oil from various countries, including Saudi Arabia, and exports more than half of its product to the northeast United States.[40] It has a 320,000 barrel-per-day capacity and is the largest refinery in Canada.[41] North Atlantic Refining at Come By Chance, Newfoundland and Labrador, sources its oil from offshore Newfoundland as well as global sources, and exports to the US market. Before COVID impacted global oil prices, the site could produce 115,000 barrels per day.[42] In 2021, the refinery was sold to be used for biodiesel production.[43]

On 13 August 2015, the *Alpine Hibiscus*, docked in Mexico, was expected to travel up the Atlantic coast to the port of Halifax, arriving between 17 and 21 August. In Mexico, it was found that the fuel was "off spec," meaning it did not meet quality specifications. It is industry practice that all fuel is quality tested before departure, as well as upon arrival, as contamination can occur en route, such as water entering the product. Fuel is required to meet a variety of specifications related to vehicle safety, such as preventing corrosion, as well as for environmental protection, such as emissions. The fuel load was treatable but would arrive late.

Upon hearing of the delay, Imperial Oil in Nova Scotia took two courses of action. First, it restricted the volume of fuel available to its customers. Distributors were allocated only 90 per cent of their original order volume. Second, it ordered two additional shipments. The *New England* was nearby but carried a small fuel load. The *Acadian* carried a large fuel load but was travelling from Europe and would take longer to arrive. Imperial Oil executives estimated that, between reducing fuel allocations and ordering alternate fuel supplies, service would return to normal in hours. Residents and officials would not be aware there was even a disruption. This, however, was not how events played out.

The *New England* arrived with its smaller cargo on 24 August. This gave Imperial Oil a few extra days' worth of product. On 27 August, Imperial Oil officially informed its terminal customers to expect a short-term fuel outage, meaning there was no available fuel at the terminal. On 28 August, as projected, the terminal ran out of fuel. Imagine, then, the relief with which the *Alpine Hibiscus* was met when it arrived from Mexico later that day, followed less than twelve hours later by the *Acadian* from Europe.

Fuel cannot be used immediately. After unloading it needs to be held on-site for several hours to allow water accumulated en route to settle. The fuel also needs to be tested to ensure it meets specifications. It was found that the fuel load carried by the *Alpine Hibiscus*, despite being corrected prior to departure, had been contaminated in transit. Further, while the *Acadian* was unloading, Imperial Oil received waylaid test results based on a cargo sample taken prior to departure. Its fuel load was also off spec. In a rare coincidence, the cargoes of both ships were contaminated. Note that this view of contamination is based on water polluting oil, not as commonly understood oil polluting water such as in the BP oil spill. Though fuel was in port, it could not be used until treated. Imperial Oil officials said that they had never heard of two tankers in a row arriving off spec. "The conjunction was unthinkable," wrote MacNeil and Keefe, "until it happened." 44 Imperial Oil was familiar with how to treat the cargo of the *Acadian*, but not as readily that of the *Hibiscus*. The *Acadian* required additives from Montreal that arrived on 30 August. Fuel was available again to terminal customers on 31 August. Mobility infrastructure disruptions highlight how the risk of immobility is embedded in mobility. Further, this case highlights the role of secondary supply chains, such as additives, that enable primary supply chains.

Between 27 and 31 August, Imperial Oil revised its estimates seven times as to when fuel would again be available. A series of mundane and unlikely events resulted in a much longer disruption than anticipated. Imperial Oil experienced a fuel outage, which translated into a public fuel shortage. Fuel was technically available in the province, but inaccessible. A station in a rural community might still carry product, for example, but urban gas stations were empty. The recovery took more than three days to be felt around the province as fuel required redistribution. The shortage officially ended on 3 September.

Other factors complicated the fuel shortage. It occurred during the last weekend of summer when many people travel. Fuel prices coincidentally dipped below one dollar for the first time in over six months. Media accounts of the fuel shortage caused car owners to top-up their vehicles and spare tanks.[45] The result of this confluence of unusual factors was empty gas pumps. The independent review panel later determined that the "shortage was caused by the three-day outage at the [terminal] rack. The price drops did not cause the outage and neither did stockpiling. But together price and panic made a bad situation worse."[46] These impacts parallel the fuel shortages experienced after Hurricanes Juan and Igor, as well as indicate a shared social response in the face of fuel disruption.

Societal Disruption

The impact was greater than just frustrated summer vacationers. A variety of essential services rely upon commercial fuel supplies, including police, fire, and ambulance. While all have contingency plans for severe weather and power outages, none planned for a fuel shortage. Fire services were not impacted as their vehicles run on diesel, which was not affected by the Imperial Oil fuel outage. However, police vehicles run on gas. In response, police opted not to carry out low-priority patrols, assigned two officers to each vehicle to avoid using additional vehicles, and patrolled by bike and on foot where possible. Police did not respond to low-priority calls, such as minor property damage, to conserve fuel in case a more pressing emergency arose.[47]

Hospitals, and the health-care system at large, are also dependent on fuel, including patients accessing care, staff getting to work, and transporting supplies like food, pharmaceuticals, and laundry.[48] Of 181 ambulances in the province, all but 6 run on gas. To compensate for the shortage, paramedics avoided idling. They called gas stations directly in search of fuel as there was no overall sense of where fuel was and was not available. Some had to drive far out of their service area to find fuel. This risked compromising the goal that ambulances respond to 911 emergency calls within nine minutes, 90 per cent of the time. In 2015, 28,000 Nova Scotians received home care, ranging from minor support to nursing, for a total of 242,000 home visits – by car – per month. These services were not disrupted during the shortage, but the degree to which health-care delivery is intertwined with fossil fuel availability is notable.

Given this tight coupling, the lack of severe impacts in the face of disrupted fuel supplies was remarkable. A Halifax hospital reported only one patient cancellation due to the shortage.[49] There was a consensus that the fuel shortage was a close call, and had it extended beyond three days, conditions would have quickly eroded. If a major incident had occurred, such as a hurricane, the lack of fuel would have been acutely felt; likewise if the outage had occurred mid-week when demand runs higher. If the fuel shortage had continued for several days *and* a significant event had occurred, the results could have been catastrophic.

Overview of Mobility Disruptions

The Nova Scotia fuel shortage was a relatively mundane event in terms of both cause and impact. It was an almost-emergency, a close call that could have easily tipped into catastrophic immobility. No lives were lost. It demonstrated the precarity of global just-in-time supply chains and low inventories that render the fuel system vulnerable to mobility disruptions. Such disruptions are not unusual. Newfoundland experienced an even more disruptive energy event around the same time. In January 2014, rolling blackouts impacted residents. At the time, temporary power outages were planned to allow for utility upgrades. Unplanned outages resulted when a substation caught fire and a generating station and its backup failed – echoing the back-to-back contaminated fuel shipments that occurred during the Nova Scotia fuel shortage: a conjunction that was unthinkable "until it happened."[50] As a result, almost 300,000 Newfoundland Power customers lost service over the course of a week. Newfoundlanders lacked heat and electricity at a time when temperatures reached lows of minus 18°C, with wind chill making it feel like minus 35°C.[51] The event triggered mobility within communities as individuals and families sought to find warm accommodation for themselves and others. Then premier of Newfoundland and Labrador Kathy Dunderdale resigned in part due to the rolling blackouts.[52]

Disruption is not uncommon, whether in the form of record-breaking storms or mundane supply chain interruptions. MacNeil and Keefe observe, "Fuel is a bulk commodity and exposed to all the risks entailed in transportation – everything from perils of the sea to snowbound roads. Terminals and service stations depend on electricity. The Imperial terminal has its own generators, but the Panel was told that few if any service stations have generators and without electricity they cannot pump fuel."[53] As with other jurisdictions in and beyond Canada, Nova Scotia's fuel supply chain is increasingly lean. A lack of backup generators means that fuel cannot be pumped even if it is physically present on-site.

The number of gas stations is also decreasing. In 1973, there were 1,413 gas retailers in Nova Scotia. In 2015, there were 385. In 2013, Imperial Oil closed its refinery, first opened in 1918. It was converted to the terminal at the centre of the Nova Scotia fuel shortage. In 2016, Irving Oil reopened its Halifax terminal, which had closed in 2002. Overall, Nova Scotia's fuel supply chain is increasingly consolidated. "The reality for Nova Scotia," write MacNeil and Keefe, "is that Atlantic Canada is a small market with little redundancy."[54] And yet, emergency and health services are premised on fuel availability.

The fact that Nova Scotia is on the Atlantic Ocean offers more flexibility than landlocked locales. Fuel tankers, more so than pipelines, can be redirected in the case of disruption.[55] At the same time, Nova Scotia is more vulnerable to the impacts of a changing climate on oceans, including rising sea levels and warming waters that fuel hurricanes. Nova Scotia is vulnerable to both fuel supply chain disruptions and climate change impacts, that is, it is vulnerable to both fuel and climate emergencies. Fuel resilience emerges as a pressing societal concern at the same time as climate scientists and advocates emphasize the need to transition away from fossil fuels.

FUEL, HEALTH, AND CLIMATE EMERGENCIES

I don't want you to be hopeful, I want you to panic and act as if the house were on fire.

Greta Thunberg, climate activist[56]

What insights do the Nova Scotia fuel shortage and Hurricanes Juan and Igor offer in terms of fuel resilience? Nova Scotia and Newfoundland and Labrador are reliant on fossil fuels. And yet, between lean global supply chains, gas station consolidation, and the lack of backup systems for remaining gas stations, the fuel system is fragile. The system endures because of technological lock-in resulting from decades of infrastructural investment and cultural buy-in to fossil-fuelled mobility. The fuel system is both precarious and persistent. It is in this context that communities are confronted with the need to stop using fossil fuels to protect the global climate and public health. Energy supply needs to be improved as society transitions to post-carbon mobilities.

Climate change is a threat multiplier. It exacerbates existing issues like the reliance of global supply chains on fossil fuel and the vulnerability of supply chains to increasingly extreme weather. Fuel shortages hinder provision of health care, eroding quality of life and life chances, and climate change yields a range of health impacts, from increased rates of disease transmission to anxiety. In this section, I discuss the relationship between fuel, health, and climate emergencies. The three spheres of fuel, health, and climate can be framed as emergencies but are not necessarily experienced as emergencies across a given population. Depending on such factors as location, budget, transport options, fuel availability, and community health, climate change is experienced differently by different individuals, communities, and countries.

The links between fossil fuel use, health, and climate change are explicit. The triad threatens to damage the health of humans and animals. There is a sense that a fundamental redraft is needed. Geographer Peter Adey theorizes the "inescapable pairs" of emergency and mobility as exemplified by temporary evacuation due to wildfires in Alberta and permanent moves by Syrian refugees, by rapid Ebola response in Africa and prolonged physical distancing during COVID.[57] Mobility and emergency are entwined and everywhere. Adey describes emergency mobilities: "whether in flight or in response, emergencies demand highly intensive forms of movement that radically transform one's life chances and quality of life."[58] Such emergencies can range from events that fall within everyday governance to states of exception, from local to global.

The governance of emergency mobilities tries to get things moving again.[59] Adey and colleague Ben Anderson define emergency as an "interval after an event, where life and death are at stake, outcomes are uncertain and timely action is demanded."[60] They are spaces for action and intervention, when critical decisions need to be made to prevent disaster. Klein writes: "Treating an emergency like an emergency means all our energies can go into action."[61] An emergency is typically a temporary state that either contracts and resolves or expands into catastrophe, hence its applicability to climate change. Declaring a state of emergency, formally and informally, creates time and space to intervene. In this section, I juxtapose three different emergencies – fuel, health, and climate – to highlight different facets of emergency mobility.[62]

Fuel Emergency

Fuel disruption is an acknowledged basis for emergency through Canada's *Energy Supplies Emergency Act*. Implemented in 1978, when Canada was a net energy importer and in response to a series of oil market crises, the act "provides a means to conserve the supplies of energy within Canada during periods of national emergency."[63] An Energy Supplies Allocation Board, chaired by the minister of natural resources, administers the act. The board can have up to six members, but currently only has a chair.[64] The act applies to fossil fuels, such as gas and diesel, as well as alternative fuels and electrical power. Notably, the act has never been used to address disruption to energy supply. This is in part because Canada is a net producer of energy, and in part because the act is geared toward longer-term, national-scale disruptions, rather than shorter-term, localized disruptions, such as the Nova Scotia fuel shortage.[65] This suggests that there is scope to update the act in the face of a changing climate where severe weather may contribute to short-term as well as longer-term energy disruptions, including fuels sources used for zero-emission vehicles such as electricity.

The two central mechanisms in the act are allocating and rationing fuel supplies. Just as Imperial Oil imposed an allocation limit during the Nova Scotia fuel shortage, the Government of Canada can impose allocation limits to wholesalers and suppliers. Rationing can apply to any fuel type, volume, and user. It might involve issuing fuel vouchers and establishing regional boards to administer rationing. Other powers under the act include waiving environmental regulations, permitting exemptions from the *Competition Act*, and rerouting fuel supplies carried by rail, ship, truck, and pipeline to areas of Canada in need. This connects to political, economic, and social questions about Indigenous, provincial, and federal relations, such as the Trans Mountain pipeline transporting oil from Alberta to coastal British Columbia as well as safety issues, such as the 2013 Lac-Mégantic, Quebec, disaster that resulted in forty-seven deaths when a train carrying crude oil derailed. Current fuel networks are geographically diffuse and feature lean supply chains and just-in-time delivery. These systems are also politically contentious, whether sourced from Saudi Arabia with its human rights violations or Alberta with its entrenched commitment to fossil fuel extraction.

Fuel is tightly coupled with mobility, which in turn is tightly coupled with all aspects of contemporary life in Canada, including key social services, such as health care and education. Thus, fuel shortages can disrupt all types of services. Environmental engineer Samuel Markolf and colleagues describe such cases as indirect pathways of disruption. Whereas direct pathways of disruption include physical damage, such as road washouts, indirect pathways of disruption result from knock-on impacts of interconnected infrastructure where "complexities within and interconnections between the transportation system and other critical infrastructure, social, and ecological systems" are exposed and damaged.[66] It is insufficient to have a road that can withstand flooding. The other transport systems and social services that are connected to and reliant upon that road also require protection.

This interconnection will only intensify with a transition to zero-emission vehicles where disruptions in the electricity grid translate even more directly to mobility disruptions. This does not deter from the merit of such a transition, but rather highlights how resilience will need to be woven into the transition. Given the impact of Hurricanes Juan and Igor on both electricity and mobility, the potential for disruption is significant. Looking forward, relying on globally and even nationally sourced fuel in the context of greater climate disruption is a blueprint for disaster. (In chapter 8, I explore how to create a looser coupling of fuel and mobility.) Next, I situate a fuel emergency in the context of health and climate emergencies.

Health Emergency

The health of human and other species faces the dual threats of fuel and climate emergencies. As shown in the case of the Nova Scotia fuel shortage, the provincial health system is built around fossil-fuelled mobility. It relies on gas and diesel for powering ambulances responding to emergencies, transporting home care workers, and conveying patients to appointments. The transport of medical supplies, food, laundry and more, requires fuel. While the impacts of the 2015 fuel shortage on patient care were minimal, administrators and health practitioners recognized the precarity of the system. If the shortage lasted more than three days or if a mass casualty event occurred, such as a bus crash, the health system and other emergency services were ill-prepared to respond. Further, reliance on fossil fuels impacts the health of Nova Scotians through air pollution and acute and chronic climate impacts, such as intensified severe weather events and increases in vector-borne disease like Lyme disease transmitted by ticks. To this end, there are efforts in and beyond Nova Scotia to "green" health care through net-zero initiatives.[67]

This blind spot puts key infrastructures at risk, like hospitals susceptible to flooding and storm damage. For example, an analysis conducted in Sackville, New Brunswick, found that a local ambulance depot is at risk of being islanded by flood waters.[68] While the fuel shortage in Nova Scotia was an acute, short-term event, climate science and lived experience demonstrate more frequent and severe weather events, which disrupt mobility. Vulnerable to increasingly rough conditions at sea, Nova Scotia's weekly fuel shipments could again be delayed, causing shortages that impact health services. Further, the delivery of other medical supplies and pharmaceuticals could also be impacted. This is just one way in which the climate emergency is also a health emergency.

The World Health Organization calls climate change the "greatest health threat of the 21st century."[69] In Canada, climate change poses diverse health risks. The Canadian Association of Physicians for the Environment (CAPE), a coalition of Canadian health-care providers, including the Canadian Medical Association and the Canadian Public Health Association, notes that mental and physical health are already being impacted by climate change due to the stress and disruption caused by temporary or permanent evacuation due to floods, poor air quality due to forest fires, and suffering resulting from heat waves.[70] Extreme weather contributes to physical and mental injury, even death. Heat and smoke from wildfire activity aggravate pre-existing conditions, such as asthma and heart disease. Ticks and mosquitoes are flourishing in a warmer climate, increasing the range and prevalence of vector-borne diseases such as

Lyme disease and West Nile virus.[71] Water and food quality are compromised by both flood and drought conditions.[72] Closer physical contact between humans and animals due to habitat loss and population redistribution as a result of warmer temperatures is a risk factor for transmission of viruses, such as COVID.[73] Further, some groups are more impacted than others, such as people with disabilities and chronic illnesses, people with low-incomes, people who are pregnant, people who are older, people who work outdoors, as well as First Nations, Inuit, and Métis communities.[74]

Short-term evacuation, damage to and destruction of homes, and long-term displacement cause significant mental stress and trauma, contributing to anxiety and depression. Health geographer Ashlee Cunsolo, for example, describes, a range of mental health impacts, such as "sadness, distress, despair, anger, fear, helplessness, hopelessness and stress; elevated rates of mood disorders, such as depression, anxiety, and pre- and post-traumatic stress; increased drug and alcohol usage; increased suicide ideation, attempts and death by suicide; threats and disruptions to sense of place and place attachment; and loss of personal or cultural identity and ways of knowing."[75] These impacts highlight the importance of social-ecological relationships, which are too often taken for granted.

Despite this bleak prognosis, CAPE, echoing the World Health Organization, argues that climate emergency is also the "greatest health opportunity of the century" as the transformative actions needed to address climate change yield many other benefits related to health, community, and equity.[76] One example is using clean energy. In Canada, air pollution from fossil fuel use contributes to 7,000 premature deaths annually. In addition to local pollution, due to prevailing continental wind conditions, Nova Scotia receives transboundary air pollution from central Canada and the eastern United States. Switching to cleaner forms of energy, such as wind, solar, and geothermal could decrease incidences and associated health-care costs of heart disease, asthma, and lung cancer.[77]

Chronic diseases, such as diabetes, osteoarthritis, and anxiety disorders, cost Canadians almost $200 billion per year in treatment and lost work time.[78] Investment in safe, convenient, and enjoyable walking, cycling, and other active transport infrastructure brings two key benefits. First, it reduces emissions that contribute to climate change and related health impacts. Second, it promotes health through physical activity. It gets people moving, yielding a plethora of health benefits, including reducing the rates and severity of chronic disease. In short, action on climate change has the potential to yield far-reaching benefits at individual, community, and global levels. Climate change enters the sphere of health in many ways, from transport disruption to heat stroke. These intertwined entry points offer a range of possibilities for simultaneously addressing environmental and human health.

Climate Emergency

The IPCC warns that humanity has less than one decade to dramatically curb emissions if a profusion of dangerous health, environment, and economic impacts are to be avoided, with communities around the world already experiencing severe impacts. Global society has a decade to halve carbon emissions, and three decades to decarbonize.[79] The World Meteorological Organization observes that the impacts of global warming are speeding up.[80] Such acceleration was experienced in summer 2021, when British Columbia residents endured a heat dome whereby temperatures were significantly higher than any previous records, illustrating non-linear changes to which humans and animals struggle to adapt. Action needs to be taken now to ensure emissions reductions are achieved in the coming decade, or humanity will trigger a dangerous and irreversible tipping point in the Earth's ability to support life. There is a strong sense among climate advocates that this decade is a last opportunity to change course. Such responsibility is difficult to fathom, let alone act upon. Global society is experiencing a chronic climate emergency.

A federal climate report states that Canada is warming at a magnitude double the global average, increasing the risk of heat waves, droughts, and wildfires.[81] In June 2019, Parliament passed a resolution declaring a climate emergency.[82] The day after, Parliament voted in favour of the Trans Mountain pipeline, indicating a conflict between climate action and fossil fuel investment. Climate change was a central issue in the 2019 and 2021 federal elections, a notable shift from previous elections. The actions of the federal government need to align with Canada's commitment to the 2015 Paris Climate Agreement, which commits 194 signatory countries to keep emissions "well below" 2.0°C and, as advocated by the IPCC, to prevent an increase over 1.5°C.[83] Current and proposed actions, such as investments in clean power and zero-emission vehicles, are significant but not sufficient.[84]

Municipally, in response to the 2018 IPCC report, Halifax city council unanimously passed a resolution declaring a climate emergency. It is one of more than 500 Canadian communities to do so since 2018, including Mahone Bay and Wolfville in Nova Scotia and St. John's in Newfoundland. The declaration of a climate emergency is a way to intervene in and act on the global climate crisis. Halifax's declaration acknowledges that climate change poses an urgent threat: "the breakdown of the stable climate and sea levels under which human civilization developed constitutes an emergency."[85] Actions proposed as part of the declaration include reaching net-zero carbon emissions before 2050; achieving net negative carbon emissions in the second half of the century; developing a carbon budget that defines and allocates remaining permitted emissions; and establishing a working group that prioritizes those "most vulnerable to climate impacts and most in need of support in transitioning to renewable energy."[86]

The goal of such a declaration is, with the effort of city staff, to leverage the focus and action that comes with being in a state of emergency. To this end, in 2020, Halifax adopted a climate plan and, in 2022, was the first region in Canada to create a dedicated climate action tax. The earmarked funds support mitigation measures such as purchasing electric buses, installing electric vehicle chargers, and investing in an "all ages, all abilities" cycle network, as well as adaptation measures such as implementing the urban forest master plan and buying backup generators for emergency comfort centres – all measures that reflect an ecological approach to mobility.[87]

Emergency Mobilities

Adey and Anderson argue that reflecting on emergency and mobility prompts questions about the "relation with life that is enacted, or promised, as decisions are made and taken."[88] This applies equally to the climate emergency and an ecological approach to mobilities. Juxtaposing three different but interrelated emergencies – fuel, health, and climate – highlights different scales, authorities, techniques, and ethics of emergency mobility.[89] Fuel emergencies, as experienced in Nova Scotia, are the most contained of the three. While fuel was sourced globally, the impacts were local. At the same time, potential impacts were far-reaching within the province, impacting health care, education, and the economy. The direct response to the Nova

Scotia fuel shortage was coordinated by the private sector using strategies such as ordering new shipments and restricting allocations to distributors. At the federal level, allocating and rationing are key strategies within the *Energy Supplies Emergency Act*. A state of emergency was not declared, but fuel distributors, health professionals, and others experienced precarity. The guiding ethic was to return to normal as quickly as possible (chapter 7).

If Nova Scotia's fuel emergency was acute, then the health emergency is chronic. Climate change compounds ongoing challenges to health-care delivery in Canada, and globally, it increases risk of illness, disease, injury, and death due to myriad physical and mental impacts related to acute weather events, transmission of vector-borne diseases, and chronic changes in water and food quality. It disrupts the fuel and medical supply chains upon which health-care delivery relies, as well as the mobilities of patients and health-care professionals. The scale of health impact and the means to recover from such impacts are highly differentiated globally, as well as within and between Canadian communities. In addition to ongoing investments in and reflections on health-care delivery, CAPE frames the climate emergency as an opportunity to implement larger policy and infrastructure changes that benefit the environment and human health beyond reducing carbon emissions. Authority comes from health practitioners, informed by the experiences of their patients and the communities in which they practice. The guiding ethic is transformative.

In turn, the climate emergency is global, intergenerational, and game-changing. There are numerous players pushing for and against substantive climate action. For example, technical authority is exerted from the top down by the IPCC, an international scientific body that uses modelling and scenario-building as key tools for anticipation and communication. The Paris Agreement is the culmination of international political negotiations to address the climate crisis and is a central strategy for managing the emergency, which in turn shapes government responses. The guiding ethic is pragmatic, based on scientific and political consensus, and radical in its call for decarbonization and climate justice. In contrast, moral authority is exerted from the bottom up in the form of global youth activism spurred by the Fridays for the Future movement and activists such as Isra Hirsi (United States), Vanessa Nakate (Uganda), and Greta Thunberg (Sweden), among many more. Also informed by science, the guiding ethic is urgency. The climate emergency, as declared by hundreds of Canadian municipalities and the federal government, is a legal-political measure with performative and aspirational dimensions. Some communities will seize the opportunity to act, while others may persist with fossil fuel investments with limited legal or political consequence.

The impacts of fuel immobility in the aftermath of Hurricanes Juan and Igor in Atlantic Canada, as well as Hurricanes Sandy in New York, and Hurricane Maria in Puerto Rico, share surprising similarities, notably acute societal disruption. Further, the 2015 fuel shortage in Nova Scotia highlighted the reliance of health-care and emergency services on fossil fuel. Fuel, health, and climate emergencies are intertwined, with fossil fuel contributing to Anthropogenic climate change and resultant health emergencies, while at the same time Canadian communities rely upon fossil fuels to deliver health care. Although distressing, emergency can also be productive, offering insights into overlooked vulnerabilities and values. The examples of fuel, health, and climate change demonstrate different approaches to emergency and how such approaches "emerge, co-exist and change," and are held in tension.[90] Each is disruptive in its own way and results in a "chaotic remaking of the here and now."[91] In the next chapter, I examine areas of resilience and vulnerability in mobility, exploring three types of resilience: transport, social-ecological, and infrastructure.

Transport Resilience

We recruited sturdy lawn chairs and consulted
an architect before placing them on the shore.

Our aim was simple, we wanted to welcome
what the ocean had to tell us and make amends

with it. We wanted the chairs to display our willingness
but also our resolve. We would not be pushed around.

We could only find eight lawn chairs that stood the test
of tide. We advertised it as a master class of listening.

Sue Goyette, "Twenty-Eight," in *Ocean*

BOUNCING BACK BETTER

Hurricanes Juan and Igor demonstrate the simultaneous rigidity
and adaptability of mobility systems. Hurricanes vary, with different conditions exposing different resiliencies and vulnerabilities. As
described, in the face of the approaching storms, human movement
contracted. During the storm, static ribbons of infrastructure such
as roads were vulnerable, almost as if under attack. This demonstrates the social-ecological principle of highly optimized tolerance,
whereby specific infrastructure designs are functional and flexible
within a daily range of experience but falter and fail under less
frequent and more extreme events.[1] In the context of the Iceland
ash cloud event, urban theorist Ole B. Jensen refers to the tension
between "normal use" and an "abnormal situation."[2] In terms of
infrastructure resilience, architect Hillary Brown describes the risk

posed by "optimizing the various parts of complex systems [that] may undermine the sustainability of the whole."[3] For example, roads in Newfoundland are designed to withstand snowstorms but are less suited for intense rainfall.

This chapter has two sections. First, I detail a suite of measures used for managing mobility before, during, and after Hurricanes Juan and Igor, as well as in the longer term. Then I describe three interrelated types of resilience: transport, social-ecological, and infrastructure. Transport resilience focuses on human mobility, while social-ecological and infrastructure resilience address larger environmental considerations, such as carbon emissions and flows of stormwater. I dive into these different facets of resilience to illustrate how each relate to climate change and mobility and to demonstrate the need for even further transformative thinking.

JUAN AND IGOR

Hurricanes Juan and Igor differed in key respects: Juan was defined by an urban epicentre subjected to high winds, Igor by extensive flooding of rural areas. Despite these differences, important parallels exist, suggesting a commonality of social response to events experienced under climate change. In both Mi'kma'ki/Nova Scotia and Ktaqmkuk/Newfoundland, the impacts of the hurricanes were perceived as devastating, with analogies of war, such as bombs, battles, and arsenal, used to describe the effects.[4] In both storms, officials observed that it felt like the weather tracked over key infrastructure: the backbone of the electrical transmission system in Nova Scotia and the main highway in Newfoundland. The overlap was so uncanny that it was perceived by infrastructure managers in both provinces to be intentional, as if the environment targeted critical infrastructure. In reality, the storms reveal the vulnerability of systems on which communities rely.

Transport managers and other officials use many strategies to navigate weather-related mobility disruptions like Hurricanes Juan and Igor. These can be broadly categorized as managing mobility before, during, and after the storm as well as with a view to the longer term. Preparing for the storm includes measures such as battening down the hatches and fuelling generators. Managing during the storm focuses on delivering emergency services. Recovering after the storm includes immediate measures like removing debris,

Table 7.1 Measures for managing mobility before, during, and after
Hurricanes Juan and Igor

Before: Preventing mobility	During: Minimal mobility	After: Restoring mobility	Future: Building resilience
Preparation	*Response*	*Restoration*	*Mitigation*
Activate emergency plans, including Emergency Operations Centre	Evacuate residents and patients	Activate alternate mobilities	Analyze risk
Advocate caution (e.g., stay indoors, stay off roads)	Assess situation (i.e., Emergency Operations Centre)	Assess progress	Build-in redundancies (e.g., backup equipment)
Batten down hatches (e.g., tying up boats)	Ready for response as needed	Contain and allow flooding	Conduct research (e.g., generate data and statistics)
Barricade roads	Respond to 911 calls	Cope with political tensions (e.g., federal/provincial)	Develop early warning systems
Charge cell phones	Shelter residents and patients	Distribute relief (i.e., water, food)	Evaluate responses
Clean catch basins and create berms		Provide shelter	Expand existing departments
Declare states of emergency		Reconnect roads and transit	Invest in equipment and technology (e.g., radios)
Evacuate residents and patients		Repurpose transport (e.g., buses as shelters)	Maintain infrastructure and equipment
Fuel generators		Detour, reroute, resume, etc.	Manage retreat of development from flood-prone areas
Implement operating standards (e.g., wind threshold policy)		Search and rescue	Manage storm water (e.g., *Urban Forestry Strategy*)
Monitor weather		Waive normal approval processes (e.g., environmental assessments)	Mitigate greenhouse gas emissions
Pre-position personnel and goods		Use temporary structures (i.e., bridges)	Update construction standards (e.g., culvert diameter)
Reschedule, postpone, close, cancel, etc.			

while longer-term measures include creating redundancies and implementing more robust standards. These loosely align with the disaster response cycle.[5] There is an iterative relationship between the phases, characterized by ongoing learning, with past experiences shaping future preparation and response measures.

In Nova Scotia and Newfoundland, there was a cultural instinct to batten down the hatches, a term so pertinent that I use it liberally in my discussion. This nautical expression refers to closing access points to prevent vessels from swamping during storms. During Juan and Igor, the idiom emerged as cultural shorthand to describe preparations made in anticipation of the coming storm. Steps taken ranged from storing lawn furniture, which can transform into dangerous projectiles, to mooring ships at sea so they did not crash into wharves and other coastal infrastructure.

Thorough but not exhaustive, table 7.1 lists diverse strategies employed in Nova Scotia and Newfoundland that relate directly and indirectly to mobility. Mimi Sheller's description of the "demobilizations, remobilizations and unique (im)mobilities" brought about by disaster is apt.[6] Both regions implemented these measures to varying degrees and in varying combinations, revising practices based on local conditions. The measures revolve around the interrelated spheres of managing people, infrastructure, and information. To this end, these measures may be transferable to different regions and different contexts. In contrast to the charismatic mobility of the storm and the charismatic immobility created by storm damage, these measures are, with some exceptions, mundane but valuable interventions that promote safety.

Before Storm: Preventing Mobility

Before both Juan and Igor, within a window of approximately seventy-two hours, officials took diverse steps to prevent storm damage. One primary activity was monitoring the weather and the course of the approaching storm. Focus was on materials, including minimizing the potential damage by battening down the hatches. These efforts ranged in scale from tying down loose objects such as barbecues to clearing dead tree branches to mooring ships at sea. Government emergency services and non-profit relief organizations stockpiled goods such as cots, blankets, and bottled water to ensure availability across affected regions.

Just as objects were attended to, so too was energy. Residents and officials charged cell phones and fuelled generators, allowing communication, lighting, and heating to continue in the short term should other infrastructure systems fail. Work crews attended to physical infrastructure, such as clearing catch basins to maximize the flow of stormwater. Small berms, that is, mounds made of dirt and gravel, were created in coastal areas to mitigate the impacts of potential flooding. Roads prone to washouts were barricaded to prevent use in the storm aftermath.

Municipalities, transport providers, and organizations such as seniors' homes activated emergency plans. In anticipation of the damage, Halifax Regional Municipality declared a state of emergency before Juan. Nearby East Hants County and Colchester County also declared states of emergency. Declaring a state of emergency triggered diverse formal and informal mobilities and immobilities, including advising that residents stay at home and off the roads and evacuating residents from flood-prone coastal regions, as well as rescheduling medical procedures; postponing flights; closing stores; and cancelling bus services. It was not until White Juan struck six months later that the Province of Nova Scotia declared its first ever state of emergency. In contrast, more than thirty communities declared states of emergency after Igor hit, though the provincial government did not. In the early hours after the storm, Premier Danny Williams said, "We don't feel at this point in time there is a general need for a state of emergency ... We do obviously have a serious situation, but it appears to be very much in control."[7] This approach may have reflected the idea of the resilient Newfoundlander who is accustomed to handling challenges in isolation (chapter 5), as well as ongoing political friction between Premier Danny Williams and Prime Minister Stephen Harper.[8]

During Storm: Minimal Mobility

During Hurricane Juan itself, mobility was limited to a small essential workforce of emergency response officials, while ecological mobilities of wind, waves, and rain moved with speed and intensity. On the day before the storm, officials from all three levels of government, as well as relevant agencies and corporations, started working out of the designated Emergency Measures Organization headquarters in Dartmouth, some staying for a week or more.[9] Efforts included evacuating and sheltering residents and patients, gathering information on the impact and severity of storm conditions, and having emergency responders on hand. In K'jipuktuk/Halifax, a paramedic lost his life when a tree fell on his ambulance, illustrating the extreme conditions and personal risk this indispensable work-force faced. Likewise, in Newfoundland leading up to Hurricane Igor efforts were made to minimize mobility by closing schools and evacuating workers from offshore oil platforms, while emergency mobilities were anticipated by setting up shelters and assembling the Canadian Forces in Nova Scotia to deploy, if needed.

After Storm: Restoring Mobility

Within twenty-four to forty-eight hours of Hurricanes Juan and Igor hitting, both regions shifted from finding it difficult to pro-cess the scale of the storm – "we've never seen anything like it" – to mobilizing at all levels to cope with the disruption and return to normal as quickly as possible. The first steps included assess-ing the damage to understand the scale of impact, using first- and second-hand accounts to piece together an overall picture of dis-ruption. In Newfoundland, road manager Phil first gathered infor-mation via word of mouth from staff, based on how far they could, or could not, travel into work. In the days after the storm, helicop-ters established an aerial perspective on the extent of damage. All this information was fed into the provincial Fire and Emergency Services command centre. This situational awareness allowed offi-cials to manage disaster response.

As a first course of action, government officials and non-gov-ernmental organizers attended to community members in need. This involved activating shelters; distributing relief, such as food and water, through formal and informal means; and in the case of Newfoundland, activating search and rescue teams to respond to a man swept away by flood waters. In Nova Scotia, 60 people needing medical attention received travel assistance and 200 Red Cross vol-unteers "provided 5,000 meals, distributed 40,000 bottles of juice and water, and conducted 70 food drops in 45 different locations" assisting 30,000 people in the province.[10]

As immediate human needs were attended to, officials pushed to restore infrastructure. Mobility was repurposed, as when buses were used to shelter evacuees and transport work crews in Halifax.

In Newfoundland, ferries were rerouted to deliver fuel. Scrambled mobilities emerged based on repurposing old cabin roads and improvising alternate transport modes, such as boats and quads. In Nova Scotia, short-term infrastructure restoration involved clearing roads of downed trees and power poles. Residents reconfigured their existing mobility, walking, biking, and driving as required and as feasible to meet their needs, assist others, survey the damage, and experience first-hand charismatic immobility. In Newfoundland, reconfiguring mobility entailed rebuilding and reconnecting roads. To this end, temporary structures such as Bailey bridges were used and normal approval procedures, including tendering processes and environmental assessments, were waived.

Coordinating with other organizations was common to all three stages in both storms. In the capital cities of Halifax and St. John's, the respective provincial EMO coordinated efforts of all three levels of government, emergency responders, non-governmental and volunteer organizations, and the private sector. The debriefing that followed Hurricane Juan found that communication required improvement between agencies, such as the province and the military, and between officials and the public. In Newfoundland, there was a sense of pride that people from diverse organizations pulled together to repair damage and restore normalcy.

Future Storms: Building Resilience

The timeline for increasing resilience to future storms is much longer than that of the immediate preparation and response phases, which can be measured in hours. It is an ongoing process that includes knowledge-gathering, ecological measures, and infrastructural interventions. There are two main measures related to knowledge-gathering. First, evaluating the overall storm response. In Nova Scotia, emergency responders participated in a debriefing that led to a report, whereas in Newfoundland, community consultations were held, though the resulting report was not made public.[11]

Second, risk analyses related to aspects of the physical environment, such as peak stream flows and rates of sea level rise, were incorporated into ongoing research. This permits the use of statistics and guidelines that can be incorporated into local planning and scenario-building. Geographer Joel Finnis uses such data to project climate change impacts in Newfoundland, providing detailed data on criteria such as daily maximum temperatures and precipitation, which can be used by communities to tailor climate adaptation.[12] Ecological measures include managing retreat of development from zones prone to flooding through often contentious community planning efforts; creating means to reduce and manage storm water runoff, such as in Halifax's *Urban Forestry Strategy*; and promoting living shorelines, as was done in Nova Scotia, to build up natural buffers in coastal communities to protects against storms and sea level rise (chapter 8).

Finally, there are traditional infrastructure interventions, such as ensuring backup equipment is available and updating construction standards, for example, installing larger culverts as a matter of routine. Governments in both regions invested in new equipment like additional radios as well as recommitted to maintaining existing infrastructure and equipment, such as regularly clearing catch basins. In some cases, the storm led to expanding the capacity of existing departments. Newfoundland and Labrador Fire and Emergency Services grew from five to twenty-seven positions between 2008 and 2012.[13] In Nova Scotia, there are efforts to increase fuel resilience, though these were motivated not by Hurricane Juan but by the 2015 fuel shortage (chapter 6).

RESILIENCE

In this section, I describe three interrelated types of resilience: transport, social-ecological, and infrastructure. These are not exhaustive but in juxtaposition help us understand current trends related to mobility and resilience. Transport resilience focuses on ensuring continual circulations of people, goods, and services in the face of disruption, particularly severe weather events. The measures used in Nova Scotia and Newfoundland before, during, and after Hurricanes Juan and Igor are grounded in transport resilience. As currently practised, it quickly restores everyday mobility upon which societies rely. Social-ecological resilience originates in ecological studies of population dynamics and is used to manage and protect specific ecosystems. It is useful in conceptualizing an ecological approach to mobilities that includes human and non-human components. For example, a social-ecological approach may be used in a coastal community where tensions exist between protecting animal migration patterns and attracting tourists. Infrastructure resilience, particularly a next-generation approach, builds infrastructure that reflects changing conditions, including extreme weather, carbon constraint, and limited financial means. These three approaches are useful in thinking through mobility in a changing climate, and how disruption can be anticipated and accommodated in communities. In sum, they highlight the need for a transformational approach that questions status quo mobility practices and reimagines what it means to be mobile in the midst of a climate crisis.

Transport Resilience

In short, resilience is the "capacity to rebound after a shock, indicated by the degree of flexibility, persistence of key functions, or ability to transform."[14] Resilience is a response to vulnerability. Vulnerability refers to the predisposition of a transport system, or any of its parts, to negative external forces.[15] In the transport resilience context, vulnerability is linked to non-operability. The terms *resilience* and *vulnerability* are used by researchers and practitioners to understand how to respond to a disrupted transport system.

Transport resilience aims to minimize economic disruption. As economists Aura Reggiani, Peter Nijkamp, and Diego Lanzi detail, in the field of transport resilience the term *resilience* has connotations of robustness, connectivity, and accessibility.[16] *Robustness* refers to the physical ability of infrastructure to withstand storm impacts, such as building a bridge to new specifications to reflect increased flooding intensity and frequency.[17] *Connectivity* refers to the ability to link between two or more points in a spatial system, and *accessibility* is the ability to obtain goods and services and reach desired destinations. To this list, Samuel Markolf and colleagues add *flexibility* and *agility*.[18] In terms of sea level rise, flexibility means adapting to a projected estimate of one metre of sea level rise, whereas agility refers to adapting to drastic sea level rise beyond what is expected, such as three metres. For all of these terms, versatility is a shared value.

CANADA
At the national level, Transport Canada is concerned with resilience in the context of climate change and its impacts on roads, rail, seaports, and airports. Its approach emphasizes the need for quick recovery to minimize economic disruption. The goal of transport resilience is to sidestep costly delays as well as to protect the "safety,

efficiency, and reliability" of Canada's transportation systems.[19]
Transport Canada, in a funding announcement for a climate change
vulnerability assessment for the Port of Toronto states, "Canada's
trade moves through ... the St. Lawrence Seaway, major ports, airports, and land border crossings. These are vital to the country's
trade and economic competitiveness. In an era of rapidly moving
global supply chains, federal assets are part of a transportation system that must be reliable, efficient and resilient to such things as
changing climate and weather."[20] In this way, transport resilience is
synonymous with the resilience of commerce. It was partly because
of the economic role of Canada's rail network that in winter 2019
the Wet'suwet'en people and allies set up countrywide rail blockades to proposed construction of a natural gas pipeline project on
traditional lands.[21]

In Canada, risk to physical infrastructure is a pressing concern,
including "damage to homes, buildings, and critical infrastructure
from heavy precipitation events, high winds, and flooding; increased
probability of power outages and grid failures; and an increasing
risk of cascading infrastructure failures."[22] The 2013 Alberta floods,
for example, destroyed more than 1,000 kilometres of road. The
2021 landslide in British Columbia blocked a short but critical
stretch of highway, resulting in widespread transport and supply
chain disruption. In coastal communities, risks include damage to
marine infrastructure due to erosion, sea level rise, and storm surges,
demonstrated by the 2021 road washouts in Newfoundland and
Nova Scotia.

The Canadian North is a "hotspot" of rapid climate change
with heating of up to 8°C anticipated by the end of the century.[23]
Permafrost accounts for about half of Canada's total land mass,
and widespread melting of this formerly permanent frost compromises all infrastructure in northern communities. Impacts include
melting of seasonal ice roads, as well as disruption to airport run-
ways, pipelines, power lines, water and sewage connections, and
buildings. In response, the Government of Canada implemented an
ongoing Northern Transportation Adaptation Initiative, which con-
ducts research and implements initiatives to adapt with widespread
changes that impact all aspects of life in northern communities,
including hunting and importing food.[24] There are also efforts to
benefit from environmental changes, such as increasing areas of nav-
igable waters due to melting sea ice. In the case of the Canadian

North, new shipping routes are possible due to climate change. Irving Shipbuilding in Nova Scotia received a $2 billion contract to build six Arctic patrol vessels and the order may be increased.[25]

Ironically, climate change is exposing the Arctic and its people to increased international tourism, shipping, military manoeuvres, and resource extraction; for instance, travel through the Northwest Passage increased 70 per cent in the past decade.[26] These activities worsen climate change and introduce the risk of marine accidents in an ecologically and culturally sensitive area. In sum, transport resilience is the most conventional of the three types of resilience under discussion in this chapter. It is about ensuring flows of goods and people, often with an economic motivation. While this is important, the overall ethic is restorative, not transformative.

Social-Ecological Resilience

Social-ecological systems theory originates from the field of ecology where C.S. (Buzz) Holling used it to describe variable dynamics in complex ecological systems.[27] It emphasizes the reciprocal impacts between social and ecological systems, highlighting the potential for adaptive and transformative change.[28] Social-ecological systems are defined as having three trajectories: resilience, adaptability, and transformability. *Resilience* refers to returning to a normal state as quickly as possible, that is, getting things back to normal or bouncing back, echoing the Nova Scotia and Newfoundland case studies.[29] *Adaptability* and *transformability* refer to leveraging disruption as an opportunity to implement systemic changes that reflect a greater consideration of ecological limits. Adaptability occurs within the dominant paradigm, while transformability shifts to a new paradigm, aligning with a post-carbon mobility transition.[30]

Of the three forms of resilience, social-ecological is closest to and most useful in thinking through an ecological approach to mobilities in a changing climate.[31] In opposition to notions of equilibrium, social-ecological systems theory recognizes and incorporates cycles of "organization, collapse, and renewal," that is, disruption and adaptation.[32] Extreme weather, such as hurricanes, provide windows of opportunity to navigate transitions, such as switching from high-carbon to zero-carbon trajectories.[33]

Social-ecological systems theory argues that experimentation and intervention at all scales can have knock-on effects that precipitate adaptive and transformational change on broader scales.[34] This spirit of experimentation is captured by the concept of climate routing, where measures like revolutionizing mobility and thinking flex are about working with, not despite, the climate to realize broader societal benefits. Such adaptation and transformation may be supported or hindered by social constraints, for example identities, values, and budgets.[35] Leveraging the charisma entailed in ecological mobilities, like restoring an urban waterway, can increase the appeal of a given initiative.

Infrastructure Resilience

Infrastructure resilience is an effort to build structures that reflect changing conditions, including extreme weather, carbon constraint, and government budgets. It is an applied field that complements the work of geographer Stephen Graham and political scientist Timothy Luke on the disruption of large social-technical infrastructure systems, such as cascading collapses of North American electricity infrastructure.[36] Within infrastructure resilience, architect professor and former New York assistant commissioner Hillary Brown is a proponent of *next-generation infrastructure*.[37] She uses the impacts of Hurricane Sandy (2012) to frame the problem:

> The extreme vulnerability of single-purpose, aging infrastructure was highlighted once again when Hurricane Sandy churned its way across the northeast United States. Inundating New York City's vital arteries, floodwaters overwhelmed tunnels and sewers; closed bridges; shut down the electrical substations that control mass transit; curtailed gas supplies; and destroyed streets, buildings, and whole neighborhoods. For days and on into weeks, failures triggered by floodwaters deprived millions of electricity, heat, and water services. How can our complex, interdependent utilities support an urbanizing world, subject to carbon constraints and the impacts of climate change?
> How might these critical networks be made more efficient, less environmentally damaging, and more resilient?[38]

From this perspective, infrastructure systems are tightly coupled with each other, for example, electricity and fuel (chapter 6), as well as with ecological processes and, by extension, potential environmental harms. This resonates with and informs the concept of an ecological approach to mobilities.

In the past, in line with conventional approaches to transport, politicians and planners "presumed an inexhaustible supply of cheap energy, the efficacy of simple and single-purpose solutions to complex problems, and the necessity of brute-force mastery of nature, all executed with bullet proof confidence in endless economic growth on a finite planet."[39] Next-generation infrastructure offers a post-industrial perspective that views infrastructure as "nested" within global ecological systems; it works with rather than dominates ecological systems. Brown raises the possibility of a "future-proof" public works that will withstand climate change impacts.[40] She identifies five guiding principles to reimagine society's approach to infrastructure:

1 Systems should be multipurpose, interconnected, and synergistic;
2 Infrastructure should contribute few or no carbon emissions;
3 Infrastructure should work with natural processes;
4 Infrastructure should improve social contexts and serve local constituencies; and
5 Infrastructure should be resilient and adapt to predicted changes brought along by an unstable climate.[41]

This wide-ranging interpretation reflects technical, social, and environmental concerns. Next-generation infrastructure attempts to decouple climate breakdown and infrastructure breakdown, building flexible infrastructure systems that are adaptable to a changing climate. For example, Brown describes a ten-kilometre traffic tunnel in Kuala Lumpur, Malaysia. Most of the time the tunnel is a major transport route, diverting traffic from the city centre and reducing travel time and related emissions by up to three-quarters. As needed, the tunnel retains stormwater, diverting up to 90 per cent of water during severe rainfall events. By using one site to deliver "seemingly incompatible uses," project costs and disruption are reduced.[42] The project was recognized by the United Nations for its approach to multiple urban design challenges.[43]

Similar examples exist, such as underground parking facilities in the Netherlands and public parks in Brazil that double as flood reservoirs. Next-generation infrastructure acknowledges the need to manage transport demand, emphasizing local and regional supply chains.[44]

However, the examples provided from Malaysia, the Netherlands, and Brazil focus on large projects that, while having merit, do not fundamentally question the role of mobility in society. This echoes a "predict-and-provide" tendency in transport management that emphasizes infrastructure provision.[45] The projects Brown profiles accommodate existing mobility demand in a more environmentally sensitive manner and offer a means to adapt to climate change, but they do not radically reconsider the mobility status quo. By contrast, an ecological approach to mobilities and climate routing embrace more transformative paradigms, not just greening the current mobility system but experimenting with different mobility paradigms altogether (chapter 8).

Officials and community members used a range of measures to manage mobility before, during, and after Hurricanes Juan and Igor, as well as in the longer term. The central motivation was to get things moving again, from critical emergency services to the economy. This is an expression of transport resilience, which aims to ensure continual circulations of people, goods, and services in the face of disruption, particularly severe weather. Infrastructure resilience, such as next-generation approaches, creates systems where human and ecological needs are accommodated and reflects the spirit of social-ecological resilience. In the next chapter, I enlarge conversations around resilience, questioning assumptions about societal reliance on fossil fuel intensive circulation to meet basic needs. An ecological approach to mobilities provides leverage to discuss the human and more-than-human circulations. What emerges is a more all-encompassing conception of resilience.

8

Climate Routing

Life, we voted, would be easier
if we knew what was going to happen. This was the biggest

flaw and became the complaint that motored
many meetings. Exactly who was in charge?

And why weren't they letting us prepare?

Sue Goyette, "Nineteen," in *Ocean*

CLIMATE ROUTING

In the marine sector, weather routing involves optimizing the course
of a ship in relation to environmental conditions, such as wind and
waves. As one Newfoundland mariner stated, "We'll weather route to
allow us to maintain the maximum speed with the minimum amount
of energy."[1] The goal is to decrease fuel use and by extension increase
profit. This mobility practice offers lessons that, if transferred to a
consciousness of carbon emissions that contribute to climate change,
could transform contemporary mobility. I introduce the concept of
climate routing to imagine how society might chart a course toward
decarbonizing mobility, while at the same time building resilience in
communities experiencing the impacts of a changing climate.

What might human mobility look like if it were deeply and
authentically responsive to the threat of climate change? Climate
routing reflects on and intervenes in an ecological approach to
mobilities. Primary considerations include questioning status quo
mobility practices, increasing social and ecological resilience, and
improving quality of life. Under the umbrella concept of climate
routing, I explore five ideas for shifting the social imaginary around

Table 8.1 Climate routing measures with select examples

Revolutionize mobility	• Reimagine mobility by working with, rather than against, climate. • Create interdisciplinary mobility working groups to explore and enact climate routing measures, disaster planning, and just transition.
Prioritize vital mobility	• Prioritize movement of goods, people, and services that impact life chances. • Invest in telemedicine as alternate to in-person mobility.
Embrace green and blue	• Invest in programs, such as Living Shorelines, that enhance ecosystems and the storm defences they provide. • Invest in climate and weather monitoring technology, including citizen science.
Rebrand redundancy	• Support redundancies across multiple scales, including roads, generators, and batteries. • Embrace a "root cellar approach" to strategically pre-position goods, energy, and expertise.
Think flex	• Develop community disaster preparedness plans that allow for prompt and flexible response and, if needed, evacuation. • Build flexibility into everyday mobilities, from commuting to supply chains.

Five recommendations are based on input and ideas garnered through research interviews in impacted communities.

ecological mobilities: revolutionize mobility, prioritize vital mobility, embrace green and blue, rebrand redundancy, and think flex. I move from larger scales, revolutionizing mobility at national levels, to smaller scales, taking a flexible approach to individual travel planning. The five ideas are interconnected, embracing a shift to an ecological approach to mobilities.

These ideas come out of my fieldwork in Mi'kma'ki/Nova Scotia and Ktaqmkuk/Newfoundland and related research. They are generative rather than exhaustive: concepts that need to be tailored to local conditions and circumstances. My goal is to create a framework to transform the mobility status quo.[2] They indicate significant social reorientation that layers on top of and extends much needed sustainable mobility measures, such as increasing investment in public transit and interprovincial bus and rail, as well as transitioning to zero-emission vehicles.[3] Ideally, the measures will entail and contribute to a renewed appreciation for charismatic mobilities, reconnecting humans with ecological cycles and forces. In addition, by decarbonizing mobility and increasing community resilience, ideally there will be reduced potential for catastrophic mobilities both locally and globally.

This chapter targets transport managers, planners, policy-makers, and community organizers in addition to informing the work of mobilities scholars and environmental sociologists. Through the overarching concept of *climate routing*, I invite readers to reflect on mobility from both professional and personal vantage points. Through the underpinning concept of an *ecological approach to mobilities* – which emphasizes that non-human environmental dynamics, including the climate, need to be considered in lockstep with human mobility – I want to reorient the way policy-makers and community organizers think about, feel through, and act on the interrelated issues of mobility, climate crisis, and disruption in order to realize a more just and equitable society.

REVOLUTIONIZE MOBILITY

Society is confronted with radical changes in the climate, as well as radical changes to political, economic, and cultural systems required to prevent more planetary heating and to cope with the global heating already baked in.[4] Revolutionizing mobility raises key questions: What different mobility futures are possible? What counts as "appropriate movement" in a decarbonized society?[5] What will mobility look like in the face of frequent and severe weather? Globally, but particularly in a country as large as Canada, our relationship with mobility needs to be markedly reoriented. Mimi Sheller links the global and the local: "changing global energy cultures at the largest scale requires attention to how we relate to each other in immediate, embodied ways ... how we build our homes, how we move around our neighborhoods ... and even what moves through our bodies."[6] Drawing on the cases of Nova Scotia and Newfoundland, this also includes how we obtain fuel, how we supply electricity, and how we prepare for and respond to severe weather disruption. Further, it entails relations within and between communities, such as energy projects that involve Indigenous communities and territories. Such wide-ranging change requires tools that facilitate thinking deeply and differently.

Sociologist Ruth Levitas imagines utopian futures to reorient the present. The task, as Levitas describes, is to use our imaginations to envision more sustainable ways of living and moving that "enable deeper and wider human happiness."[7] Levitas contends that sociologists must "reclaim utopia," by understanding systemic connections and mapping alternatives.[8] In a similar vein, Anna Lowenhaupt Tsing argues that to cope with the unpredictability and precarity of the Anthropocene, "we need to reopen our imaginations."[9] This call for a utopian turn is radical given our collective starting point: climate disruption is happening today. From this disadvantageous starting point, how can environmentally and socially preferable futures be realized?

Utopia as method includes focusing on hypothetical scenario-building. Reimagining is an "expression of creative resistance" that transcends all five climate routing measures.[10] John Urry uses scenario-building as a technique to think through potential future mobilities and immobilities. Urry's work is premised on the inevitability of climate change and the pervasiveness of climate impacts.[11] He outlines four scenarios: resource fights, magic bullet technology, digital lives, and low-carbon society.[12] These are imagined as potential outcomes of a society shaped by carbon constraint, oil scarcity, and extreme weather.[13] Each scenario implies vastly different social, political, and material futures. Regional resource fights are dystopian, defined by "plummeting standards of living, relocalization of mobility patterns, [and] increasing emphasis upon local warlords controlling recycled forms of mobility and weaponry."[14] Omar El Akkad describes such a dystopia in his novel *American War*. The book paints a picture of the southern United States shrunk by sea level rise and regularly under threat from Category 6 hurricanes – an extension of the current hurricane scale – impoverished and engaged in civil war over fossil fuel use.[15] By contrast, Urry's second scenario, is the antithesis of disruption. Magic bullet technology centres on the intervention of one or a combination of technologies like zero-carbon air travel, carbon capture and storage, and geo-engineering. These technological remedies allow society to carry on the status quo and require minimal change in human cultures and economies. Social injustices endure.

Between these two extremes, Urry examines digital lives and low-carbon society. Digital lives consist of diverse, lightweight, and flexible mobilities including car sharing, ride sharing, walking, biking, and mass transit all integrated into physical and virtual networks.[16] Human mobility produces zero-carbon, and transport managers regard the component parts as neutral and interchangeable. Residents tailor their own mobility based on age, ability, budget, and more. While mobility functions differently, society functions much as it did before. By contrast, low-carbon society is transformative. It hinges on localization of mobility, energy, and food. The Transition Network, for example, emphasizes community self-sufficiency in response to the threats of climate change and peak oil.[17] In terms of mobility, this means minimizing supply chains by growing, producing, and investing locally. Another related concept is that of the :15 CITY where a resident can access all necessities within a fifteen-minute walk or bike ride from home. Urbanist Dan Luscher argues access rather than mobility is the true goal – a point I reference below in the context of rebranding redundancy.[18]

Urry's four scenarios – resource fights, magic bullet technology, digital lives, and low-carbon society – may appear to be esoteric thought experiments, but contemporary policy-making and community organizing are faced with imagining and navigating desirable futures. Beyond local communities, there are other efforts to revolutionize mobility, from resurrecting sailing schooners to designs for wind-powered cargo vessels.[19] There is also a global initiative, of which Canada is a signatory, to develop zero-emission green shipping corridors by mid-decade.[20] Likewise, there is a global initiative, also signed by Canada, to green the aviation sector, which centres on increasing plane fuel efficiency and shifting to sustainable fuels.[21] These brief references mask myriad technical, economic, and social challenges. For example, a demand for biofuel in the aviation sector could, without appropriate checks, compete with food production. There is also a risk of techno-optimism, that is, relying on the prospect of yet-to-be-proven future technologies, delaying the need for both immediate emission reductions and a transformed societal relationship with mobility.[22]

Just Transition

As others look to the future, there are aspirations for a "just transition" away from a fossil-fuelled society toward a zero-carbon society. In Canada, in an effort to meet its Paris Agreement, there are initiatives in and beyond the transport sector to implement carbon pricing, switch to electric vehicles, and green the grid.[23] Initiatives include a carbon tax reaching fifty dollars per tonne by 2022, zero-emission vehicles accounting for 100 per cent of all new cars sold in 2035, and generating 90 per cent of energy from clean sources by 2030. Indicating the scale of the challenge, these measures fall short of Canada's climate commitments by 30 per cent.[24] Even more revolutionary change is necessary, indicating the need to reimagine society's relationship with mobility through climate routing measures. Before the COVID pandemic, such transformative change and investment were difficult to fathom but now feel more feasible; however, it is up to community and political leaders to frame such transformation as charismatic, not catastrophic.

One specific expression of such a just transition is the Green New Deal. The goal of a Green New Deal is to reorient a country's economy away from polluting sectors and transform it environmentally, economically, and socially into a more equitable, inclusive, and livable society. In Canada, there are efforts to create a Green New Deal that includes, for example, a transition to 100 per cent renewable energy, one million green jobs, and phase out of the oil and gas sector.[25] However, this concept has gained even greater traction in the United States, where it was the basis for a congressional climate resolution that proposes a ten-year mobilization on the scale of World War II.[26] In scope and spirit it echoes the New Deal implemented by President Franklin D. Roosevelt between 1933 and 1936 in response to the Great Depression. The original New Deal included massive public works projects and introduced social security programs. In line with IPCC recommendations, the congressional resolution sets a goal of limiting climate heating to 1.5°C by cutting carbon emissions in half by 2030 and achieving net-zero emission by 2050. This IPCC target is more ambitious than the Paris Agreement, which aims to limit global heating to well below 2.0°C. The resolution frames this present moment in time with global heating of 1.1°C as a "historic opportunity" to create green jobs, generate economic prosperity and security, and increase social security and justice.[27] Rather than focusing on a specific sector or technology, it describes and supports system-wide change.

The Green New Deal envisions guaranteeing each resident with a "job with a family-sustaining wage, adequate family and medical leave, paid vacations, and retirement security," and has, for some, utopian aspirations.[28] In the face of a daunting climate crisis, it is an effort to "go bold rather than give up."[29] In an excerpt from a short film that takes place in a future shaped by a Green New Deal, congressperson Alexandria Ocasio-Cortez narrates, "We didn't just change the infrastructure. We changed how we did things. We became a society that was not only modern and wealthy, but dignified and humane, too. By committing to universal rights like health care and meaningful work for all, we stopped being so scared of the future. We stopped being scared of each other. And we found our shared purpose."[30] Actions in the Green New Deal include increasing community resilience to severe weather; repairing and upgrading infrastructure; generating all energy from renewable sources; and upgrading building and housing stock. The resolution proposes decarbonizing transport through investment in zero-emission vehicles, public transit, and rail.[31]

Some critics view the Green New Deal as an oppressive intervention of government in the lives of Americans, while other critics are concerned about implementation costs and the political feasibility of the resolution passing a Senate vote. Naomi Klein positions it as politically viable because it unites ecological and economic concerns:

> Nothing about its framework forces people to choose between caring about the environment and the end of the month. The whole point is to design politics that allow us to care about both, policies that simultaneously lower emissions and lower the economic strain on working people – by making sure that everyone can get a good job in the new economy, that they have access to basic social protections like health care ... There will certainly have to be a price on carbon, but it has a much better chance of survival if the people who pay the increased costs are not hanging on by their fingernails.[32]

In 2019, all Democratic presidential candidates endorsed the Green New Deal and the concept infuses President Joe Biden's beleaguered infrastructure bill. There are now Green New Deal movements around the world, including a European Green Deal that aims to be the first climate neutral continent by 2050. To this end, Sheller adds a sobering note of caution that such initiatives, if carried out in conventional ways, risk reproducing climate coloniality through top-down neo-liberal policies that entrench racial and global divisions.[33] Looking forward, journalist Robinson Meyer calls for the same spirit of experimental pragmatism that shaped Roosevelt's New Deal to shape a just transition away from fossil fuels toward green energy.[34]

Working Groups

At the provincial scale, in Nova Scotia and Newfoundland, in the wake of Hurricanes Juan and Igor, transport managers felt a sense of trepidation as they tried to meet primary mandates, such as the delivery, and often growth, of transport services, in the face of peripheral but pressing concerns about infrastructure investment, emissions management, and disaster preparedness. Discussing the status of emergency measures in Newfoundland, Norm Catto and Stephen Tomblin identify barriers to reform that apply to numerous communities in terms of climate action:

> Renewing governance and transformation are influenced by
> the levels of perceived crisis but also by the power of inherited
> processes and mechanisms when compared with new paradigms
> or visions. In small NL communities, without the expertise,
> personnel, financial resources, and institutional support required
> to effect major reforms, promote integration, construct a via-
> ble alternative, or even to cope with events as they unfold, any
> reform will be slower than in places where the prospects for
> change are better.[35]

There is a need to create time, space, and capacity for conversations that bring together different scales of thinking, such as short-term infrastructure investment and long-term climate change trends.

Peter Adey argues for the "slowing down of deliberation," to allow space and time to do things differently, rather than reactively, particularly with a view to mobility justice.[36] One Newfoundland transport manager suggests the creation of a "provincial think tank" to provide practical direction on how to move forward.[37] Such a body – a working group, commission, or citizen assembly – would create space for interdisciplinary consideration of, and experimentation with, an ecological approach to mobilities.[38] In the aftermath of Hurricanes Juan and Igor, organizations in both Nova Scotia and Newfoundland worked together, coordinating multiple levels of government, the Canadian Forces, non-profit organizations, and communities to restore mobility, illustrating a robust resilience in terms of getting things back to normal. The emancipatory potential of catastrophe appears in these cases to be gradual. In the months and years following the event, it is processed by residents and decision-makers and incorporated to some degree into emerging policies. While the aspirations of lower-carbon transport are often stated and increasingly entrenched in law, a working group would create time and space to consider how to navigate a just and inclusive mobility transition in the spirit of a Green New Deal, facilitate public discussion and debate, and following social-ecological systems theory, implement experimental interventions (i.e., pilot projects) that may lead to adaptive and transformational change on broader scales.

Big picture questions such as safety, over-dependency on mobility, and climate change mitigation and adaptation could augment ongoing conversations pertaining to engineering and maintenance. Geographers Tim Schwanen, David Banister, and Jillian Anable ask, for example, "What is the kind of world that we would like to live in and find desirable and how should mobility be configured in that world? Is mobility in principle a right to which people are entitled"?[39] More forcefully, sustainability professor Jem Bendell proposes a deep climate change adaptation agenda centred on *resilience* (i.e., "How do we keep what we really want to keep?"), *relinquishment* (i.e., "What do we need to let go of in order to not make matters worse?"), *restoration* (i.e., "What do we need to let go of in order to not make matters worse?"), and *reconciliation* (i.e., "With what and whom can we make peace with as we face our mutual mortality?").[40] In short, it is a process of connecting human material needs to the carrying capacity of the Earth. Another approach is that of blue urbanism. It asks, "How do we want to live with the ocean?"[41] An ecological mobilities approach, in turn, asks how the ocean and broader environment need us to live with them. These are reflective questions that go far beyond the shared instinct to restore normalcy as quickly as possible in the face of societal disruption.

Yet another fundamental question is how communities can accommodate changing human mobilities within and beyond national borders? The "interplay of disturbance and organization" – or flow and turbulence – could be a guiding theme for such a working group.[42] Such big picture questions would leverage the emancipatory potential of disruptive events, like the 2015 fuel shortage. An interdisciplinary approach, including but by no means limited to scientists, service providers, and the public who represent diversity in terms of race, age, and income, would create a pool of lived experience from which to draw.

The ideal time to create such a working group may be in the aftermath of an extreme event, from severe weather to the COVID-19 pandemic, to garner political will and momentum that will foster a permanent culture shift. A time-limited format might facilitate the transfer of conditions permitted in times of crisis – intense focus on one common goal, interdepartmental co-operation, regulatory support, and major financial resources – to be leveraged. Such an approach was used with success in the development of British Columbia's carbon tax, implemented in one year by a Climate Action Secretariat.[43] Potential outputs, informed by public consultations, could include developing a climate routing vision and plan, developing and implementing carbon budgets, and developing disaster response plans with a strong focus on mobility.

PRIORITIZE VITAL MOBILITY

When Category 5 Hurricane Maria hit Puerto Rico, it impacted health care on and beyond the island. Power outages resulting from the hurricane shut down a major producer of saline solution.[44] This solution is the mundane but vital substance used in IV bags to dilute and transport all other medications into the bodies of patients. Lack of production in Puerto Rico translated into shortages in the mainland United States. As a result, nurses administered medication directly into patient IV lines, an approach which is comparatively time-consuming and risky.[45] Hurricane Maria exposed vulnerabilities in and beyond Puerto Rico. It raised questions about which mobilities, like electricity and saline solution, are vital to health-care delivery and need to be prioritized and safeguarded, especially in the case of disruptive events.

Vital mobilities are external circulations that enable internal bodily circulations necessary to life. Of myriad global mobilities, these are simultaneously the most required and in high-income contexts the most taken for granted until they are absent and the "infrastructural backstage of ... life becomes startlingly visible."[46] Assessments of Canada's top climate change risks find that "damage to physical infrastructure (e.g., buildings, roads, power grids) can also lead to lack of access to medical care, pharmacies, and social services, putting people further at risk."[47] Climate change will widen existing gaps in the provision of both mental and physical health care. Approximately five million Canadians – 16 per cent of the population – do not have access to a regular health-care provider.[48]

Vital mobilities were disrupted in Nova Scotia and Newfoundland. During the night of Hurricane Juan one paramedic died, while in the aftermath of the storm, home care workers and other medical professionals travelled to work in harrowing conditions. The Nova Scotia fuel shortage was a close call, highlighting the tight coupling of fossil fuels, mobility, health care, and emergency response. In Newfoundland, following Hurricane Igor, people struggled to access insulin, home oxygen tanks, and methadone. During the rolling blackouts in 2014, family and friends carried senior citizens down flights of stairs when apartment elevators stopped working. From the movement of emergency responders to residents to medications, disasters highlight the importance of vital mobilities.

The term *vital* draws on three concepts: vital signs, vital systems, and vital materialism. Vital signs refer to the observation of and, if necessary, intervention in the key indicators of life: respiration rate, pulse rate, body temperature, and blood pressure.[49] The performance of cardiopulmonary resuscitation (CPR), where air is transferred and circulated from one human to another, is a basic and intimate expression of vital mobilities.[50] Vital systems security focuses on maintaining critical infrastructure.[51] The field is a product of Cold War preoccupation with the vulnerability of large-scale and inter-linked infrastructure systems – transport networks, power grids, and water supplies – to intentional, accidental, or environmental disasters. Vital systems security draws on measures, such as stockpiling goods, decentralizing services, and building in redundancy, to ensure vital flows. Vital materialism highlights the role materials play in shaping society. Jane Bennett looks at the agency of food that sustains life, like omega fatty acids from fish oil that regulates human mood, as well as stem cells that repair life. She describes these as vibrant materialities that course "alongside and inside humans."[52] Bennett softens conceptual boundaries between body and environment, as well as between life and matter in the same way as an ecological approach to mobilities considers the movements of the abiotic and biotic non-human environment in relation to human mobility. Bringing together the concepts of vital signs, vital systems, and vital materialities, I introduce vital mobilities as an extension of the mobilities paradigm apt for a time of growing disruption heightened by climate change and global inequalities.

Anthropologist Peter Redfield uses the term *vital mobility* to frame the movement of humanitarian goods.[53] I expand the concept to include goods such as oxygen, saline IV solution, insulin, vaccines, and EpiPens; people such as patients, home care workers, utility crews, aid workers, and refugees; and information such as patient records, votes, early warning systems, and telemedicine. In addition to what is being moved, vital mobilities can be categorized by circumstances that trigger mobility: acute medical conditions like avian flu or COVID19;[54] chronic medical conditions like tuberculosis;[55] need for human tissues such as blood;[56] search and rescue deployments;[57] social services such as food banks;[58] and utilities like water, sewage, and gas lines.[59]

The cases of Hurricanes Juan and Igor, as well as subsequent events such as the Nova Scotia fuel shortage and the Newfoundland blackouts, raise critical questions. For instance: How do vital mobilities of goods, people, and services, including information, circulate in everyday circumstances? What are actual and potential sources of disruption? What are the impacts of disruption? How might disruptions cascade and compound? What contingencies are possible? In the face of mobility scarcity, how are vital mobilities prioritized? How might vital mobilities be reconfigured to enhance life chances, both locally and globally, more equitably?[60]

In Nova Scotia and Newfoundland, as well as across Canada, there is a need to consider alternate approaches to vital mobilities. There are, for example, widespread shortages of both family doctors and specialists. A vital mobilities approach complements and informs ongoing discussions about the provision of health care in Canada, including COVID response, as well as climate action. One option to alleviate the shortage is the provision of telemedicine, that is, consulting with medical practitioners via video call. Although not ideal in isolation from the continual care of a family doctor, it is an option in the context of the everyday where communities are unable to retain medical professionals and during disruptive crises where communities are physically inaccessible.[61] In the Canadian North, drones are being used to transport food, mail, as well as medical tests and results, including HIV and hepatitis C blood tests, providing an alternative to increasingly unstable winter road conditions.[62] Similarly, a drone was used to deliver an EpiPen and naloxone six kilometres across open water from Vancouver Island to Salt Spring Island.[63] Both telemedicine and drones are technological interventions that can help overcome physical inaccessibility, and change, for better or worse, the culture of health-care delivery. In chapter 9 I discuss other, nontechnical approaches to ensuring vital mobilities, but for now I turn from flows of goods and knowledge to ecological flows.

EMBRACE GREEN AND BLUE

Revolutionizing mobility requires embracing an ecological mobilities approach that reconceptualizes the relationship between human and non-human mobility. In this section, I address how to grow, accommodate, and monitor green stands of trees and blue flows of water. *Embrace green and blue* is a catchall term that captures ecological mobilities on land, in water, and in the atmosphere. It is a simplified conceptual hook for complex ecological mobilities such as water – blue – and trees – green. As a Nova Scotian who lived for a time in Newfoundland, I know that water is oh so many shades, from tea-brown lakes to steel-grey ocean, and that deciduous trees spend much of the year as sculptures without any foliage. It is even counterintuitive to think of trees as mobile until one shifts temporal and spatial scales to consider seasonal flows of sap, unseen reaches of roots, and the snap and crash of a branch during a storm. Blue and green also serve as a proxy for the five domains of life: archaea, bacteria, animals, fungi, and plants, and the resulting biodiversity.[64] Ulrich Beck refers to "new maps of the world where the key lines are not traditional boundaries between nation-states and social classes, but rather elevation above sea – a whole different way of conceptualizing the world and the 'life' chances, the chances of survival within it."[65] My intention through a focus on the green and blue is to highlight charismatic ecological mobilities to promote a sustained engagement with the environment and climate in daily life and policy-making.

Grow

Communities in New York (traditional territory of the Lenape) are cultivating one billion oysters, and they successfully planted one million trees (chapter 2). These are examples of eco-disaster risk reduction measures, which aim to protect communities from the impacts of hazards, like hurricanes and sea level rise, through the restoration of environments.[66] By investing in ecosystem-based solutions, such as the capacity of oyster reefs to buffer storm surges that accompany hurricanes and the shade trees provide during heat waves, these initiatives work with the environment to protect humans from severe weather. The Canadian government, for example, committed to planting two billion trees by 2030. Such targets are deceptively simple, making for engaging headlines and tweets, but need to be followed through on, in environmentally and culturally sensitive ways, ensuring that conserving intact habitat is the highest priority.[67] In terms of meeting its goal, the Canadian government stated there is difficulty in sourcing seedlings, indicating another facet of ecological mobilities.[68]

In Nova Scotia, Living Shorelines is a public education project coordinated by the Ecology Action Centre, an environmental non-profit organization.[69] The project centres on stabilizing coastal areas by preventing erosion due to wind, waves, storms, and sea level rise. Typically, hard infrastructure approaches, such as building rock sea walls, are used by property owners. In addition to being costly, these approaches shift erosion down the shore to adjacent properties, reduce habitat, and block beach access. The Living Shorelines approach advocates for softer methods that result in more robust coastal ecosystems, reduced slope grade, and added biomass.[70] Coastal ecosystems are diverse and dynamic. In Nova Scotia alone they include "oyster reefs and eelgrass meadows in shallow waters, salt marshes in the intertidal zones, beaches, dunes, vegetated slopes, and upland coastal forests."[71] Each contributes to preventing erosion and buffering flood waters.

Accommodate

Following Hurricane Juan, an urban planner reflected on how to manage a stretch of coastal highway: "One of my areas of key concern is sections of Highway 107 along the eastern shore ... there's all sorts of salt marsh complexes in through there, and the highway has no room to move. And so that's more of a question for provincial transport planners. There's no sense of retreat there. I guess it would have to be putting in a causeway or a bridge or I don't know."[72] With sea level rise, such spatial pressures will only increase. Infrastructure wends among ecological systems, such as rail tracks built along coastal zones and roads shaded by the urban tree canopy. Increasing attention is being paid to how to accommodate ecological mobilities by explicitly including environmental considerations, such as water, trees, and climate, into human mobility. The goal is to work with, rather than stifle, nature – a significant challenge of attunement compounded by the fact that climate change is characterized by uncertainties and extremes.[73]

Eco-disaster risk reduction advocates for the restoration of environments to prevent and alleviate hazards, such as reforesting slopes to avoid flooding and restoring wetland habitat to buffer storm surges. The elegance of such solutions is that they mitigate disaster through softer and less expensive ecological measures rather than, solely, harder and costlier engineering approaches.[74] One response implemented in the Netherlands was to prioritize the spatial needs of the non-human environment over those of human society. The Room for the River project is a nation-wide, multicomponent initiative to allow rivers greater latitude (chapter 2). It is guided by asking how water needs to circulate. This initiative is illustrative of Hillary Brown's next-generation infrastructure approach in that it works with natural processes and adapts to changes already experienced in a more extreme climate (chapter 7).[75]

Blue urbanism is a similar approach that proposes a more meaningful relationship between cities and the ocean.[76] It is a counterpart of green urbanism, which creates communities that benefit people and the land. Developed by Timothy Beatley, blue urbanism focuses on acknowledging and embracing the often-disregarded role of the ocean in the lives of cities, both coastal and inland, from urban design to sustainable seafood, from parks to aquariums. Coastal communities embrace different approaches to living with water and the threat of flooding. There is a focus on creating more flood-tolerant and water-permeable urban environments. Beatley describes the possibility of floating cities where there is a "softer edge" between cities and the ocean. So, while in some circumstances retreat from the ocean might be optimal, in other cases embracing the ocean is preferable. Beatley describes an initiative in Bangladesh – a country that could lose up to one-third of its land to sea level rise – that uses boats to provide "floating schools, libraries, and health centers." Similarly, in the Netherlands, traditional houseboats are being expanded to include floating homes in "water neighbourhoods."[77] In Nova Scotia, such aqua infrastructure includes floating docks on the K'jipuktuk/ Halifax waterfront and, to be launched in 2022, a floating tidal energy array.[78] The next iteration of asking how water needs to circulate is, How can humans adapt to such circulations and surges?

Monitor

Surveillance is key to accommodating green and blue flows. Carbon emissions are tracked and accounted for in regular audits.[79] Sea level rise and stream flow volume are monitored. Humans are drawing on increasingly sophisticated meteorological techniques to reduce the uncertainty involved in predicting hurricanes. Monitoring the weather involves complex socio-technical assemblages, extending from ocean buoys to satellites.[80] Knowledge of the environment, in the form of meteorological and climatic data, emerges as a form of human power. Whereas previously, knowledge was associated with power in the form of control or strength, as epitomized by the *Titanic*, due to shifting social-ecological dynamics, power can now be equated with identifying and preparing for hazards so that they do not tip into disaster. The IPCC bases its reports and recommendations on climate science that relies on a global network of climate data. In 2012, Hurricane Sandy was predicted "at least six days in advance. By 2025, they are expected to be able to detect high-impact events two weeks into the future."[81] Greater knowledge of pending extreme weather will allow for better preparation.

Charles Perrow emphasizes that even monitoring instruments can fail.[82] Due to the force of Hurricane Juan, a weather buoy at the mouth of Halifax Harbour snapped its moorings, illustrating the relative powerlessness of human surveillance relative to the environment. Nonetheless, intimate familiarity with weather conditions is invaluable in the transport sector. Just as Global Positioning Systems can provide real-time information on transport, forecasting provides real-time data on the movement of weather systems, with both transport managers and meteorologists anticipating the intersection of human and ecological mobilities. With the manifestation of climate change and the socio-economic centrality of mobility, meteorological data will only grow in import. Journalist Hannah Fry reflects on how weather forecasting "requires armies of people all over the globe collecting and sharing data, exquisite mathematical modeling, and staggering computer power. The weather doesn't respect political or geographic boundaries: we're all living under the same sky. And so weather prediction has been a marvel not only of technology but also of international cooperation."[83] A changing climate system complicates weather prediction; the Anthropocene is a post-normal era.[84]

There are also efforts to develop early warning systems by increasing the number of weather buoys. In part due to the experience of Hurricane Juan, the Halifax Port Authority, Dalhousie University, Environment Canada, and other organizations, partnered to fund the installation of a 1.5 metric tonne "smart" ocean data collection buoy. It is possible for members of the public to track such live data.[85] More buoys mean more information and therefore more power to adequately prepare for storms. However, cost is a limiting factor. As with burying power lines, the cost may be more palatable after the expense and disruption incurred by storms.

On Canada's west coast, Ocean Networks Canada, based in Victoria, British Columbia, maintains an extensive network of undersea observatories gathering seismic, oceanographic, and biological data, as well as a tsunami warning system. The organization also has a station at Cambridge Bay, Nunavut.[86] More buoys, as well as more weather stations and more satellite data, means further enabling communities to adequately prepare for storms.

Such monitoring infrastructure and data can be complemented by citizen science. The Smartfin Project encourages surfers to replace one of their surfboard fins with a technologically enabled version.[87] On the water, the Smartfin collects data, such as carbon dioxide and acidity levels. Oceans absorb carbon in the atmosphere, increasing acidity and damaging ocean habitat. When uploaded and compiled with data from other surfers, a picture is created of conditions in each region. Such individual approaches collect finer grain data from the near shore coastal zone, where buoys are not feasible due to wave conditions. While the surfing community in Nova Scotia and Newfoundland is small, Smartfin raises the possibility of other boaters, from kayakers to sailors, as well as coastal property owners, contributing to data collection. Such an approach extends and deepens the relationships with charismatic ecological mobilities, from awe at the size of crashing waves before a storm to an ongoing, daily engagement with the non-human environment.

REBRAND REDUNDANCY

Redundancy gained a bad reputation in recent decades, synonymous with bureaucratic inefficiency. From public hospitals and schools to private gas stations and banks, there are efforts to minimize costs by centralizing services. Pressures are constant to streamline government and business. While there are efficiencies to be gained, if too many cuts are made, strategic redundancies risk being lost. Moves to centralize health-care services and schools mean that transport is built into the DNA of health care and education. Disruptions to transport translate into disruptions in the lives of medical professionals and patients, teachers and students. Hurricane Juan led to the disruption of surgical schedules, extending already lengthy wait times. In winter 2015, so many snow days cancelled school in Nova Scotia that the issue was raised of how to make up for days of school lost, including extending the school year and holding classes on Saturdays.[88]

Redundancy means having a backup plan. Strategic decentralization, both of services as well as electrical grids, may allow for faster resumption of services in the face of disruption. Creative and flexible means of delivering key services, such as health and education, need to be the focus of exploration and experimentation. The push to centralize services under the justification of cost savings needs to be re-evaluated. Since climate change impacts are more apparent, redundancy needs to be conceptualized as desirable and strategic. In Nova Scotia, a provincial debriefing session after Hurricane Juan noted that while schools can serve as community centres, most do not have backup power supplies.[89] This scenario echoes the lack of backup power supplies at gas stations (chapter 6).

Redundancy is needed at multiple scales. In Newfoundland, during Hurricane Igor old cabin roads and retired bridges turned out to be a valuable, if unexpected, form of redundancy, allowing different, scrambled mobilities to emerge. Ideally there would be greater redundancy of routes, modes, and fuels in mobility systems so that communities are not reliant upon one route or fuel type to meet all their supply and emergency needs. This is not to advocate for more roads, but rather more access points, whether by land, air, or water. A case in point: the availability of alternate mobilities, such as boats and off-road vehicles, as well as the skills to use them, were a source of redundancy that proved valuable in the aftermath of Igor.

With the decline of the fisheries in Newfoundland outport communities, mobility infrastructure and related skills and knowledge may be less readily available – a reminder that mobility and concomitant disaster planning are continually shifting. Active transportation skills such as biking, canoeing, cross-country skiing, snowshoeing, and even swimming, in both urban and rural environments, may characterize post-disaster mobility in future. Likewise, alternate technological configurations may arise, including existing and emerging technologies, such as autonomous and electric vehicles, snowmobiles, Sea-Doos, off-road vehicles, drones, and the internet. Food delivery apps, for example, could be expanded to include delivery of medical supplies and other vital goods.

A related area in need of attention is that of the resilience of fuel supplies. Fuel resilience emerged as an issue during both Hurricanes Juan and Igor, as well as during the Nova Scotia fuel shortage. While sustaining fuel supplies may appear at odds with a transition away from fossil fuels, the experience of both hurricanes revealed the vulnerability created by relying on one fuel source. Possible actions include updating the *Energy Supplies Emergency Act* to accommodate short-term fuel disruptions that may increase due to climate-related disruption, as well as requirements for backup generators at strategic fuelling stations. More broadly, diversifying the fuel supply to include zero-carbon products with a goal of full transition to zero-carbon fuel sources, paired with decreasing fuel and mobility demand, would benefit societal resilience during disruption.

Root Cellars

There is a need at the community level for backup equipment, such as generators, pumps, batteries, chainsaws, radios, and medical supplies. In Canada, emergency managers recommend having a household supply of food that will last three days. Given lean just-in-time supply chains, Canadian communities need to ensure food provisions, for example aiming for a ten-day supply in contrast to the five-day supply in Newfoundland commercial food stores. One versatile concept may be that of root cellars. Traditional root cellars are underground structures, accessible via above-ground doors, which are used to store root crops, such as potatoes, carrots, and onions, to keep them cool in summer and prevent freezing in winter without relying on electricity. Early settlers relied on root cellars to preserve subsistence crops needed for survival. Until recently, root cellars were common with many homes having some form of alternate food storage. With the rise of refrigerators, freezers, and deep freezers, root cellars fell out of use. Today, the town of Elliston, Newfoundland, population 308, calls itself the Root Cellar Capital of the World. It has 135 historic root cellars, many of which are still in use and celebrated as part of Roots, Rants and Roars, an annual culinary festival.[90]

At the household and community level, the root cellar – or parallel storage practices from Indigenous traditions – is an idea worth sharing widely.[91] Contemporary mobility relies on lean supply chains and just-in-time delivery practices that are ineffective in the face of disruption. There is a need to cultivate a culture of more robust supply chains, reliable delivery schedules, and local provisioning, especially for essential services. Root cellars as a metaphor are a means of community self-sufficiency that is transferable to a range of goods, from bottled water to cots, from fuel to temporary bridges. In addition, acquiring goods specifically designed for humanitarian contexts, from personal water filtration systems to incubators that do not require electricity, would be low-cost investments with potentially life-saving impacts.[92]

A root cellar approach is a way of strategically pre-positioning goods. They create moorings that reduce reliance on longer-distance supply chains. The concept can also be applied to services, such as ensuring that communities have trained personnel like nurse practitioners available without travelling long distances. It can apply to energy, such as making sure there are local sources of power like solar panels and wind turbines that allow the community to function should the central grid fail. While various organizations, such as government and non-profits, already routinely pre-position some supplies as part of disaster preparedness efforts, there is a need for a broader cultural shift toward a root cellar approach. Nova Scotia's *Choose How You Move: Sustainable Transportation Strategy* advocates policies that involve driving shorter distances, providing access to "employment and essential services," and creating "locally designed, regionally integrated solutions."[93] Likewise, :15 CITY is an urban initiative that promotes being able to access necessities within a fifteen-minute walk or bike ride. It is based on the premise that geographically proximate communities can achieve "zero carbon, zero poverty, zero exclusion."[94] Perhaps regions like Nova Scotia and Newfoundland and Labrador could pioneer a parallel initiative that adds public transit and zero-emission car sharing to the mix (e.g., :45 RURAL)?

THINK FLEX

Higher winds speeds mean more destructive hurricanes, though lower wind speeds can also bring significant damage, as seen with Hurricanes Juan and Igor. During hurricanes, most of the affected population is immobilized in the short term. They are encouraged, but not necessarily persuaded, by official advisories and mandatory evacuations to slow down, stay at home and off the roads. In contrast, essential workers, such as emergency managers and power crews, are in a state of intense mobility, travelling between impacted sites, and working long hours under strenuous conditions. This prompts consideration of what a more climate-centric mobility might look like. Under a changing climate, hurricanes will be more severe.[95] Movement may be more fractured as complex human mobility systems, operating at top speed, are subject to more frequent and intense ecological mobilities like hurricanes. There are tight human and ecological timelines in the form of supply chains and emission reduction targets. There is a push to keep things moving and growing, and to recover from disruption quickly (chapter 7). A shift is needed whereby minimizing disruption to the climate is a primary focus, with the realization that this will reduce societal disruption in the long term.

Deep structural shifts in the global carbon cycle are disturbing human mobility. Aspirations for seamless connectivity need to be abandoned in the face of increased mobility disruptions.[96] A paradigm shift is needed, such that smooth mobility is considered the exception and turbulence the rule. Adey and Anderson observe that "decisions are almost always taken at the limits, edges, or just inside established, previously exercised, plans or protocols."[97] Climate routing assists with accommodating assumptions centred on turbulent mobilities, rather than assumptions of laminar flow.[98] A greater expectation for, and accommodation of, turbulence in the movement of people, goods, and services is justified. The same applies

to movements of flora and fauna as their species range shifts with a
changing climate, as well as vector-borne diseases such as West Nile
virus, malaria, and Lyme disease. Ghassan Hage observes that crisis
no longer feels unusual but is a new normal defined by a "permanent
state of exception."[99] Turbulence needs to be expected and accommodated.[100] This is especially the case for complex and interconnected
mobility systems. Samuel Markolf and colleagues suggest that the
"ultimate goal should not necessarily be to rebound as quickly as
possible or be as robust as possible, but to incorporate concepts of
flexibility and agility."[101] A narrow focus on speed – in daily life and
in disaster recovery – needs to be replaced by a shift to enduring and
equitable solutions implemented in a timely way.

This requires a cultural shift. A motto attributed to the United
States Postal Service epitomizes a dated mentality: "Neither snow
nor rain nor heat nor gloom of night stays these couriers from the
swift completion of their appointed rounds." Such dedication to
service provision promotes a heroic dependability that recalls the
resilient Newfoundlander. In the face of growing climatic extremes,
moderated expectations and greater focus on flexibility in terms of
both supply and delivery are needed. This ranges from everyday
mobilities, from walking to school to flying for work, where backup
travel plans, including timing and location as well as familiarity with
cancellation policies, will be the new norm. The global COVID pandemic prompted a crash course in immobility through lockdowns
alongside learning how to think flexibly about mobility due to ongoing cancelling, rescheduling, and last-minute scrambling.

Sheller reflects, "Have we reached the limits of the fast life and
evermore accelerated mobility? Is it possible to transform a culture
of energy-consuming speed into a culture of energy conservation and
valuation of slowness?"[102] Further, how can a shift to slowness align
with the rapid responses needed in emergencies where lives are at
stake?[103] This might even apply to evacuation in the case of extreme
weather, where speed of evacuation and slowness of living in shelters and waiting for information are juxtaposed. The frequency of
extreme weather across Canada indicates that evacuation skills are
increasingly necessary.

In High River, Alberta, sociologist Eva Bogdan, in collabora-
tion with town planners and community organizers, spearheaded a
neighbourhood disaster-planning pilot project called We're Ready.[104]
The project was developed in response to the 2013 Alberta floods,

which caused the evacuation of 80,000 residents and incurred more than $6 billion in damage.[105] Given the widespread upheaval caused by disasters, particularly in the first days, We're Ready was intended to build the resilience of communities to address their needs within the first seventy-two hours of an event. Increased community organization means that finite first responder capacity can in turn focus on the highest priority situations in each community. There is a balance to be struck between developing community resilience and ensuring critical reflection on community disaster preparedness and climate change adaptation.

Bogdan and her team helped communities, based on geography and ethnicity, in designing and implementing their own disaster plans. These plans included developing hazard and evacuation maps, communication plans, and community capacity inventories. They used community-building activities, such as identifying community resources and a mock disaster game, to engage participants and design the needed tools. The goal was that these communities would maintain, update, and practice their plans on their own and that, in case of another emergency, there would be greater community capacity to respond promptly and flexibly as needed. They are, to some extent, empowered to govern their own mobility in the face of safety warnings and calls for evacuation. Critically, this community capacity needs to be supported by staff as well as matched by effective policy measures, such as land-use and community design, as well as climate change mitigation and adaptation, which position citizens for success.

Such initiatives are emerging across Canada. Halifax Regional Fire and Emergency, formerly the EMO, coordinates a model of community disaster planning, whereby a standing committee made up of community members meets monthly to learn about and plan for disaster response in their community. Their roles include planning for emergencies, coordinating comfort centres, and providing status updates to the EMO.[106] The support of staff and ongoing volunteer involvement are critical to the viability of such a model. At the household level, the Canadian government recommends emergency preparedness measures such as packing a grab-and-go bag that includes items like food, water, flashlight, clothes, medications, cash, copies of key documents, and more. It also recommends that communities work with more vulnerable members to learn how they can be supported in case of emergency and evacuation.[107] These examples indicate the preparedness culture that is needed in the climate emergency.

Climate routing shifts the social imagination. These five ideas – revolutionize mobility, prioritize vital mobility, embrace green and blue, rebrand redundancy, and think flex – are a starting point. These measures are dependent upon high-quality implementation of innovative ideas. They require a balance between courageous, transformative leadership and the need to gain public confidence to co-develop and support these measures through active participation.

9

Changing Course

We realized then that we lived on a peninsula and the rocking
for water surrounding us was actually the ocean

slurping.

Sue Goyette, "Fifteen," in *Ocean*

November 2021
It is a grey Glasgow morning and I sit feeling foggy on a train
shuttling me to the international climate negotiations, known as
COP26. I am planning my day, thinking about which sessions
are most strategic to attend and whether I can connect with that
reporter about the recommendations of our working group.[1]
Then a blur of colour. My head whips round to catch a fleeting sight: eight protestors dressed in red robes wearing white
face paint standing silently in a row holding hands on a train
platform. I let out a gasp and a man near me looks up from his
phone, but they are now out of sight. This flash of red was the
Red Rebel Brigade, a group of performance artists who combine
astute aesthetics with silence in a way that is mesmerizing and
haunting – a charismatic expression of the potential for climate
catastrophe.[2] Of five days attending COP26 talks and negotiations, this momentary soundless encounter made the greatest
impression on me, the touching solidarity of these performers
representing an alienating future that is to be avoided.

November 2021
The video clip shows a man on the near shore speaking to a person
on the far shore using a walkie-talkie.[3] Between them is a rushing

river where a thirty-metre steel bridge used to be. Strung across the river is a wire that supports a pulley system that will allow a blue milk crate loaded with supplies to shuttle back and forth, supplying thirteen people stranded on the far shore. This is a scene from Tarbotvale, Nova Scotia, where an unnamed rainstorm resulted in widespread road and bridge washouts. This scene is both inspiring and humbling. It is an expression of community resilience in the face of daunting challenges. However, the community members' efforts appear modest in the face of the global climate crisis. Just as the Red Rebels hold hands, the members of this community reach out to forge the physical and emotional connections that are the lifeline of community. The scene, which centres on a bobbing blue milk crate, is charismatic. However, if instead the focus was a flashing red ambulance siren stuck at the edge of a washout with no viable alternate route, the tenor would be catastrophic. This is the prospect for which communities across Canada need to prepare.

MOBILITY IN THE CLIMATE CRISIS / JUAN AND IGOR

References were made to the disturbing sensory experience of both Hurricanes Juan and Igor: the sound of cracking trees, the noise of streams turned into rushing rivers, and the sight of massive tree falls and flooded homes. These experiences included embodied sensations of movement, ranging from pleasure to pain, from welcomed to resented, from charismatic to catastrophic. Residents mourned the loss of beloved trees and the death of community and family members. There was disbelief at the scale of impact, pride in the recovery effort, and anxiety about how to proceed.

The scale of both storms surprised residents and authorities. One town manager recalled, "I'd never seen anything like it that severe."[4] In the aftermath of both storms, reinstating mobility was the priority. Getting back to normal meant re-establishing systems proven vulnerable. There was tension between the response "we've never seen anything like it" and the instinct to "get things back to normal as quickly as possible." While infrastructural and societal upheaval provides an opportunity to navigate a mobility transition, the understandable collective reflex was to return to the status quo. Power lines toppled by Juan were replaced. Roads and bridges washed out by Igor were rebuilt.

In both provinces, when electricity was lost so too was the capacity to pump fuel. Today, electrical and fuel systems remain intertwined. This fact was highlighted by Hurricane Dorian which hit Mi'kma'ki/Nova Scotia in September 2019. Category 2 winds once again toppled the power grid, incurring three times as much damage and impacting 100,000 more customers than Hurricane Juan.[5] While ongoing tree clearing and trimming along key infra- structure corridors resulted in less damage than otherwise might have been the case, the impact of the storm indicates the need for a radical rethink of the electrical grid rather than incremental interventions, recalling Hillary Brown's push for next-generation infrastructure, where she argues for future-proofing public utili- ties by adapting to actual and anticipated changes brought by an unstable climate (chapter 7).

Officials in both provinces encouraged residents to stay at home and off the roads while providing regular updates on the status of infrastructure reconnections: electricity in Nova Scotia and roads in Ktaqmkuk/Newfoundland. In Nova Scotia, officials expressed frustration at residents' urge to experience the approaching storm, charismatic mobility, as well as the storm impacts, charismatic immobility. In the big picture, officials understood the storm as an opportunity to plan for things to come, part of a larger series of events to impact the province, from the Swissair crash to the threat of SARS, all of which centre on mobility. By contrast, Newfoundland officials commended the resilience of community members, divert- ing attention from larger issues such as public safety, infrastructure design and maintenance, and climate change mitigation and adap- tation (chapter 5). Compared to Nova Scotia, successive floods in Newfoundland were framed as isolated events, not part of a larger trend. These issues emerged again when Newfoundland was hit by a record-breaking storm nicknamed "Snowmageddon" in January 2020, leaving many people isolated, without power, and experienc- ing food insecurity.[6]

These two examples respectively reinforce and contradict Ulrich Beck's argument that climate change, though catastrophic, can have an emancipatory effect, shocking society into what Tim Schwanen, David Banister, and Jillian Anable describe as durable reconfigura- tion (chapter 1).[7] I introduce the concepts of an ecological approach to mobilities and climate routing to empower researchers, officials, and the public alike, to think through the relationships between

mobility, disruption, and climate with a view to improving community well-being. Canada is warming at twice the rate of other
countries; it is set to experience ten times as many heat waves and
twice as many extreme rainstorms.[8] Halifax and St. John's are
among many Canadian cities to declare a permanent state of climate emergency. Rising emissions combined with alterations in
storm track, intensity, and timing, will result in more extreme events
in Atlantic Canada. If Hurricane Juan made landfall just two hours
earlier, it would have coincided with the high tide. The resulting
storm tide would have reached four metres instead of three metres,
causing far greater damage.

In addition to the cases of Hurricanes Juan and Igor, I drew on
wider comparisons and juxtapositions beyond Atlantic Canada,
including the impacts of Hurricane Sandy on New York (Lanape
territory), Hurricane Katrina on Bulbancha/New Orleans, and
Hurricane Maria on Boriken/Puerto Rico. For example, one storm
impact experienced as far north as Hurricane Igor in Newfoundland
and as far south as Hurricane Maria in Puerto Rico is the vulnerability of fuel systems to disruption (chapter 6). Without electricity,
fuel cannot be pumped, posing knock-on effects on health care, education, and the economy. I also juxtaposed the North American ice
storm and the Icelandic ash cloud, which disrupted human activity
across huge areas, illustrating the interconnectivity of human mobility and the non-human environment (chapter 2).

The overall picture is a fossil-fuelled mobility geared toward speed,
volume, and connectivity that, like a finely tuned race car, is vulnerable when exposed to less-than-optimal conditions. Mobility is
perceived as desirable, with disruptions viewed as temporary incon-
veniences. The climate is communicating, but the collective human
body is, if listening, not sufficiently responsive.[9] Goyette describes a
"master class of listening" where humans heed the ocean.[10] In the
same vein, what might mobility look like if communities were deeply
and authentically responsive to the climate crisis? Instead of moving
as if the results of mobility are neutral, with no external impacts on
the environment or the global community, an *ecological approach to
mobilities* and *climate routing* emphasize that to harm the climate is
to harm ourselves and others.

REIMAGINING MOBILITY IN THE
CLIMATE CRISIS / 2022

In this poem, Goyette observes the vulnerability entailed in coastal living,

> The trick to building houses was making sure
> they didn't taste good. The ocean's culinary taste
> was growing more sophisticated and occasionally
> its appetite was unwieldy.[11]

The ocean has proven itself: it is not a scenic background nor a peripheral actor, but rather an active participant in contemporary life. Blue urbanism (chapter 2) asks, "How do we want to live with the ocean?" Alex Colville's painting *Woman, Dog and Canoe* depicts a paddler who could be asking, "How do you need me to live with you?" Guided by this question, I introduce concepts that encourage reimagining human mobility. I use disasters and disruption, namely Hurricanes Juan and Igor, as a portal to think and feel through social and ecological resilience, climate and mobility justice, and quality of life.

Two linked concepts frame this book, an *ecological approach to mobilities* and *climate routing*. An ecological approach to mobilities emphasizes that environmental dynamics, including the climate, need to be considered in lockstep with human mobility. Climate routing is an umbrella concept for shifts in thinking and doing that align with such an approach: *revolutionize mobility*, *prioritize vital mobility*, *embrace green and blue*, *rebrand redundancy*, and *think flex*.

Hurricanes are an intense and charismatic source of disruption that expose how easily the human desire to control the environment is thwarted. It is this illusion of control that Zygmunt Bauman claims humans will "miss most" in future.[12] At the same time, disruption is a reminder that communities can, to some extent, function "without mobility and vast resources."[13] As mentioned, Tim Cresswell emphasizes the role disruption plays in revealing the working parts of overlooked and ubiquitous mobilities: the moment when that which is "taken-for-granted becomes suddenly visible."[14] Sparking creative reorderings, disruption allows improvised and repurposed mobilities to take centre stage, temporarily altering mobility. In Nova Scotia, residents navigated streets blocked by fallen trees and power lines,

Figure 9.1 *Woman, Dog and Canoe*, Alex Colville, 1982

climbing over trunks and using alternate streets. In Newfoundland, new water, air, and land routes were forged replacing asphalt highways washed out by rivers that were themselves carving new routes or returning to old ones.

Satya Savitzky calls these *scrambled mobilities* to indicate both the rush to restore disrupted mobilities, as well as the interconnected or scrambled-up nature of broader social, technical, and ecological systems.[15] But given that the mobility status quo is problematic, scrambled mobilities can suggest new possibilities. The scramble can generate new connections, both in terms of mobility and community. On a broader scale, Savitzky argues that a prolonged scramble to extract fossil fuels is being replaced by a scramble to transition to renewable energy sources, where ecological mobilities of solar, tidal, and wind energy are translated into electricity that powers human mobilities.

An ecological approach to mobilities encapsulates the tight coupling of human movement, fuel, and the environment, emphasizing that changes in one component cause changes in the other components, extending John Urry's work on the relationship between mobility, peak oil, and climate change (chapter 1). In a similar vein,

Pete Adey and Ben Anderson's theorization of the governance of emergency mobilities serves as a jumping-off point for juxtaposing the interrelated emergencies of fuel, health, and climate, again highlighting the acute interconnections entailed in an ecological approach to mobilities (chapter 6). In the face of mobility disruption, the collective instinct is to re-establish mobility systems, which through their reliance on fossil fuels exacerbate disruptive weather events that destroyed these systems in the first place. Windows of opportunity like hurricanes can be better leveraged to enact more systemic, transformational mobility shifts.

Climate routing is a metaphor for navigating and enacting change that centre on five measures: revolutionize mobility, prioritize vital mobility, embrace green and blue, rebrand redundancy, and think flex. It is an expression of deep climate change mitigation and adaptation that transforms the mobility status quo.[16] Though the five measures range in scale from national to individual, what is common to all of them is the push to reduce social, ecological, physical, mental, and economic vulnerability by prioritizing the health of the human and non-human environment.

Revolutionizing mobility refers to transformative interventions that protect the environment and increase social well-being, from sweeping Green New Deals to local interdisciplinary mobility working groups that prioritize a just transition away from fossil-fuelled to sustainable societies. These efforts prioritize vital mobilities that impact life chances, such as emergency response and health-care delivery. From the 2015 Nova Scotia fuel shortage, which caused emergency services to ration fuel (chapter 6), to Hurricane Maria, which caused 4,500 deaths in Puerto Rico due to a lack of medical care (chapter 4), disasters highlight the vulnerability of vital mobilities. These are matters of life and death. Further, residents of Canada are increasingly inundated with experiences and news of extreme weather. In the past, it was difficult to understand and act on the interscalar connections between climate change and everyday mobilities. Fossil-fuelled transport contributes to climate change, and severe weather, intensified by climate change, disrupts transport. By embracing green and blue this circularity must be a central consideration in policy through measures that support and privilege ecological mobilities, from rivers to forests.

Climate routing reframes societal responses. Through government, communities, and households, we are attuned to think of how to minimize investments of money and time. This aptitude needs to be channelled into a mobility transition that eliminates carbon emissions at the same time as it mitigates the social inequities worsened by disruption. Relying on fossil fuels that both cause and are susceptible to climate disruption is a formula for catastrophe, underscoring the relationship between mobility, oil, and climate change. Rebranding redundancy needs to be a central planning approach, from roads to batteries. Similarly, thinking flex needs to be the new norm in terms of how individuals and communities approach everyday travel plans and disaster-related evacuation. Ideally, the five climate routing measures entail and contribute to a renewed appreciation for charismatic ecological mobilities, connecting humans with ecological dynamics and forces. In addition, by decarbonizing the economy, increasing local community resilience, and empowering global communities to redress historic and contemporary climate coloniality, there will be reduced potential for catastrophic ecological mobilities, as well as greater capacity to welcome those forced to move, whether partially or wholly, due to a changing climate.

CARING MOBILITIES IN A CHANGING CLIMATE

Looking back over the many experiences that shaped this short book on a long project, there is one conversation in particular that stays with me. It was an interview with a disaster responder in Newfoundland who commented simply that she needed to get goods, like cots and bottled water, from "here to there." This seemingly simple and mundane task was made almost insurmountable by extensive road and bridge washouts. There was something in her voice that struck me – a combination of both overwhelm and matter-of-factness. In retrospect, it was the tone of an individual grappling with how to address the local expression of the global climate crisis.

This brings me to thoughts on care – for the climate and for communities. The climate is changing, and the scale of change this means for communities is something even social and natural scientists are only beginning to understand. From hurricanes to heat waves, from floods to forest fires, intensity and frequency are altering. Communities from coast to coast to coast will need robust and ongoing support to weather storm after storm after storm. While individuals play a role in disaster preparedness, the nature and magnitude of challenge is societal. According to climate routing

– which questions status quo mobility practices, increases social and ecological resilience, and improves quality of life – care for the climate must be a central consideration in policy-making. However, even with dramatic immediate cuts in carbon, a significant level of global heating is already locked in during our lifetimes. And so climate routing needs to be paired with care for communities. This ranges in scope from neighbours checking in on each other to local disaster preparedness initiatives to a health-care system that is resourced to cope with the impact of the climate crisis on health and health-care delivery.

This was demonstrated in summer 2021, when the British Columbia heat dome resulted in sustained temperatures over 40°C. Consequently, there were hundreds of additional deaths, disproportionately impacting those over age seventy. This raises the question of how an ecological approach to mobility can be tailored to vulnerable populations, including senior citizens, people with disabilities, and individuals with insufficient income, among many others. In the K'emk'emelay/Vancouver area, families and support workers who called 911 waited to get an answer and waited even longer, to get an ambulance, if one came at all. This was immobility, not caused by infrastructure disruption but by increased demand for emergency health services due to the direct impact of heat on humans. Although there are specific calls for heat response plans, this experience and others across Canada – from forest fire evacuations in Alberta to road washouts in Nova Scotia and Newfoundland – speak to the need to address broader issues of health equity and care in a changing climate.

Appreciating and acting on the intersections between health and climate need to traverse multiple scales. Starting at the level of the body, actions need to include regular care and check-ins on people who are vulnerable to monitor health and build community, and then move through the levels of home design (e.g., insulation) and provisioning (e.g., air conditioners), through to communities (e.g., comfort centres that provide heating and cooling), and bolstering emergency service capacity (e.g., increasing numbers of paramedics and ambulances). In the spirit of a just and sustainable societal transition, efforts to decarbonize could be paired with investments and initiatives that promote caring communities prepared for the physical, mental, emotional, as well as infrastructural, economic, and cultural impacts of severe weather on health and health-care delivery.

The COVID-19 pandemic reveals strains on health-care delivery and provides a glimpse into a lower-carbon and differently mobile world, from reallocating street space to bicycles to the provision of guaranteed basic income, from the experience of a slower and more local lifestyle to the possibility of a green economic transition in line with a just transition. Such ongoing learning applies both to the consequences of Earth's changing climate and the profound reorientation society needs to reduce its climatic impact and contend with environmental change already under way. We exist in relation to the climate and must be guided by an ethic of care – for the climate and for each other.

Notes

PREFACE

1 IWK Foundation, "Land Acknowledgement," 2021, https://iwkfoundation. org/land-acknowledgement, n.p. Also included are Prince Edward Island, part of New Brunswick, the Gaspé region of Quebec, part of Maine, and southwestern Newfoundland.
2 Canadian Association of University Teachers, "Guide to Acknowledging First Peoples & Traditional Territory," 2021, https://www.caut.ca/content/ guide-acknowledging-first-peoples-traditional-territory.
3 Liboiron, *Pollution Is Colonialism*.
4 Robert Booth, "UK More Nostalgic for Empire than other Ex-Colonial Powers," *Guardian*, 11 March 2020, https://www.theguardian.com/ world/2020/mar/11/uk-more-nostalgic-for-empire-than-other-ex-colonial-powers.

ACKNOWLEDGMENTS

1 See https://stephaniesodero.weebly.com/book.html.

INTRODUCTION

1 The Chronicle Herald, *Hurricane Juan*.
2 The Telegram, *Hurricane Igor*.
3 Climate Action Tracker, "Canada," 15 September 2021, https://climateactiontracker.org/countries/canada/.
4 Beck, *Risk Society*.
5 *Quad* is a regional term for off-highway vehicles or all-terrain vehicles.

6 Government of Canada, "Canada-Kazakhstan Relations," 2020, https://
www.canadainternational.gc.ca/kazakhstan/bilateral_relations_bilaterales/
canada_kazakhstan.aspx?lang=eng.

7 Stephanie Sodero, Leana Garrison, and Jennifer Powley, *Green Mobility
Strategy for Nova Scotia*, 2008, https://ecologyaction.ca/files/images-
documents/file/Transportation/GMG.pdf.

8 National coverage: *Globe and Mail*, *National Post*; provincial coverage:
Chronicle Herald, *Telegram* (St. John's); and local coverage: *Coast*, and
Packet).

9 Goyette, "One," in *Ocean*, n.p.

10 This refers to diverse self-identities, including lesbian, gay, bisexual,
transgender, queer and/or questioning, intersex, asexual, and two-spirit.

11 Bærenholdt, "Governmobility."

12 Lee Pitts, "Hurricane Igor: What It Was Like on the Ground During, and
After, the Storm," CBC News, 21 September 2015, https://www.cbc.ca/
news/canada/newfoundland-labrador/hurricane-igor-what-it-was-
like-on-the-ground-during-and-after-the-storm-1.3234201.

13 Goyette, book jacket, *Ocean*.

CHAPTER ONE

1 Risseeuw, *The Fish Don't Talk About the Water*, quoted in Cresswell, *In
Place/Out of Place*.

2 Urry, *Societies Beyond Oil*.

3 Beck, *Risk Society*.

4 Sheller, "Islanding Effects," 87.

5 International Federation of Red Cross and Red Crescent Societies, *Cost of
Doing*.

6 Six greenhouse gases are tracked by the government of Nova Scotia:
carbon dioxide, methane, nitrous oxide, hydrofluorocarbons, perfluoro-
carbons, and sulphur hexafluoride. Source: Government of Nova Scotia,
Environmental Goals and Sustainable Prosperity Act.

7 Beck, "Emancipatory Catastrophism," 78.

8 Birtchnell and Büscher, "Stranded," 7.

9 Hage, *Waiting*.

10 Tim Cresswell, "Mobility: The Lifeblood of Modernity."

11 Environment and Climate Change Canada, *Canada's Changing Climate
Report Executive Summary*," 2019, https://www.nrcan.gc.ca/sites/www.
nrcan.gc.ca/files/energy/Climate-change/pdf/CCCR_ExecSumm-EN-
040419-FINAL.pdf.

12 IPCC, "Summary for Policymakers," in *Global warming of 1.5°C*.
13 World Meteorological Organization, "Multi-agency Report Highlights Increasing Signs and Impacts of Climate Change in Atmosphere, Land and Oceans," 10 March 2020, https://public.wmo.int/en/media/press-release/multi-agency-report-highlights-increasing-signs-and-impacts-of-climate-change.
14 IPCC, "Summary for Policymakers," in *Global warming of 1.5°C*.
15 IPCC, *Climate Change 2014*.
16 Transport Canada. "Minister of Transport Advances Canada's Efforts to Fight Climate Change at COP26," 10 November 2021, https://www.canada.ca/en/transport-canada/news/2021/11/minister-of-transport-advances-canadas-efforts-to-fight-climate-change-at-cop26.html.
17 Transport Canada, "Building a Green Economy: Government of Canada to Require 100% of Passenger Car and Truck Sales be Zero-Emission by 2035 in Canada," press release, 29 June 2021, https://www.canada.ca/en/transport-canada/news/2021/06/building-a-green-economy-government-of-canada-to-require-100-of-car-and-passenger-truck-sales-be-zero-emission-by-2035-in-canada.html.
18 For example, see review by Hussain and Musilek, "Resilience Enhancement."
19 Environment and Climate Change Canada, *Canada's Changing Climate Report Executive Summary*, 2019.
20 IPCC, "Summary for Policymakers," in *Managing the Risks*.
21 BBC, "What's the Difference between Hurricanes, Cyclones and Typhoons?," BBC (website), 10 August 2019, https://www.bbc.co.uk/newsround/24879162.
22 Hyndman, Hyndman, and Catto, *Natural Hazards and Disasters*.
23 Environment and Climate Change Canada, "7.4 Marine Winds, Storms, and Waves," in "Chapter 7: Changes in Oceans Surrounding Canada," 2019. https://www.nrcan.gc.ca/sites/www.nrcan.gc.ca/files/energy/Climate-change/pdf/CCCR-Chapter7-ChangesInOceansSurroundingCanada.pdf, 377. See also, IPCC, *Climate Change 2021*.
24 IPCC, "Summary for Policymakers," in *Managing the Risks*. See also, IPCC, *Climate Change 2021*.
25 IPCC, *Climate Change 2021*, 41.
26 Environment and Climate Change Canada, "7.4 Marine Winds, Storms, and Waves," 377. And IPCC, "Climate Change: New Dimensions," in *Managing the Risks*.
27 Oliver Milman, "Extreme Atlantic Hurricanes Now Twice as Likely as in 1980s," *Guardian*, 13 April 2022, https://www.theguardian.com/

world/2022/apr/13/hurricanes-atlantic-climate-change-tropical-cyclones?
CMP=Share_AndroidApp_Other.

28 IPCC, "Sea Level Change," in *Climate Change 2013*.

29 Sobel, *Storm Surge*.

30 Joseph Stromberg, "What Is the Anthropocene and Are We in It?,"
Smithsonian, January 2013, https://www.smithsonianmag.com/science-nature/what-is-the-anthropocene-and-are-we-in-it-164801414/.

31 Elizabeth Kolbert, "'Louisiana's Disappearing Coast," *The New Yorker*,
25 March 2019, https://www.newyorker.com/magazine/2019/04/01/
louisianas-disappearing-coast.

32 Potter and Romano, *Doing Recent History*, 3.

33 Sheller and Urry, "New Mobilities Paradigm."

34 Cowen, *The Deadly Life of Logistics*, 10–11.

35 Sheller, "Mobility."

36 Hannam, Sheller, and Urry, "Editorial: Mobilities, Immobilities and
Moorings."

37 Schwanen, Banister, and Anable, "Scientific Research."

38 Sheller, "Mobility."

39 Bauman, *Globalization*.

40 Sheller, "Mobility."

41 Salter, "To Make Move."

42 Urry, *Mobilities*.

43 Spaargaren, Mol, and Bruyninckx, "Governing Environmental Flows."

44 Sheller, "Mobility."

45 Gwyn Topham, Matthew Weaver, and Haroon Siddique, "Runway
Reopens after Days of Drone Disruption at Gatwick," *Guardian*,
20 December 2018, https://www.theguardian.com/uk-news/2018/dec/20/
tens-of-thousands-of-passengers-stranded-by-gatwick-airport-drones.

46 Cresswell and Martin, "On Turbulence."

47 Cresswell and Martin, 525.

48 Adey, "Emergency Mobilities."

49 Adey.

50 Sheller, *Mobility Justice*, 103.

51 Budd et al., "Fiasco of Volcanic Proportions."

52 Sheller, *Mobility Justice*.

53 Cresswell, "Towards a Politics of Mobility," 26.

54 Cresswell, 26.

55 Klein, *This Changes Everything*, 3.

56 Chariandy, *Brother*, 17.

57 Klinenberg, *Heat Wave*.

58 Klinenberg, 15.
59 Sheller, "Mobility."
60 UN Sustainable Development Goals, *Nature's Dangerous Decline.*
61 Trainor, et al., "Environmental Injustice."
62 Giddens, *Runaway World.*
63 Gramling and Freudenburg, "Century of Macondo."
64 Due to widespread development of hydraulic fracking, US energy
    imports have declined since 2005. Clifford Krauss, "Oil Prices: What's
    Behind the Drop? Simple Economics," *New York Times*, 20 August 2015,
    https://www.nytimes.com/2015/01/13/business/energy-environment/
    oil-prices.html.
65 Gramling and Freudenburg, "Century of Macondo."
66 Freudenburg, Erikson et al., *Catastrophe in the Making.*
67 Freudenburg, Kai et al., "Organizing Hazards," 1015.
68 Freudenburg, Kai et al., 1015.
69 Giddens, *Runaway World.*
70 Beck, *Risk Society.*
71 Beck.
72 Giddens, *Runaway World.*
73 National Geographic, "Causes of Global Warming, Explained," 17
    January 2019, https://www.nationalgeographic.com/environment/
    global-warming/global-warming-causes/.
74 Beck, *Risk Society.*
75 Beck, "Emancipatory Catastrophism," 79.
76 Beck, *Risk Society.*
77 Tsing, *The Mushroom.*
78 CBC News Edmonton, "Fort McMurray Wildfire Remains Out of Control
    After City Evacuated," CBC, 3 May 2016, https://www.cbc.ca/news/
    canada/edmonton/fort-mcmurray-wildfire-remains-out-of-control-
    after-city-evacuated-1.3563977.

CHAPTER TWO

1 See Szerszynski, "Planetary Mobilities."
2 Catto and Tomblin, "Multilevel Governance," 96.
3 Claudia Mora, "Tree Rings Provide a 200-Year Old Hurricane
   Record," National Science Foundation, press release, 19 September 2006,
   https://www.nsf.gov/news/news_summ.jsp?cntn_id=108010&preview=
   false.
4 Latour, *Politics of Nature.*

5 Boas et al. in "Environmental Mobilities: An Alternative Lens" (2018), use the term *environmental mobilities* to refer to the governance of human and non-human movements. I opt for ecological mobilities to highlight the interactions between humans and other living organisms, such as animals and trees.

6 Uexküll, *A Foray*.

7 Tsing, *The Mushroom*, 152.

8 On economic impacts of hurricanes in Cuba, see Peréz, *Winds of Change*.

9 Graham Readfearn, "Climate Change in Deep Oceans Could be Seven Times Faster by Middle of Century, Report Says," *Guardian*, 25 May 2020, https://www.theguardian.com/environment/2020/may/26/climate-change-in-deep-oceans-could-be-seven-times-faster-by-middle-of-century-report-says.

10 Cresswell, "The Two Magicians," in *Plastiglomerate*, 31–3.

11 Bennett, *Vibrant Matter*, 116.

12 Foucault quoted in Usher, "Veins of Concrete," 558.

13 Usher, 558.

14 Goyette, "Twenty-Eight," in *Ocean*, n.p.

15 Kolbert, "Louisiana's Disappearing Coast."

16 Freudenburg, Erikson et al., *Catastrophe in the Making*.

17 Room for the River, "Making Room for Safety," 2019, https://issuu.com/ruimtevoorderivier/docs/uk_rvdr_making_room_for_safety.

18 Room for the River, "Highlights of Our Programme," 2019, https://www.dutchwatersector.com/news/room-for-the-river-programme.

19 Freudenburg, Erikson et al., *Catastrophe in the Making*.

20 PBS Newshour, "Dutch Homeowners Move to Make Room for the River," video (2:16 min.), 29 October 2013, https://www.youtube.com/watch?v=XrYWVJKjvRU.

21 Million Trees NYC, "NYC's Urban Forest," 2019, https://www.milliontreesnyc.org/html/about/forest.shtml.

22 Million Trees NYC, "NYC's Urban Forest." After a severe 1888 blizzard, New York buried its power lines, preventing future entanglements of trees and power lines. See Museum of the City of New York, "Living on the Grid: Wires above Ground: The Blizzard of 1888," 2015, http://thegreatestgrid.mcny.org/greatest-grid/the-underground-grid/317.

23 Billion Oyster Project, "Billion Oyster Project," 2019, https://billionoysterproject.org/#.

24 Beatley, *Blue Urbanism*, 80.

25 Billion Oyster Project, "Billion Oyster Project."

26 Beatley, *Blue Urbanism*.

27 Klein, *The Battle for Paradise*, 34.

28 Pacific Marine Environmental Laboratory's Carbon Program, "Ocean Acidification's Impact on Oysters and Other Shellfish," National Oceanic and Atmospheric Administration (NOAA), 2019, https://www.pmel.NOAA.gov/co2/story/Ocean+Acidification%27s+impact+on+oysters+and+other+shellfish.

29 NOAA's PMEL Carbon Program.

30 Alex Gollner, "Bringing the Thames Back to the London Tube Map," 16 September 2009, https://blog.alex4d.com/2009/09/16/thames-on-tube-map/.

31 Craig Kanalley, "New York Subway Map Post-Sandy: Limited Service Plans Revealed," *Huffington Post*, 31 October 2012, https://www.huffingtonpost.ca/entry/new-york-subway-post-sandy-map_n_2053407?ri18n=true.

32 Szerszynski, "Planetary Mobilities," 620.

33 Bissell, *Transit Life*, xix–xx.

34 Cambridge Dictionary, "Ecosystem," 2019, https://dictionary.cambridge.org/dictionary/english/ecosystem.

35 Sheller, *Mobility Justice*, 137.

36 Sheller, *Island Futures*.

37 Whyte, Talley, and Gibson, "Indigenous Mobility Traditions," 320.

38 Cresswell, "Mobilities III."

39 Urry, *Societies Beyond Oil*.

40 Baldwin, Frölich, and Rothe, "From Climate Migration."

41 Adey, "If Mobility Is Everything."

42 Jim Day, "Construction of Mi'kmaq Canoe Helps Elder Connect with the Past," *Chronicle Herald*, 8 October 2019, https://www.thechronicleherald.ca/news/canada/construction-of-mikmaq-canoe-helps-elder-connect-with-the-past-361624/.

43 Sheller, *Aluminium Dreams*.

44 Angel Moore, "'The Trees are Dying' Climate Change Affecting a Mi'kmaq Tradition says Canoe Maker," APTN National News, 10 July 2019, https://aptnnews.ca/2019/07/10/the-trees-are-dying-climate-change-affecting-a-mikmaq-tradition-says-canoe-maker/.

45 Holling, "Resilience and Stability."

46 Beck, *Risk Society*.

47 Latour, "From Multiculturalism to Multinaturalism," 3.

48 Latour, 4.

49 Latour, *Aramis, or the Love of Technology*, 139.
50 Murdoch, "Ecologising the Social"; and Sodero, "Greenhouse Gases, Pine Beetles, and Humans."
51 Murdoch, 113.
52 Bennett, *Vibrant Matter*, 112.
53 Murdoch, "Ecologising the Social," 111.
54 Murdoch, 114.
55 Latour, *Politics of Nature*.
56 Rutland and Aylett, "Work of Policy."
57 Markolf et al., "Transportation Resilience."
58 Goyette, "Thirty-One," in *Ocean*, n.p.
59 Goyette, book jacket, *Ocean*.
60 Elliott and Urry, *Mobile Lives*, 18–19.
61 Barnes, *The Nature of Power*, 1.
62 Murphy, "Disaster or Sustainability," 254.
63 Marilla Steuter-Martin and Loreen Pindera, "Looking Back on the 1998 Ice Storm 20 Years Later," CBC News, 4 January 2018, https://www.cbc.ca/news/canada/montreal/ice-storm-1998-1.4469977.
64 Murphy, *Leadership in Disaster*, 194.
65 Howard Schneider, "Close Call Spurs Disaster Plan Review," *Washington Post*, 25 January 1998, https://www.washingtonpost.com/wp-srv/inatl/longterm/canada/stories/montreal012598.htm.
66 Giddens, *Runaway World*, 30.
67 Murphy, *Leadership in Disaster*.
68 Murphy.
69 Murphy, "Disaster or Sustainability," 255.
70 Murphy, quoting *New York Times*, in *Leadership in Disaster*, 139. Emphasis added.
71 Andre Mayer, "Quebec Ice Storm: Why it's Impossible to Storm-Proof the Power Grid," CBC News, 5 January 2015, https://www.cbc.ca/news/technology/quebec-ice-storm-why-it-s-impossible-to-storm-proof-the-power-grid-1.2890371.
72 Budd et al., "Fiasco of Volcanic Proportions."
73 O'Regan, "On the Edge of Chaos."
74 Birtchnell and Büscher, "Stranded."
75 Jensen, "Emotional Eruptions," 68.
76 Barton, "People and Technologies as Resources."
77 Barton, 64.
78 BBC, "New Rules to Aid Ash Flight Chaos," BBC, 17 May 2010, http://news.bbc.co.uk/1/hi/uk/8685913.stm.

79　Budd et al., "Fiasco of Volcanic Proportions," 31.

80　Budd et al.

81　Volcanoes are a small source of global carbon emissions, but the massive amounts of ash emitted during eruptions deflect the sun, resulting in global cooling. However, this cooling effect is outpaced by human carbon pollution that contributes to global heating (National Aeronautics and Space Administration, "What Do Volcanoes Have to Do with Climate Change?," n.d., https://climate.nasa.gov/faq/42/what-do-volcanoes-have-to-do-with-climate-change/).

82　Climate Action Network and International Coalition for Sustainable Aviation, "Contribution of the Global Aviation Sector to Achieving Paris Agreement Climate Objectives," n.d., https://unfccc.int/sites/default/files/resource/156_CAN%20ICSA%20Aviation%20TD%20submission.pdf, 1.

83　Budd et al., "Fiasco of Volcanic Proportions."

84　Appleyard, "Environmental Quality of City Streets."

85　Marshall, "Challenge of Sustainable Transport"; and Banister, "Sustainable Mobility Paradigm."

86　Banister, "Sustainable Mobility Paradigm."

87　Sheller, *Mobility Justice*.

88　Skeggs quoted in Sheller, *Mobility Justice*, 52.

89　Sheller, *Mobility Justice*.

90　Appleyard, *Livable Streets*.

91　Appleyard.

92　Institute for Transportation and Development Policy quoted in Sheller, *Mobility Justice*, 165.

93　Caroline Rodier, "The Effects of Ride Hailing Services on Travel and Associated Greenhouse Gas Emissions," National Center for Sustainable Transportation, 2018, https://ncst.ucdavis.edu/research-product/effects-ride-hailing-services-travel-and-associated-greenhouse-gas-emissions.

94　Canadian Climate Action Network, *Getting Real about Canada's Climate Plan*, 2019, https://climateactionnetwork.ca/wp-content/uploads/2019/06/CAN-RAC_ClimatePlanExpectations_EN-1.pdf.

95　Adam Vaughan, "Electric Cars Won't Shrink Emissions Enough – We Must Cut Travel Too," *New Scientist*, 20 March 2019, https://www.newscientist.com/article/2197211-electric-cars-wont-shrink-emissions-enough-we-must-cut-travel-too/.

96　Baldwin, Frölich, and Rothe, "From Climate Migration," 1.

97　Clark and Yusoff, "Geosocial Formations and the Anthropocene."

98　Castells, *Communication Power*.

99　Lockie, "Why Environmental Sociology," 2.

100 Cresswell, "Towards a Politics of Mobility," 27.
101 Baldwin, Frölich, and Rothe, "From Climate Migration," 2.
102 Sheller, *Mobility Justice.*
103 Uexküll, *A Foray.*

CHAPTER THREE

  1 Government of Nova Scotia, *Toward a Greener Future,* 3.
  2 To see a gallery of Hurricane Juan and Igor images, visit https://stephanie-
      sodero.weebly.com/book.html.
  3 Alex Tesar, "Reserves in Nova Scotia," *The Canadian Encyclopedia,*
      Historica Canada, article published 15 June 2018; last edited 19 October
      2020, https://www.thecanadianencyclopedia.ca/en/article/reserves-in-
      nova-scotia.
  4 Richard leBrasseur, "Why Nova Scotia Has to Take Environmental Racism
      Seriously," *The Conversation,* 24 March 2020, https://theconversation.
      com/why-nova-scotia-has-to-take-environmental-racism-seriously-132052.
  5 Government of Nova Scotia, "Coastal Protection Legislation:
      Consultation Document," 2018, https://novascotia.ca/coast/Coastal-
      Protection-Consultation-en.pdf.
  6 Alex Whalen and Jairo Yunis, "Investors Souring on Nova Scotia's Oil
      and Gas Sector," Fraser Institute Blog, 22 January 2021, https://www.
      fraserinstitute.org/blogs/investors-souring-on-nova-scotias-oil-and-
      gas-sector.
  7 The viability of a ferry service between Nova Scotia and Maine is a subject
      of continual debate. See, for example, Canadian Press, "Delay Means
      Ferry Season between Nova Scotia and Maine now in Question, Minister,"
      Global News, 20 June 2019, https://globalnews.ca/news/5412445/delay-
      means-ferry-season-between-nova-scotia-and-maine-now-in-question-
      minister/.
  8 Beazley et al., "Road Density and Potential Impacts."
  9 Hugh Morley, "Halifax Expands as Eastern Canada Volume Gains
      Outpace West," *Journal of Commerce* online, 11 September 2018, https://
      www.joc.com/port-news/international-ports/port-halifax-expands-eastern-
      canada-volume-outpaces-west-coast_20180911.html.
 10 Statistics Canada, "Commuters Using Sustainable Transport in Census
      Metropolitan Areas," 29 November 2017, https://www12.statcan.gc.ca/
      census-recensement/2016/as-sa/98-200-x/2016029/98-200-x2016029-
      eng.cfm.

11 Cruise Halifax, "Cruise Industry in Halifax Continues to Grow,"
    4 February 2019, https://www.cruisehalifax.ca/cruise-industry-in-halifax-
    continues-to-grow/.

12 Wayne Groszko, "Which Way Forward? A Public Transit Map of Nova
    Scotia," 2010, https://ecologyaction.ca/files/images-documents/transit_
    forward_groszko.pdf.

13 Government of Nova Scotia, *A Report on the Emergency Response to
    Hurricane Juan*, 2003, https://www.halifaxexaminer.ca/wp-content/
    uploads/2019/09/report_on_the_emergency_response_to_hurricane_juan.pdf.

14 Government of Nova Scotia.

15 Government of Nova Scotia.

16 Government of Nova Scotia, 1.

17 Government of Nova Scotia, 1.

18 "Empty Gas Tanks Leave Drivers Fuming," *Chronicle Herald*,
    30 September 2003.

19 Environment Canada, "Hurricane Juan Storm Summary," 18 June 2015,
    http://ec.gc.ca/ouragans-hurricanes/default.asp?lang=En&n=0D496835-1.

20 John Gillis and Gerrie Grevatt, "Province Braced for Juan: Surging Tides
    Big Threat as Hurricane Approaches N.S.," *Chronicle Herald*,
    29 September 2003.

21 Research interview with transport professional, 14 February 2014.
    All interviews were conducted in confidentiality, and names are withheld
    by mutual agreement. Pseudonyms are used for research participants.

22 Research interview with transport professional, 13 December 2013.

23 Research interview with risk professional, 17 February 2014.

24 Becky Little, "Why are Hurricanes Classified by Category?," *History*
    newsletter, 12 April 2019, https://www.history.com/news/why-are-
    hurricanes-classified-by-category.

25 Research interview with meteorologist, 1 November 2013.

26 Canadian Hurricane Centre, "Hurricane Juan Storm Summary," n.d.,
    https://www.ec.gc.ca/ouragans-hurricanes/default.asp?lang=En&n=
    B1A7B85A-1.

27 Environment Canada, "Hurricane Juan Storm Summary," 18 June 2015,
    http://ec.gc.ca/ouragans-hurricanes/default.asp?lang=En&n=0D496835-1;
    and "Empty Gas Tanks Leave Drivers Fuming," *Chronicle Herald*,
    30 September 2003.

28 Environment Canada, "Hurricane Juan Storm Summary." 18 June 2015.

29 Government of Nova Scotia, "*A Report on the Emergency Response to
    Hurricane Juan*," 1.

30 Government of Nova Scotia, 6.

31 Government of Nova Scotia, 69.

32 Government of Nova Scotia.

33 "Empty Gas Tanks Leave Drivers Fuming."

34 For account of hospital evacuation during hurricane, see Fink, *Five Days at Memorial.*

35 Government of Nova Scotia, *A Report on the Emergency Response to Hurricane Juan*, 5.

36 Government of Nova Scotia. On how Halifax hospitals coped in the storm aftermath, see Fulmore and Russell, "After the Flood: Surviving Hurricane Juan."

37 Nova Scotia Legislature, *Debates and Proceedings*, 22 October 2003, Hansard 03–18, 1524.

38 Government of Nova Scotia, *A Report on the Emergency Response to Hurricane Juan*, 4.

39 Government of Nova Scotia.

40 UN News, "Climate Change Recognized as 'Threat Multiplier,' UN Security Council Debates its Impact on Peace," 25 January 2019, https://news. un.org/en/story/2019/01/1031322.

41 Paul McLeod, "Halifax Guilty of Juan-chalance; Many Humbled by Severity of Hurricane," *Chronicle Herald*, 1 October 2003.

42 Simpson, *Journeys through Eastern Old-Growth Forests.*

43 Nova Scotia Lands and Forestry, "Wildlife and Birds of Nova Scotia: Kingdom Animalia: Vertebrates," Department of Natural Resources, 2018, https://novascotia.ca/natr/wildlife/wns/wns7f.asp.

44 McLeod, "Halifax Guilty of Juan-chalance."

45 Research interview with urban planner, 11 December 2013.

46 Research interview with emergency manager, 4 February 2014.

47 Research interview with meteorologist, 1 November 2013.

48 Research interview with transport professional, 14 February 2014.

49 Research interview with transport operator, 21 February 2014.

50 Research interview with transport professional, 14 February 2014.

51 Government of Nova Scotia, *A Report on the Emergency Response to Hurricane Juan.*

52 Kevin Cox, "Felled Trees Slow Return of Power in N.S.," *Globe and Mail*, 4 October 2003.

53 Research interview with urban planner, 11 December 2013. In contrast, one study found that no particular tree type was more susceptible to Hurricane Igor, see Wiersma et al., "Hurricane Igor Impacts."

54 Amy Pugsley Fraser, "Juan Took Destructive Walk in Parks; City Official says Damage to Trees Worst 'Since Halifax Explosion,'" *Chronicle Herald*, 30 September 2003.

55 McLeod, "Halifax Guilty of Juan-chalance."

56 Pugsley Fraser, "Juan Took Destructive Walk in Parks."'

57 Research interview with transport professional, 13 December 2013.

58 Halifax Regional Municipality, *Urban Forest Master Plan*.

59 Halifax Regional Municipality, xiii–xiv.

60 Research interview with transport professional, 14 February 2014.

61 Research interview with transport professional, 14 February 2014.

62 Research interview with transport professional, 14 February 2014.

63 Research interview with transport professional, 14 February 2014.

64 Research interview with emergency manager, 4 February 2014.

65 On internal rhythms, see Lefebvre, *Rhythmanalysis*.

66 Government of Nova Scotia, *A Report on the Emergency Response to Hurricane Juan*.

67 Research interview with emergency manager, 4 February 2014.

68 Research interview with transport professional, 14 February 2014.

69 For accounts of how mass transit providers prepare for and respond to extreme events including 9/11, the 2003 Blackout, and Hurricane Sandy, see New York Transit Museum, "Bringing Back the City: Mass Transit Responds to Crisis," 2016, http://bringingbackthecity.com.

70 Government of Nova Scotia, *A Report on the Emergency Response to Hurricane Juan*, 6.

71 Government of Nova Scotia, 7.

72 Research interview with risk professional, 17 February 2014.

73 Nova Scotia experienced a record-breaking series of winter storms that resulted in significant damage and disruption, see MacIntyre, *Deep Freeze Winter 2015*.

74 Giddens, *Runaway World*, 35.

75 Bruce Little, "Bad-luck Year is Taking Bites Out of Canada's GDP," *Globe and Mail*, 6 October 2003.

76 Bill Spurr, "Juan for the Record; Hurricane Juan was a Sobering Test for Halifax's Lauded EMO. Officials say it Held Up Well," *Chronicle Herald*, 4 October 2003.

77 Research interview with disaster responder, 31 January 2014. Other sources states that approximately 7,000 passengers on up to fifty planes landed in Halifax on 9/11.

78 Helen Branswell, "Ten Years Later, SARS Still Haunts Survivors and

Health-care Workers," *Globe and Mail*, 11 May 2018, https://www.the-globeandmail.com/life/health-and-fitness/health/ten-years-later-sars-still-haunts-survivors-and-health-care-workers/article9363178/.

79 Davidson and Bogdan, "Reflexive Modernization," 359–80.

80 Travis Dunn, "Tragic Flood Hits Canada: Thousands of Homes are Damaged in Storms," Disaster News Network, 7 April 2003. At the same time, flooding isolated Corner Brook, Newfoundland and Labrador, for four days.

81 Grieve and Turnbull, "Emergency Planning in Nova Scotia."

82 Bill Spurr, "Hurricane Juan: Damage Left by Juan 'Worst I've Ever Seen.'" *Chronicle Herald*, 30 September 2003.

83 University of Virginia, "The Halifax Explosion: Relief from Outside Following the Halifax Explosion," 2007, http://exhibits.hsl.virginia.edu/halifax/reliefoutside/ (site discontinued).

84 Remes, *Disaster Citizenship*.

85 Government of Nova Scotia, *A Report on the Emergency Response to Hurricane Juan*, 2.

86 Grieve and Turnbull, "Emergency Planning in Nova Scotia," 77. For an account of the Halifax Explosion through the lens of disaster citizenship, see Remes, *Disaster Citizenship*.

87 Pugsley Fraser, "Juan Took Destructive Walk in Parks."

88 Goyette, "Twenty-Six," in *Ocean*, n.p.

89 Cunsolo and Ellis, "Ecological Grief."

90 Nova Scotia Legislature, *Debates and Proceedings*, 30 October 2003, Hansard 03–24, 1897.

91 Nova Scotia Legislature, *Debates and Proceedings*, 4 May 2004, Hansard 03/04–38, 3104–5.

92 Nova Scotia Power, "Underground Power Lines," 2015, https://www.nspower.ca/about-us/reliability/underground-power-lines.

93 On tensions that emerged between utility providers and homeowners following Hurricane Juan, see Kochanoff, "Trees versus Power Lines," 43–5.

94 Grieve and Turnbull, "Emergency Planning in Nova Scotia," 69.

95 Research interview with emergency manager, 4 February 2014.

96 Grieve and Turnbull, "Emergency Planning in Nova Scotia."

97 Grieve and Turnbull.

98 Urry, "Mobility and Proximity."

99 Research interview with emergency manager, 4 February 2014.

100 Government of Nova Scotia, *A Report on the Emergency Response to Hurricane Juan*.

101 Grieve and Turnbull, "Emergency Planning in Nova Scotia."

102 Government of Nova Scotia, *A Report on the Emergency Response to Hurricane Juan*, 8.

103 Government of Nova Scotia, 8.

104 Nova Scotia Legislature, *Debates and Proceedings*, 7 October 2003, Hansard 03–9, 663.

105 Grieve and Turnbull, "Emergency Planning in Nova Scotia." Power failures are a regular feature of severe weather in Nova Scotia, such as occurred during post-tropical storm Noel (2007).

106 Government of Nova Scotia, *Toward a Greener Future*, 3.

107 Government of Nova Scotia, 20.

108 Government of Nova Scotia, "Sustainable Transportation," 2018, https://novascotia.ca/sustainabletransportation/.

109 Government of Nova Scotia, "Nova Scotia Moves," 2018, https://novascotia.ca/sustainabletransportation/nova-scotia-moves.asp.

110 Tim Halman, "Bill No. 57: Environmental Goals and Climate Change Reduction Act," 27 October 2021, https://nslegislature.ca/legc/bills/64th_1st/1st_read/b057.htm.

111 Ivany Commission, "*The Report of the Nova Scotia Commission on Building Our New Economy*, Halifax: Nova Scotia Commission on Building Our New Economy, 2014, https://www.onens.ca/sites/default/files/editor-uploads/now-or-never.pdf, 18.

112 Sodero and Stoddart, "Typology of Diversion."

113 Province of Nova Scotia, "Netukulimk," Nova Scotia Curriculum, October 2020, https://curriculum.novascotia.ca/sites/default/files/documents/resource-files/Netukulimk_ENG.pdf, 1.

CHAPTER FOUR

1 Steinmetz, "Ceasarism and Parliamentarism," review of Baehr, ed., *Caesarism, Charisma, and Fate*.

2 Weber, *The Vocation Lectures*.

3 Lorimer, "Nonhuman Charisma," 915.

4 Amber Pariona, "Who Are the Charismatic Megafauna of the World?," World Atlas, 25 April 2017, https://www.worldatlas.com/articles/who-are-the-charismatic-megafauna-of-the-world.html.

5 Cocker, *Birders: Tales of a Tribe*, 915.

6 Lorimer, "Nonhuman Charisma," 921–2.

7 Goyette, "Four," in *Ocean*, n.p.

8 Wilson, *Biophilia*.

9   Ingold, "Earth, Sky, Wind, and Weather," 28.

10 Goyette, "Fifty-Six," in *Ocean*, n.p.

11 Ingold, "Earth, Sky, Wind, and Weather," 19. Emphasis added.

12 Goyette, "Seven," in *Ocean*, n.p.

13 Goyette, "Four," in *Ocean*, n.p.

14 The Chronicle Herald, *Hurricane Juan: The Story of a Storm*; and The Telegram, *Hurricane Igor: In the Eye of the Storm*.

15 Bennett, *Vibrant Matter*.

16 Ingold, "Earth, Sky, Wind, and Weather," 32.

17 Pam Frampton, "Storm Warning," *Telegram*, 25 September 2010.

18 For discussion of how Iceland leveraged the volcanic risks as an opportunity for tourists to play, see Benediktsson, Lund, and Huijbens, "Inspired by Eruptions?"

19 The Chronicle Herald, *Hurricane Juan*.

20 McLeod, "Halifax Guilty of Juan-chalance."

21 Benediktsson, Lund, and Huijbens, "Inspired by Eruptions?," 81. For public perception of and response to storm warnings, see Silver and Conrad, "Public Perception."

22 Research interview with transport professional, 26 February 2014.

23 Craig Ferguson, "Night in Black," *The Coast*, 2 October 2003. On tactics of walking, see de Certeau, *The Practice of Everyday Life*.

24 Spurr, "Hurricane Juan: Damage Left."

25 Ed Hewitt, "Disaster Tourism: Why Tragedy Draws Tourists Together," Smarter Travel, 19 June 2017, https://www.smartertravel.com/disaster-tourism-tragedy-draws-tourists/. On disaster tourists who travelled to New Orleans to view the damage after Hurricane Katrina, see Pezzullo, "Tourists and/as Disasters."

26 Pugsley Fraser, "Juan Took Destructive Walk in Parks."

27 McLeod, *Hurricane Juan: The Unforgettable Storm*.

28 Davene Jeffrey and Amy Pugsley-Fraser, "Hurricane Hammers Halifax; Juan Surges Ashore with Teeming Rain, Furious Wind," *Chronicle Herald*, 29 September 2003.

29 Research interview with emergency manager, 4 February 2014.

30 Grieve and Turnbull, "Emergency Planning in Nova Scotia."

31 Jeffrey and Pugsley-Fraser, "Hurricane Hammers Halifax; Juan Surges Ashore."

32 Research interview with disaster responder, 31 January 2014.

33 Government of Nova Scotia, *A Report on the Emergency Response to Hurricane Juan*.

34 The Chronicle Herald, *Hurricane Juan: The Story of a Storm*.

35 Bærenholdt, "Governmobility."

36 Adey, "Emergency Mobilities," 32.

37 Foucault, "Governmentality," in *The Essential Foucault*.

38 Manderscheid, Schwanen, and Tyfield, "Introduction to Special Issue."

39 Bærenholdt, "Governmobility," 25.

40 Bærenholdt, 24.

41 Foucault, "Governmentality."

42 Sheller, "Mobility."

43 By contrast, see Murphy, *Leadership in Disaster* for a discussion of the fatality and injury rates that resulted from the North American ice storm.

44 Spurr, "Juan for the Record."

45 Research interview with environmental advocate, 21 November 2013.

46 Research interview with transport operator, 21 February 2014.

47 Sheller, *Mobility Justice: The Politics*, 96.

48 Milnes and Haney, "'There's Always Winners and Losers.'"

49 Murphy, *Leadership in Disaster*.

50 Birtchnell and Büscher, "Stranded."

51 Grieve and Turnbull, "Emergency Planning in Nova Scotia."

52 Michael Tutton, "Nova Scotia is One 'Perfect Storm' Away from Being Cut Off from Canada," CBC, 30 March 2019, https://www.cbc.ca/news/canada/nova-scotia/storm-maritime-provinces-1.5075448.

53 Anderson and Adey, "Governing Events and Life," 26.

54 National Hurricane Center and Central Pacific Hurricane Center, "Saffir-Simpson Hurricane Wind Scale," n.d., https://www.nhc.noaa.gov/aboutsshws.php. Emphasis added.

55 Kelman, *Disaster by Choice*.

56 Fothergill and Peek, *Children of Katrina*.

57 Fothergill and Peek, 1.

58 Fothergill and Peek, 2–3.

59 Fothergill and Peek, 44.

60 Fothergill and Peek, 61.

61 Boas et al., "Climate Migration Myths."

62 Klinenberg, *Heat Wave: A Social Autopsy*.

63 Sheller, "Islanding Effects: Post-Disaster Mobility Systems."

64 Baldwin, Frölich, and Rothe, "From Climate Migration to Anthropocene," 3.

65 Sou and Douglas, *After Maria*.

66 Sou and Douglas, 24.

67 Sou and Douglas.

68 Klein, *The Battle for Paradise*.

69 Sheller, *Mobility Justice*.

70 Klein, *The Battle for Paradise*, 15.

71 Klein, *The Battle for Paradise*.

72 Patricia Mazzei and Frances Robles, "Ricardo Rosselló, Puerto Rico's Governor Resigns after Protests," *New York Times*, 24 July 2019, https://www.nytimes.com/2019/07/24/us/rossello-puerto-rico-governor-resigns.html.

73 Klein, *The Battle for Paradise*.

74 Mark Fishetti, "Climate Change Hastened Syria's Civil War," *Scientific American*, 2 March 2015, https://www.scientificamerican.com/article/climate-change-hastened-the-syrian-war/.

75 United Nations High Commissioner for Refugees, "Syria Emergency," n.d., https://www.unhcr.org/uk/syria-emergency.html; and Statistics Canada, "Results from the 2016 Census: Syrian Refugees who Settled in Canada in 2015 and 2016," 12 February 2019, https://www150.statcan.gc.ca/n1/pub/75-006-x/2019001/article/00001-eng.htm.

76 World Bank, "Climate Change Could Force over 140 million to Migrate within Countries by 2050: World Bank Report," press release, 19 March 2018, https://www.worldbank.org/en/news/press-release/2018/03/19/climate-change-could-force-over-140-million-to-migrate-within-countries-by-2050-world-bank-report.

77 Boas et al., "Climate Migration Myths," 901.

78 Boas et al., 902.

79 Nail, "Forum 1: Migrant Climate."

80 Baldwin, Frölich, and Rothe, "From Climate Migration to Anthropocene," 291.

81 Boas et al., "Climate Migration Myths," 902.

82 Sheller, *Mobility Justice*, 136.

83 Budd et al., "Fiasco of Volcanic Proportions," 39.

84 Sheller, *Mobility Justice*, 141.

85 Oliver Laughland, "Barbados PM: 'We Are on the Front Line of the Consequences of Climate Change,'" *Guardian*, 5 September 2019, https://www.theguardian.com/world/live/2019/sep/05/hurricane-dorian-carolinas-latest-live-updates-bahamas-us?page=with:block-5d714f768f08143ee1ae0e09#block-5d714f768f08143 ee1ae0e09.

86 Worldometer, "Carbon Dioxide (CO_2) Emissions by Country," Worldometer.info, n.d. https://www.worldometers.info/co2-emissions/co2-emissions-by-country/.

87 Sheller, *Island Futures*, 9.

88 Sheller, 12.
89 Whyte, Talley, and Gibson, "Indigenous Mobility Traditions," 326.
90 Weber, *The Vocation Lectures.*
91 Sheller, Island Futures, 64.

CHAPTER FIVE

1 Research interview with transport professional, 8 November 2013.
2 To see a gallery of Hurricane Juan and Igor images, visit https://stephanie-sodero.weebly.com/book.html.
3 Amber Pariona, "The Coastline of Canada, The Longest in the World," World Atlas, 11 June 2019, https://www.worldatlas.com/articles/the-coast-line-of-canada-the-longest-in-the-world.html.
4 CBC News, "Thought to be Extinct, Beothuk DNA is Still Present in N.L. Families, Genetics Researcher Finds," CBC, 8 May 2020, https://www.cbc.ca/news/canada/newfoundland-labrador/beothuk-dna-steven-carr-1.5559913.
5 Ralph T. Pastore, "Aboriginal Peoples," Heritage Newfoundland and Labrador, 1997, updated July 2021, https://www.heritage.nf.ca/articles/aboriginal/aboriginal-peoples-introduction.php.
6 Sandra Clarke, Harold Paddock, and Marguerite MacKenzie, "Language," Heritage Newfoundland and Labrador, 1999, updated July 2021, https://www.heritage.nf.ca/articles/society/language.php.
7 Government of Newfoundland and Labrador, "Provincial Healthy Aging Policy Framework," n.d., https://www.releases.gov.nl.ca/releases/2007/health/0711n04HA%20Policy%20Framework.pdf.
8 Trevor Bell, "Avalon Forest," Heritage Newfoundland and Labrador, 2002, https://www.heritage.nf.ca/articles/environment/avalon-forest.php.
9 Luke, "On the Political Economy of Clayoquot Sound."
10 Cresswell, "Newfoundland," *Plastiglomerate*, 41.
11 Valdivia, "'Petro-Capitalism.' Green Politics," 312. See also Altvater, "Capitalist Energy System."
12 Research interview with elected official, 31 October 2013.
13 Catto and Tomblin, "Multilevel Governance Challenges," 96.
14 Research interview with transport professional, 8 November 2013.
15 Research interview with municipal administrator, 28 October 2013.
16 Environment Canada, *Vigorous Igor*, 2017, https://ec.gc.ca/meteo-weather/default.asp?lang=En&n=BDE98E0F-1.
17 Courage, "Physical, Social and Economic Impacts of Hurricane Igor."
18 Environment Canada, *Hurricane Igor: 2010.*

19 Courage, "Physical, Social and Economic Impacts of Hurricane Igor." For discussion of the impacts of disaster on children, including long-term absence from school, see Fothergill and Peek, *Children of Katrina*.

20 CBC News, "Storm Prompts Evacuation of Offshore Oil Rigs," CBC, 19 September 2010, https://www.cbc.ca/news/canada/newfoundland-labrador/storm-prompts-evacuation-of-offshore-oil-rigs-1.891700.

21 Masson, "Extratropical Transition," 631.

22 Environment and Climate Change Canada, "Top Ten Weather Stories for 2010: Story Two," modified 2017, https://ec.gc.ca/meteo-weather/default.asp?lang=En&n=BDE98E0F-1.

23 Masson, "Extratropical Transition."

24 Masson, 631.

25 Government of Newfoundland and Labrador Department of Finance, Research and Analysis Division, "Hurricane Igor. Newfoundland and Labrador Statistics Agency," 2010, http://www.stats.gov.nl.ca/maps/PDFs/HurricaneIgor.pdf. Hurricane Sandy (2012) had a diameter of 1,600 kilometres (National Oceanic and Atmospheric Administration).

26 Current Results, "Average Annual Precipitation in Newfoundland and Labrador," 2015, https://www.currentresults.com/Weather/Canada/Newfoundland-Labrador/precipitation-annual-average.php and Environment Canada, "Vigorous Igor," 2017, https://ec.gc.ca/meteo-weather/default.asp?lang=En&n=BDE98E0F-1.

27 CBC News, "Hurricane Igor Attacks Newfoundland," CBC, 21 September 2010, https://www.cbc.ca/news/canada/newfoundland-labrador/hurricane-igor-attacks-newfoundland-1.935880.

28 John Lewandowski and Alison Auld, ""Hurricane Igor Batters Newfoundland," *Globe and Mail*, 21 September 2010, https://www.theglobeandmail.com/news/national/hurricane-igor-batters-newfoundland/article4326544/.

29 Catto and Tomblin, "Multilevel Governance Challenges."

30 Masson, "Extratropical Transition."

31 The Telegram, *Hurricane Igor: In the Eye*.

32 Raphael Borja, "A River Ran Through It," *Packet*, 30 September 2010.

33 CTV.ca News Staff, "Igor Prompts States of Emergency in Newfoundland," CTV News, 21 September 2010, http://www.ctvnews.ca/igor-prompts-states-of-emergency-innewfoundland-1.555232.

34 Environment and Climate Change Canada, "Top Ten Weather Stories for 2010."

35 The Canadian Underwriters, "Aviva Canada now Offering Overland Water Protection as Add-on to Personal Property Insurance Policies,"

2 June 2015, https://www.canadianunderwriter.ca/insurance/aviva-canada-now-offering-overland-water-protection-as-add-on-to-personal-property-insurance-1003655281/.

36 Pitts, "Hurricane Igor: What It Was Like on the Ground."

37 Research interview with elected official, 31 October 2013.

38 The Telegram, *Hurricane Igor: In the Eye.*

39 Research interview with elected official, 31 October 2013.

40 Research interview with elected official, 31 October 2013.

41 Research interview with elected official, 31 October 2013.

42 Research interview with elected official, 31 October 2013.

43 Frampton, "Storm Warning."

44 Masson, "Extratropical Transition," 63.

45 Research interview with fuel distributor, 10 February 2014.

46 Research interview, 31 October 2013, 113. For discussion of the environmental adaptive capacity of truckers in Newfoundland, see Fleming, "'Roads Less Travelled.'"

47 Research interview with transport professional, 8 November 2013.

48 Research interview with elected official, 31 October 2013. *Quad* is a regional term for off-highway vehicles or all-terrain vehicles.

49 Research interview with elected official, 31 October 2013.

50 Bærenholdt, "Governmobility."

51 Cresswell, "Mobility: The Lifeblood of Modernity," 2.

52 Savitzky, "Scrambled Systems."

53 Sheller, *Mobility Justice*, 103.

54 Birtchnell and Büscher, "Stranded," 5.

55 Research interview with elected representative, 31 October 2013.

56 Government of Newfoundland and Labrador, "Minister Provides Overview of Impacts of Hurricane Igor," news release, 24 September 2010, http://www.releases.gov.nl.ca/releases/2010/ma/0924n18.htm.

57 Research interview with elected representative, 31 October 2013.

58 Barton, "People and Technologies as Resources."

59 CBC News, "Chopper Picks Up Stranded N.L. Woman, 90," CBC. 24 September 2010, https://www.cbc.ca/news/canada/newfoundland-labrador/chopper-picks-up-stranded-n-l-woman-90-1.945240/.

60 This image in isolation is reminiscent of George W. Bush looking over New Orleans from the seat from Air Force One in the aftermath of Katrina. Combined with failures in federal response, the image caused widespread concern about his apparent indifference. In contrast, Prime Minister Harper spent time on the ground meeting those affected in Newfoundland. Kenneth Walsh, "The Undoing of George W. Bush: Hurricane Katrina Badly

Damaged the Former President's Reputation. And it Still Hasn't Recovered," USA News, 28 August 2015, https://www.usnews.com/news/ the-report/articles/2015/08/28/hurricane-katrina-was-the-beginning-of-the-end-for-george-w-bush. For discussion on the role of helicopters in Hurricane Katrina relief, see Fardink, "Helicopter Response."

61   Harvey, *Condition of Postmodernity*, 240.
62   Klein, *Battle for Paradise*, 68.
63   Research interview with elected representative, 31 October 2013.
64   Research interview with elected representative, 31 October 2013.
65   Research interview with elected official, 31 October 2013.
66   Masson, "Extratropical Transition."
67   Government of Newfoundland and Labrador, "Minister Provides Overview of Impacts of Hurricane Igor."
68   Masson, "Extratropical Transition."
69   Quora, "Why Do Asphalt Plants Close for the Winter?," 22 March 2016, https://www.quora.com/Why-do-asphalt-plants-close-for-the-winter.
70   Research interview with municipal administrator, 28 October 2013.
71   Research interview with municipal administrator, 3 March 2014.
72   Research interview with elected official, 31 October 2013.
73   Research interview with elected official, 31 October 2013.
74   Masson, "Extratropical Transition," 629.
75   Catto and Tomblin, "Multilevel Governance Challenges," 101.
76   CBC News, "Igor Damage Wasn't Fixed Well," CBC, 4 October 2011, https://www.cbc.ca/news/canada/newfoundland-labrador/igor-damage-wasn-t-fixed-well-mayor-1.1077052.
77   CBC News, "Igor Damage Wasn't Fixed Well."
78   United Nations Environment Programme, *Frontiers 2018/19*.
79   CBC News, "Igor Damage Wasn't Fixed Well."
80   Frampton, "Storm Warning."
81   Research interview with municipal administrator, 28 October 2013.
82   The Telegram, *Hurricane Igor: In the Eye*.
83   Masson, "Extratropical Transition."
84   Steve Bartlett, "Survivors and Everyday Heroes," *Telegram*, 25 September 2010.
85   Catto and Tomblin, "Multilevel Governance Challenges."
86   Lindroth and Sinevaara-Niskanen, "Colonialism Invigorated?"
87   Mark Iype and Bradley Bouzane, "Newfoundland Cleans Up after Hurricane Igor," *National Post*, 22 September 2010, https://nationalpost.com/news/newfoundland-cleans-up-after-hurricane-igor.

88 David Newell, "Hurricane Igor Wrecked my Honeymoon, and I'm OK with that," CBC, 22 September 2010, https://www.cbc.ca/news/canada/newfoundland-labrador/hurricane-igor-wrecked-my-honeymoon-and-i-m-ok-with-that-1.3234457.

89 Bartlett, "Survivors and Everyday Heroes."

90 The Telegram, *Hurricane Igor: In the Eye.*

91 "'Sense of Security' from Military Involvement, Hedderson," *Telegram,* 25 September, 2010.

92 On observation that official narratives tend to focus on the upbeat and heroic, see Borins, *Governing Fables.*

93 Government of Newfoundland and Labrador, *House of Assembly Proceedings,* 2011.

94 Pitts, "Hurricane Igor: What It Was Like on the Ground."

95 Freudenburg and Alario, "Weapons of Mass Distraction."

96 Sodero and Stoddart, "A Typology of Diversion."

97 Research interview with elected official, 31 October 2013.

98 Research interview with transport professional, 4 December 2013.

99 Research interview with elected official, 31 October 2013.

100 For anticipated regional climate impacts see Catto, *Review of Academic Literature Related to Climate Change Impacts.* See also, Finnis, *Projected Impacts of Climate Change.*

101 Research interview with municipal administrator, 28 October 2013. Wind speeds of 180 kilometres are on par with a Category 3 hurricane.

102 Research interview with transport professional, 4 December 2013. Referring to Category 5 Typhoon Haiyan.

103 Research interview with transport professional, 8 November 2013.

104 Goyette, "Five," in *Ocean,* n.p.

105 Catto and Tomblin, "Multilevel Governance Challenges," 96.

106 Catto and Tomblin, 100.

107 Justin Brake, "Climate Action Won't Involve Move from Oil: Premier," *Independent,* 18 April 2015, https://theindependent.ca/news/climate-action-wont-involve-move-from-oil-premier/. Dwight Ball replaced Paul Davis as premier in December 2015. With three premiers in two years, there was also fluidity of political leadership.

108 Government of Newfoundland and Labrador, Department of Finance, Research and Analysis Division. "Gross Domestic Product by Industry 1997–2010," 2011, https://www.google.com/url?sa=t&rct=j&q=&esrc=s&source=web&cd=&ved=2ahUKEwiI1oLZ3Z_3AhXlQUEAHdaqAyoQFnoECAkQAQ&url=https%3A%2F%2Fwww.mun.ca%2Fharriscentre%2Fpolicy%2Fconferencesworkshops%2Fnora_

nordregio%2FEconomic_and_Demographic_Overview.pdf&usg=
AOvVaw2Mh3Dj2mjG9gkHg-_9XjwF.

109 Government of Newfoundland and Labrador, Municipal Affairs and
Environment, Climate Change Branch, "The Way Forward: On Climate
Change in Newfoundland and Labrador," n.d., https://www.google.com/
url?sa=t&rct=j&q=&esrc=s&source=web&cd=&ved=2ahU-
KEwjQnu-t35_3AhXTNcAKHUv9C5sQFnoECAcQAQ&url=
https%3A%2F%2Fwww.gov.nl.ca%2Fecc%2Ffiles%2Fpublications-
the-way-forward-climate-change.pdf&usg=AOvVawof2dpbZOiWud3n
ZCt2jsRC.

110 Research interview with municipal administrator, 28 October 2013.

111 Research interview with transport professional, 4 December 2013.

112 Mark Maslin, "Five Climate Change Science Misconceptions –
Debunked," *The Conversation*, 15 September 2019, https://
theconversation.com/five-climate-change-science-misconceptions-
debunked-122570.

113 Government of Newfoundland and Labrador, *House of Assembly
Proceedings*, 7 April 2011, vol. XLVI 46?, no. 12.

114 Government of Newfoundland and Labrador, *Budget Speech 2011*,
19 April 2011, 12–13.

115 Research interview with elected official, 31 October 2013.

116 Research interview with elected official, 31 October 2013.

117 Government of Newfoundland and Labrador, *Charting Our Course*, 7.

118 Government of Newfoundland and Labrador, 51.

119 Government of Newfoundland and Labrador, "The Development of a
Sustainable Transportation Plan for Labrador," consultation document,
2006, https://www.gov.nl.ca/ti/files/publications-ltp-consultation.pdf.

120 See Andrey, Kertland, and Warren, "Water and Transportation
Infrastructure in Canada."

121 Catto and Tomblin, "Multilevel Governance Challenges," 93.

122 Government of Newfoundland and Labrador, "The Way Forward."

123 CBC News, "Carbon Pricing Won't Cost N.L. as Much as the Rest of
Canada, says MP Yvonne Jones," CBC, 15 November 2018, https://www.
cbc.ca/news/canada/newfoundland-labrador/yvonne-jones-climate-change-
1.4904650.

124 Government of Newfoundland and Labrador, "The Way Forward," 28.

125 Terry Roberts, "N.L.'s Offshore Regulator to Get a New Name, Mandate
to Pursue Renewable Energy Projects," 5 April 2022, https://www.cbc.ca/
news/canada/newfoundland-labrador/offshore-regulator-renamed-
1.6408561.

126 "Provincial Healthy Aging Policy Framework," n.d., https://www.google.
com/url?sa=t&rct=j&q=&esrc=s&source=web&cd=&ved=2ahU-
KEwiK7oLD4J_3AhVloVwKHfTZCRoQFnoECBIQAw&url=
http%3A%2F%2Fwww.releases.gov.nl.ca%2Freleases%2F2007%2F-
health%2Fo711no4HA%2520Policy%2520Framework.pdf&usg=AOv-
Vaw1vg5X4IxjoLngTUZk98hg3, 12.

CHAPTER SIX

1 Research interview with fuel distributor, 10 February 2014.
2 Urry, "System of Automobility," 4.
3 Brown, *Next-Generation Infrastructure.*
4 Sheller, *Mobility Justice*, 155.
5 Normark, "Tending to Mobility."
6 Research interview with fuel distributor, 10 February 2014.
7 Research interview with transport professional, 8 November 2013.
8 On parallel reconfiguration of airspace, see Lin, "Flying through Ash
Clouds."
9 Masson, "Extratropical Transition," 629.
10 Research interview with elected official, 31 October 2013.
11 Research interview with fuel distributor, 10 February 2014.
12 Research interview with fuel distributor, 10 February 2014.
13 See Berlant, *Cruel Optimism.*
14 Research interview with transport professional, 14 February 2014.
15 Research interview with transport professional, 14 February 2014.
16 CBC News, "Gas Shortage in Nova Scotia Leads to 'Complete Insanity' for
Station Owners," CBC, 31 August 2015, https://www.cbc.ca/news/
canada/nova-scotia/gas-shortage-in-nova-scotia-leads-to-complete-
insanity-for-station-owners-1.3209691.
17 Winnie Hu, "Mayor Mandates Rationing of Gas to Ease Shortage," *New
York Times*, 8 November 2012, https://www.nytimes.com/2012/11/09/
nyregion/new-york-city-imposes-gas-rationing-to-ease-shortage.html.
18 Sabina Zawadzki and Anna Louie Sussman, "Analysis: Six Months after
Sandy, New York Fuel Supply Chain still Vulnerable," Reuters, US News,
30 April 2013, https://www.reuters.com/article/us-usa-sandy-fuel/analysis-
six-months-after-sandy-new-york-fuel-supply-chain-still-vulnerable-
idUSBRE93ToDG20130430.
19 Hu, "Mayor Mandates Rationing of Gas."
20 Hu, "Mayor Mandates Rationing of Gas."
21 Zawadzki and Sussman, "Analysis: Six Months after Sandy."

22 Jennifer McLogan, "New York Awards $12-million to Provide Generators to Gas Stations along Evacuation Route," CBS New York, 15 June 2016, https://newyork.cbslocal.com/2016/06/15/gas-station-generator-grant/.

23 Klein, *The Battle for Paradise*, 6.

24 Klein, 6–7.

25 Klein, 41.

26 Klein, 7.

27 Klein, 8.

28 Urry, "Sociology and Climate Change."

29 Hesse, "Cities and Flow"; and Sassen, *Expulsions*.

30 Brown, *Next-Generation Infrastructure*.

31 Birtchnell, Savitzky, and Urry, *Cargomobilties*. See also Cowen, *The Deadly Life of Logistics*.

32 Cowen, *The Deadly Life of Logistics*, 3.

33 Sheller, *Mobility Justice*, 98.

34 Sheller, 154.

35 Alphonse MacNeil and Douglas Keefe, *The Nova Scotia Fuel Shortage: Report of the Independent Review Panel*, http://s3.documentcloud.org/documents/2644267/Nova-Scotia-Fuel-Shortage-Report.pdf, 5.

36 Perrow, *Normal Accidents*.

37 MacNeil and Keefe, *The Nova Scotia Fuel Shortage*," 9.

38 Grace Kay, "From Toilet Paper to Coffee, Here Are Some of the Products that Could Soon be in Short Supply because of the Suez Canal Blockage," *Business Insider*, 26 March 2021, https://www.businessinsider.com/toilet-paper-coffee-products-delayed-suez-canal-blockage-impact-2021-3?r=US&IR=T.

39 "Natural Gas Vehicles – Why Aren't We Buying Them?," Compare.com, 16 October 2018, https://www.compare.com/auto-insurance/guides/natural-gas-vehicles-guide.

40 Tristin Hopper, "Why Has Canada Spent Billions of Dollars Buying Saudi Arabian Oil?," *National Post*, 8 August 2018, https://nationalpost.com/news/canada/why-has-canada-spent-billions-of-dollars-buying-saudi-arabian-oil.

41 MacNeil and Keefe, *The Nova Scotia Fuel Shortage*.

42 MacNeil and Keefe.

43 CBC News, "Come By Chance Refinery Sold, Will Become Biofuel Operation by Mid-2022," CBC, 30 November 2021, https://www.cbc.ca/news/canada/newfoundland-labrador/nl-north-atlantic-refinery-1.6267625.

44 MacNeil, and Keefe, *The Nova Scotia Fuel Shortage*, 7.

45 MacNeil and Keefe.

46 MacNeil and Keefe, 10.

47 MacNeil and Keefe.

48 MacNeil and Keefe.

49 MacNeil and Keefe.

50 MacNeil and Keefe, 7.

51 For a sampling of public response see Stephanie Sodero, "#darknl," 2014, https://darknl.tumblr.com.

52 Sue Bailey, "Newfoundland's Dunderdale on Defensive after Handling of Blackouts," *Globe and Mail*, 7 January 2014, https://www.theglobeandmail.com/news/politics/newfoundlands-dunderdale-on-defensive-over-handling-of-blackouts/article16237842/.

53 MacNeil and Keefe, *The Nova Scotia Fuel Shortage*, 36.

54 MacNeil and Keefe, 36.

55 MacNeil and Keefe, 35.

56 Greta Thunberg, "'Our House is on Fire': Greta Thunberg, 16, Urges Leaders to Act on Climate Change," *Guardian*, 25 January 2019, https://www.theguardian.com/environment/2019/jan/25/our-house-is-on-fire-greta-thunberg16-urges-leaders-to-act-on-climate.

57 Adey, "Emergency Mobilities," 32.

58 Adey, 32.

59 Adey.

60 Anderson and Adey, "Governing Events and Life," 24.

61 Klein, *On Fire*.

62 Adey, "Emergency Mobilities," 35.

63 Government of Canada, *Energy Supplies Emergency Act*, Justice Laws website, 1985, https://laws-lois.justice.gc.ca/eng/acts/E-9/.

64 Government of Canada, "Organization Profile – Energy Supplies Allocation Board," 2019, https://appointments.gc.ca/prflOrg.asp?OrgID=ESR&lang=eng.

65 Christine Siminowski, personal communication to author, 20 June 2019.

66 Markolf et al., "Transportation Resilience," 177.

67 See, for example, Dalhousie University, "National Project Involving Dalhousie University's Health Population Institute Aims to Reduce Greenhouse Gas Emissions Linked to Health Care, Create Low-Carbon 'Green' Health System," 8 June 2021, https://www.dal.ca/news/media/media-releases/2021/06/08/media_release__national_project_involving_dalhousie_university_s_healthy_populations_institute_aims_to_reduce_greenhouse_gas_emissions_linked_to_health_care__create_low_carbon__green__health_system.html.

68 Tutton, "Nova Scotia is One 'Perfect Storm' Away."
69 World Health Organization, "WHO Director-General Addresses Human
    Rights Council on Climate Change," 3 March 2016, https://www.who.int/
    director-general/speeches/detail/who-director-general-addresses-human-
    rights-council-on-climate-change.
70 Kim Perrotta, "Canada's Health Organizations Demand Actions to
    Prevent Catastrophic Climate Change," *Canada's National Observer*,
    21 February 2019, https://www.nationalobserver.com/2019/02/21/opinion/
    canadas-health-organizations-demand-action-prevent-catastrophic-
    climate-change?fbclid=IwAR2GZmzBaMOgHAR7QsJuEZXzOFQ7JdfV_
    nzrH4sodJdwI3MRsGq437JtJxw.
71 Council of Canadian Academies, *Canada's Top Climate Change Risks*.
72 Berry and Schnitter, *Health of Canadians*, 2022.
73 Martha Currie, "How Climate Change Could Make Outbreaks like
    COVID-19 More Common," CBC, 14 February 2020, https://www.cbc.ca/
    radio/day6/pipeline-protests-covid-19-sonic-the-hedgehog-cheating-astros-
    suing-juul-coachella-meets-saudi-and-more-1.5463038/how-climate-
    change-could-make-outbreaks-like-covid-19-more-common-1.5463057.
74 Berry and Schnitter, *Health of Canadians*.
75 Cunsolo and Ellis, "Ecological Grief," 275.
76 Canadian Association of Physicians for the Environment, "Climate
    Change."
77 Perrotta, "Canada's Health Organizations Demand Actions."
78 Perrotta, "Canada's Health Organizations Demand Actions."
79 IPCC, "Summary for Policymakers," in *Global Warming of 1.5°C*.
80 World Meteorological Organization, "Multi-agency Report Highlights
    Increasing Signs and Impacts of Climate Change in Atmosphere, Land and
    Oceans," press release, 10 March 2020, https://public.wmo.int/en/media/
    press-release/multi-agency-report-highlights-increasing-signs-and-
    impacts-of-climate-change.
81 *Canada's Changing Climate Report – Executive Summary*.
82 Hannah Jackson, "National Climate Emergency Declared by House of
    Commons," Global News, 17 June 2019, https://globalnews.ca/
    news/5401586/canada-national-climate-emergency/.
83 United Nations Framework Convention on Climate Change, "The Paris
    Agreement," 22 October 2018, https://unfccc.int/process-and-meetings/
    the-paris-agreement/the-paris-agreement.
84 John Paul Tasker, "Federal Watchdog Warns That Canada's 2030
    Emissions Target May Not be Achievable," CBC, 26 April 2022, https://
    www.cbc.ca/news/politics/environment-commissioner-emissions-

reduction-targets-1.6431155?fbclid=IwAR2hKwWyquR3bEuK-
gnszi9co2Oq13RLg3h19jSKN8XDMYlaUhTVDkvwORvg.

85 Richard Zurawski, "HRM - Request for Council's Consideration," 29
January 2019, https://www.halifax.ca/sites/default/files/documents/
city-hall/regional-council/190129rc1471.pdf.

86 Zurawski, 1. *Net zero* is a contentious concept in the climate community.
It refers to balancing all carbon emissions put into the atmosphere with
reductions in emissions (e.g., natural and artificial carbon sinks), in
contrast to an absolute emission reduction. *Net negative carbon emissions*
is a step beyond this where communities store more carbon than is
emitted.

87 Halifax Regional Municipality, "HalifACT: Acting on Climate Change
Together," n.d., https://www.halifax.ca/about-halifax/energy-environment/
halifact-2050-acting-climate-together#latestnews.

88 Adey and Anderson, "Event and Anticipation," 2883.

89 Adey, "Emergency Mobilities," 35.

90 Anderson and Adey, "Governing Events and Life," 25.

91 Anderson and Adey, 30.

CHAPTER SEVEN

1 Folke et al., "Resilience Thinking."

2 Jensen, "Emotional Eruptions," 70.

3 Brown, *Next-Generation Infrastructure*, 2.

4 For example, one research participant described Hurricane Juan in the
following way: "It just looked like a bomb hit down there off of the harbour. It was unbelievable. All those big old trees down covering the whole
road, and we had to detour around another way." Likewise, another
research participant described Hurricane Igor in similar terms: "It's the
closest I've ever felt to being involved in a battle, except the enemy was
the weather and it had far more in its arsenal than we did."

5 Humanitarian Innovation Fund (HIF), "Disaster Management Cycle,"
Humanitarian Innovation Guide, n.d., https://higuide.elrha.org/humanitar-
ian-parameters/disaster-management-cycle/.

6 Sheller, "Islanding effects."

7 CBC News, "Hurricane Igor Attacks Newfoundland," CBC, 21 September
2010, https://www.cbc.ca/news/canada/newfoundland-labrador/
hurricane-igor-attacks-newfoundland-1.935880.

8 CBC News, "Danny Williams Says Stephen Harper's Tactics are Borderline
Racist," CBC, 5 October 2015, https://www.cbc.ca/news/canada/

newfoundland-labrador/danny-williams-stephen-harper-election-1.3256756.

9 Government of Nova Scotia, *A Report on the Emergency Response to Hurricane Juan*, 2.

10 Government of Nova Scotia, 3.

11 Government of Nova Scotia, *A Report on the Emergency Response to Hurricane Juan*.

12 Finnis, *Projected Impacts of Climate Change*.

13 Catto and Tomblin, "Multilevel Governance Challenges," 96.

14 Reggiani, Nijkamp, and Lanzi, "Transport Resilience and Vulnerability," 7.

15 Reggiani, Nijkamp, and Lanzi.

16 Reggiani, Nijkamp, and Lanzi.

17 Markolf et al., "Transportation Resilience," 174.

18 Markolf et al., 182.

19 Transport Canada, "Government of Canada Invests in Strengthening Resilience to Climate at the Port of Toronto," news release, 4 March 2019, https://www.canada.ca/en/transport-canada/news/2019/03/government-of-canada-invests-in-strengthening-resilience-to-climate-at-the-port-of-toronto.html.

20 Transport Canada.

21 Canadian Press, "Rail Blockades Causing Containers to Pile up at Canadian Ports," CBC News, Business, 21 February 2020, https://www.cbc.ca/news/business/rail-blockade-ports-1.5471312.

22 Council of Canadian Academies, *Canada's Top Climate Change Risk*, ix.

23 Ford et al., "Climate Change and Canada's North Coast."

24 Transport Canada, *Evaluation of the Northern Transportation Adaptation Initiative*, 2015, https://www.tc.gc.ca/eng/corporate-services/des-reports-1260.htm#toc5.

25 Paul Withers, "Irving Reaches Shipbuilding Deal with Federal Government," CBC News, 16 January 2020, https://www.cbc.ca/news/canada/nova-scotia/irving-reaches-shipbuilding-deal-with-federal-government-1.2912429.

26 Transport Canada, *Evaluation of the Northern Transportation Adaptation Initiative*.

27 Holling, "Resilience and Stability."

28 Folke et al., "Resilience Thinking."

29 Holling, "Engineering Resilience versus Ecological Resilience."

30 Adger et al., "Resilience Implications."

31 Frantzeskaki et al., "Social-Ecological Systems."

32 Ommer, *Coasts Under Stress*, 14.
33 Folke et al., "Resilience Thinking."
34 Folke et al.
35 Brand and Jax, "Focusing the Meaning(s)."
36 Graham, *Disrupted Cities*.
37 Brown, *Next-Generation Infrastructure*.
38 Brown.
39 Orr in Brown, *Next-Generation Infrastructure*, xi.
40 Brown, 12.
41 Brown, 11.
42 Brown, *Next-Generation Infrastructure*, 17.
43 Brown.
44 Brown.
45 Schwanen, Banister, and Anable, "Scientific Research," 997.

CHAPTER EIGHT

1 Research interview with transport professional, 4 December 2013.
2 Brown, *Next-Generation Infrastructure*, 3.
3 Canadian Climate Action Network, *Getting Real about Canada's Climate Plan*, 2019.
4 Naomi Klein (@NaomiAKlein), "The future is radical. We face a stark choice btw radical, disruptive changes to our physical world or radical, disruptive changes to our political and economic systems to avoid those outcomes. The status quo is not one of the options on the table - get it yet 'centrists'?" Twitter, 25 February 2019, https://twitter.com/NaomiAKlein/status/1100081193960329216.
5 Cresswell, "Towards a Politics of Mobility," 27.
6 Sheller, *Mobility Justice*, 138.
7 Levitas, *Utopia as Method*, 198.
8 Levitas, 217.
9 Tsing, *The Mushroom*, 5.
10 Levitas, *Utopia as Method*, xiii.
11 Urry, "Climate Change, Travel."
12 Urry, *Societies Beyond Oil*.
13 Urry.
14 Urry, "Climate Change, Travel," 269.
15 El Akkad, *American War*.
16 Urry, "Climate Change, Travel."

17 Transition Network, "About Us," 2019, https://transitionnetwork.org.
18 Dan Luscher, "Access, not Mobility: It's not About How Fast You Can Go," *15 Minute City* (blog), n.d., https://www.15minutecity.com/blog/access.
19 Jocelyn Timperly, "This Cargo Ship Runs on Wind," Wired, 1 October 2021, https://www.wired.co.uk/article/wind-powered-cargo-ships.
20 Clydebank Declaration signatories, "Clydebank Declaration for Green Shipping Corridors," UN Climate Change Conference, 11 October 2021, https://ukcop26.org/cop-26-clydebank-declaration-for-green-shipping-corridors/.
21 "International Aviation Climate Ambition Coalition," UN Climate Change Conference, 11 October 2021, https://ukcop26.org/cop-26-declaration-international-aviation-climate-ambition-coalition/.
22 Sodero, "Blood Drones."
23 CBC News, "What Would it Take for Canada to Meet its Climate Targets?" *Front Burner*, 18 June 2019, https://www.cbc.ca/radio/frontburner/what-would-it-take-for-canada-to-meet-its-climate-targets-1.5179310.
24 CBC News, "What Would it Take?"
25 See, for example, 350.org, "Green New Deal," n.d., https://350.org/canada/gnd/.
26 United States House of Representatives, *Recognizing the Duty.*
27 United States House of Representatives, 3.
28 United States House of Representatives, 13.
29 Klein, *On Fire*, 277.
30 Klein, 278.
31 United States House of Representatives, *Recognizing the Duty*, 4–5.
32 Klein, *On Fire*, 287–8.
33 Sheller, *Island Futures.*
34 Robinson Meyer, "The Green New Deal Does Not, Strictly Speaking, Exist," *Atlantic*, 13 July 2021, https://www.theatlantic.com/science/archive/2021/07/the-green-new-deal-doesnt-exist/619424/.
35 Catto and Tomblin, *Multilevel Governance*, 93.
36 Adey, "Emergency Mobilities," 44.
37 Research interview with elected official, 31 October 2013.
38 David Farrell, "Politics-as-usual Can't Fix the Climate Crisis. Maybe it's Time to Try a Citizens' Assembly," *Guardian*, 29 August 2019, https://www.theguardian.com/commentisfree/2019/aug/28/climate-crisis-citizens-assembly-extinction-rebellion.
39 Schwanen, Banister, and Anable, "Scientific Research," 1004.
40 Bendell, "Deep Adaptation," 23.

41 Beatley, *Blue Urbanism*.

42 Brand and Jax, "Focusing the Meaning(s)," 27.

43 Sodero, "Policy in Motion."

44 Lauren Weber, "Hurricane Maria's Effects on the U.S. Health Care Industry is Threatening Lives across the U.S.," *Huffington Post*, 20 September 2018, https://www.huffingtonpost.co.uk/entry/ iv-bag-drug-shortage-puerto-rico-hurricane-maria_n_5ba1ca16e4b-046313fc07a8b.

45 Julia Wong, "Hospitals Face Critical Shortage of IV Bags due to Puerto Rico Hurricane," *Guardian*, 10 January 2018, https://www.theguardian. com/us-news/2018/jan/10/hurricane-maria-puerto-rico-iv-bag-shortage-hospitals.

46 Graham, "Disruptions," 471.

47 Council of Canadian Academies, *Canada's Top Climate Change Risk*, 22.

48 Statistics Canada, "Primary Health Care Providers, 2016. Health Fact Sheets," 27 September 2017, https://www150.statcan.gc.ca/n1/pub/ 82-625-x/2017001/article/54863-eng.htm.

49 Sell, Rothenberg, and Chapman, "Vital Signs."

50 Ikeya, "Practical Management of Mobility." See also Scarry, *Thinking in an Emergency*.

51 Collier and Lakoff, "Vital Systems Security."

52 Bennett, *Vibrant Matter*, viii.

53 Redfield, "Vital Mobility and the Humanitarian Kit."

54 Lavau, "Viruses."

55 Kiel, "Diseased."

56 Morgan et al., "Business Continuity."

57 Yarwood, "One Moor Night."

58 Davis et al., "Scheduling Food Bank Collections."

59 Graham, "Disruptions."

60 Sodero and Rackham, "Vital Mobilities."

61 Associated Press, "Telemedicine and Walk-in Clinics have Future of Family Doctor in Flux," 16 April 2019, CBC News, https://www.cbc.ca/news/ health/telemedicine-and-walk-in-clinics-have-future-of-family-doctor-in-flux-1.5100395.

62 Glauser, "Blood-Delivering Drones Saving Lives"; and Rhiannon Johnson, "Moose Cree First Nation Signs Deal for Deliveries by Drone from Moosonee," CBC News, 9 December 2017, https://www.cbc.ca/news/ indigenous/moose-factory-drone-delivery-deal-1.4937422.

63 Cheryl Chan, "Drone Carries Meds from Vancouver Island to Salt Spring Island in Historic Flight," *Vancouver Sun*, 30 August 2019, https://

vancouversun.com/news/local-news/drone-carries-meds-from-vancouver-island-to-salt-spring-island-in-historic-flight/.

64 Szerszynski, "Planetary Mobilities."

65 Beck, "Emancipatory Catastrophism," 76.

66 United Nations Environment Programme, "Ecosystem," n.d.

67 Alex Morss, "Planting Trees to Tackle Climate Change Might Feel Nice, but it Could be Doing More Harm than Good," *Independent*, 18 November 2019, https://www.independent.co.uk/voices/planting-trees-climate-crisis-environment-a9207086.html.

68 Marie Woolf, "2 years after Trudeau pledged to plant 2 billion trees, only 8.5 million have been planted," CBC News, 13 December 2021, https://www.cbc.ca/news/politics/tree-planting-update-cp-1.6284165.

69 Ecology Action Centre, *Living Shorelines: Managing Erosion while Restoring Coastal Habitat*, n.d., https://www.ecologyaction.ca/files/images-documents/file/Coastal/LivingShorelines_Brochure_Aug28-REG.pdf.

70 Ecology Action Centre.

71 Ecology Action Centre.

72 Research interview with urban planner, 11 December 2013.

73 Usher, "Veins of Concrete."

74 United Nations Environment Programme, "Eco-system Based Disaster Risk Reduction," 2013, https://www.unenvironment.org/explore-topics/disasters-conflicts/what-we-do/risk-reduction/ecosystem-based-disaster-risk.

75 Brown, *Next-Generation Infrastructure*.

76 Beatley, *Blue Urbanism*.

77 Beatley, 77.

78 AtCoMedia, "Canada Invests in Its First Floating Tidal Energy Array," *Offshore Engineer*, 6 November 2020, https://www.oedigital.com/news/483013-canada-invests-in-its-first-floating-tidal-energy-array.

79 Schwanen, Banister, and Anable, "Scientific Research."

80 Graham, *Vertical*.

81 Hannah Fry, "Why Weather Forecasting Keeps Getting Better," *New Yorker*, 24 June 2019, https://www.newyorker.com/magazine/2019/07/01/why-weather-forecasting-keeps-getting-better, 9.

82 Perrow, *Normal Accidents*.

83 Fry, "Why Weather Forecasting Keeps Getting Better," 10.

84 Fry, 10.

85 See: El Dorado Weather, "Nova Scotia, Canada Area Waters Live Buoy Observations," *El Dorado Weather*, 2022, https://www.eldoradoweather. com/buoy/Nova%20Scotia/buoy-xhtml.php.

86 Ocean Networks Canada, "About Us," 2019, http://www.oceannetworks.ca/.

87 Smartfin, "About," 2019, https://smartfin.org/about/.

88 Rebecca Lau, "Number of Snow Day School Closures Mounting in Nova Scotia," Global News, 25 February 2015, https://globalnews.ca/ news/1850739/number-of-snow-day-school-closures-mounting-in-nova-scotia/.

89 Government of Nova Scotia, *A Report on the Emergency Response to Hurricane Juan.*

90 Government of Newfoundland and Labrador, "The Root Cellars of Elliston, Newfoundland and Labrador," YouTube, 1.52 min., 2 May 2013, https://www.youtube.com/watch?v=IxWMpNouk30.

91 See Whyte, Talley, and Gibson, "Indigenous Mobility Traditions."

92 See, for example, Redfield, "Fluid Technologies."

93 Government of Nova Scotia, *Choose How You Move*, 17–18.

94 Carlos Moreno and Pierre Veltz, "The '15 Minute City': The Way Forward or an Ideological Mirage," *Mobile Lives Forum*, 11 April 2022, https:// forumviesmobiles.org/en/arguings/15541/15-minute-city-way-forward-or-ideological-mirage.

95 IPCC, "Climate Change," in *Managing the Risks of Extreme Events.*

96 Cowen, *Deadly Life of Logistics.*

97 Adey and Anderson, "Event and Anticipation," 2895.

98 Cresswell and Martin, "On Turbulence."

99 Hage, "Waiting Out the Crisis," 8.

100 Cresswell and Martin, "On Turbulence."

101 Markolf et al., "Transportation Resilience," 183.

102 Sheller, *Mobility Justice*, 144.

103 Adey, "Emergency Mobilities."

104 We're Ready, "About," 2019, http://www.wereready.org/about.html.

105 City of Calgary, "The Flood of 2013," n.d., https://www.calgary.ca/UEP/ Water/Pages/Flood-Info/Flooding-History-Calgary.aspx.

106 Halifax Regional Municipality, "Joint Emergency Management Teams," http://ns.211.ca/service/27851427_53488659/ joint_emergency_management_teams.

107 Government of Canada, "Get Prepared: Your Emergency Preparedness Guide," 2018, www.getprepared.gc.ca.

CHAPTER NINE

1 UK-Med, "Sounding the Siren," 2021, https://soundingthesiren.com/. Also, see the graphic novella here: Illustrations: Dwarka Nath Sinah, and story: Stephanie Sodero, Holly Smith, and Sophie Grattidge, "Amrita's Story," September 2021, https://soundingthesiren.com/amritas-story/.

2 Red Rebel Brigade, "Home," 2022, http://redrebelbrigade.com/.

3 Erin Pottie, "Stranded Residents of Tiny Cape Breton Community Relying on Rope, Milk Crate to Get Supplies," 25 November 2021, https://www.cbc.ca/news/canada/nova-scotia/tarbotvale-cape-breton-stranded-after-storm-1.6262548.

4 Research interview with transport professional, 28 October 2013.

5 Paul Withers, "Nova Scotia Power says Dorian was its Most Damaging Storm Ever," CBC News, 28 November 2019, https://www.cbc.ca/news/canada/nova-scotia/nova-scotia-power-says-dorian-was-its-most-damaging-storm-ever-1.5376098.

6 Alex Kennedy, "What Did Snowmageddon Teach Us About Food Insecurity?," CBC News, 26 February 2020, https://www.cbc.ca/news/canada/newfoundland-labrador/snowmageddon-food-insecurity-1.5476127.

7 Beck, "Emancipatory Catastrophism"; and Schwanen, Banister, and Anable, "Scientific Research."

8 Environment and Climate Change Canada, Canada's Changing Climate Report, 7

9 Banister, "Sustainable Mobility Paradigm."

10 Goyette, "Twenty-Eight," in Ocean, n.p.

11 Goyette, "Eight," in Ocean, n.p.

12 Bauman, Globalization: The Human Consequences, 57.

13 Birtchnell and Büscher, "Stranded," 7.

14 Cresswell, "Mobility: The Lifeblood of Modernity," 2.

15 Savitzky, "Scrambled systems."

16 Brown, Next-Generation Infrastructure, 3.

Bibliography

MEDIA SOURCES CITED

BBC News
Business Insider
CBC News
CTV News
Canadian Press
Chronicle Herald
Coast
The Conversation
Global News
Globe and Mail
Guardian
Huffington Post
Independent (Ktaqmkuk/Newfoundland)
Independent (United Kingdom)
National Post
New Scientist
New York Times
New Yorker
Packet
Reuters
Telegram
Washington Post
Wired

WORKS CITED

Adey, Peter. "Emergency Mobilities." *Mobilities* 11, no. 1 (2016): 32–48.
– "If Mobility Is Everything then It Is Nothing: Towards a Relational Politics of (Im)mobilities." *Mobilities* 1, no. 1 (2006): 75–94.
Adey, Peter, and Ben Anderson. "Event and Anticipation: UK Civil Contingencies and the Space-Time of Decision." *Environment and Planning A* 43, no. 12 (2011): 2878–99.
Adger, W. Neil, Katrina Brown, Donald R. Nelson, Fikret Berkes, Hallie Eakin, Carl Folke, Kathleen Galvin et al. "Resilience Implications of Policy Responses to Climate Change." *Wiley Interdisciplinary Reviews: Climate Change* 2, no.5 (2011): 757–66.
Altvater, Elmar. "The Capitalist Energy System and the Crisis of the Global Financial Markets: The Impact on Labour." *Labour, Capital and Society / Travail, Capital et Société* 40, no. 1/2 (2007): 18–34.
Anderson, Ben, and Peter Adey. "Governing Events and Life: Emergencies in UK Civil Contingencies." *Political Geography* 31, no. 1 (2012): 24–33.
Andrey, Jean, Pamela Kertland, and Fiona Warren. "Water and Transportation Infrastructure in Canada." In *Canada in a Changing Climate: Sector Perspectives on Impacts and Adaptation*, edited by Fiona Warren and Donald Lemmen, 233–252. Government of Canada: Ottawa, Ontario, 2014.
Appleyard, Donald. "The Environmental Quality of City Streets: The Residents' Viewpoint." *Journal of the American Planning Association* no. 35 (1969): 84–101.
– *Livable Streets*. Berkeley, CA: University of California Press, 1981.
Bærenholdt, Jørgen Ole. "Governmobility: The Powers of Mobility." *Mobilities* 8, no.1 (2013): 20–34.
Baldwin, Andrew, Christiane Frölich, and Delf Rothe. "From Climate Migration to Anthropocene Mobilities: Shifting the Debate." *Mobilities* 14, no. 3 (2019): 289–97.
Banister, David. "The Sustainable Mobility Paradigm." *Transport Policy* 15, no. 2 (2008): 73–80.
Barnes, Barry. *The Nature of Power*. Cambridge: Polity Press, 1988.
Barton, David. "People and Technologies as Resources in Times of Uncertainty." *Mobilities* 6, no. 1 (2011): 57–65.
Bauman, Zygmunt. *Globalization: The Human Consequences*. New York: Columbia University Press, 1998.
Beatley, Timothy. *Blue Urbanism: Exploring Connections between Cities and Oceans*. Washington: Island Press, 2014.

Beazley, Karen, Tamaini Snaith, Frances MacKinnon, and David Colville. "Road Density and Potential Impacts on Wildlife Species such as American Moose in Mainland Nova Scotia." *Proceedings of the Nova Scotian Institute of Science* 42, no. 2 (2004): 339–57.

Beck, Ulrich. "Emancipatory Catastrophism: What Does It Mean to Climate Change and Risk Society?" *Current Sociology* 63, no. 1 (2015): 75–88.

– *Risk Society: Toward a New Modernity.* London: Sage, 1992.

Bendell, Jem. "Deep Adaptation: A Map for Navigating Climate Tragedy." Institute for Leadership and Sustainability Occasional Paper. 27 July 2018.

Benediktsson, Karl, Katrín Anna Lund, and Edward, Huijbens. "Inspired by Eruptions? Eyjafjallajökull and Icelandic Tourism." *Mobilities* 6, no. 1 (2011): 77–84.

Bennett, Jane. *The Enchantment of Modern Life: Attachments, Crossings, and Ethics.* Princeton, NJ: Princeton University Press, 2001. Quoted in "Nonhuman Charisma." Jamie Lorimer. *Environment and Planning D: Society and Space*, no. 25 (2007): 911–32.

– *Vibrant Matter: A Political Ecology of Things.* Durham: Duke University Press, 2010.

Berlant, Lauren. *Cruel Optimism.* Durham: Duke University Press, 2011.

Berry, Peter, and Rebeka Schnitter, R., eds. *Health of Canadians in a Changing Climate: Advancing our Knowledge for Action.* Ottawa, ON: Government of Canada, 2022.

Birtchnell, Thomas, and Monika Büscher. "Stranded: An Eruption of Disruption." *Mobilities* 6, no.1 (2011): 1–9.

Birtchnell, Thomas, Sataya Savitzky, and John Urry. *Cargomobilties: Moving Materials in a Global Age.* New York: Routledge, 2015.

Bissell, David. *Transit Life: How Commuting is Transforming Our Cities.* Boston: MIT Press, 2018.

Boas, Ingrid, Carol Farbotko, Helen Adams, Harald Sterly, Simon Bush, Kees van der Geest, Hanne Wiegel et al. "Climate Migration Myths." *Nature Climate Change*, no. 9 (2019): 898–903.

Boas, Ingrid, Sanneke Kloppenburg, Judith van Leeuwen, and Machi Lamers. "Environmental Mobilities: An Alternative Lens to Global Environmental Governance." *Global Environmental Politics* 18, no. 4 (2018): 107–26.

Borins, Sandford. *Governing Fables: Learning from Public Sector Narratives.* Charlotte: Information Age Publishing, 2011.

Brand, Fridolin, and Kurt, Jax. "Focusing the Meaning(s) of Resilience:

Resilience as a Descriptive Concept and a Boundary Object." *Ecology and Society* 12, no.1 (2007): 23.

Brown, Hillary. *Next-Generation Infrastructure: Principles for Post-Industrial Public Works*. Washington: Island Press, 2014.

Budd, Lacy, Steven Griggs, David Howarth, and Stephen Ison. "A Fiasco of Volcanic Proportions? Eyjafjallajökull and the Closure of European Airspace." *Mobilities* 6, no. 1 (2011): 31–40.

Bush, Elizabeth, Nathan Gillett, Barrie Bonsal, Stewart Cohen, Chris Derksen, Greg Flato, Blair Greenan, Majorie Shepherd, and Xuebin Zhang. *Canada's Changing Climate Report – Executive Summary*. Government of Canada, 2019, https://www.nrcan.gc.ca/sites/www.nrcan.gc.ca/files/energy/Climate-change/pdf/CCCR_ExecSumm-EN-040419-FINAL.pdf.

Caletrío, Javier. "The Flying Less Movement. Mobile Lives Forum." 2019. http://en.forumviesmobiles.org/2018/07/19/flying-less-movement-12600.

– "Transition Studies. Mobile Lives Forum." 11 May 2015. http://en.forumviesmobiles.org/marks/transition-studies-2839.

Canadian Association of Physicians for the Environment, "Climate Change Toolkit for Health Professionals." 2019. https://cape.ca/blog-health-professionals/.

Castells, Manuel. *Communication Power*. Oxford: Oxford University Press, 2009.

Catto, Norm, and Steven Tomblin. "Multilevel Governance Challenges in Newfoundland and Labrador: A Case Study of Emergency Measures." In *Multilevel Governance and Emergency Management in Canadian Municipalities*, edited by David Henstra, 91–133. Montreal & Kingston: McGill-Queen's University Press, 2013.

– *Review of Academic Literature Related to Climate Change Impacts and Adaptation in Newfoundland and Labrador*. St. John's: Newfoundland and Labrador Office of Climate Change, Energy Efficiency and Emissions Trading, 2010.

Chariandy, David. *Brother*. Toronto: McClelland & Stewart, 2018.

The Chronicle Herald. *Hurricane Juan: The Story of a Storm*. Halifax: Nimbus Publishing, 2003.

Clark, Nigel, and Kathryn Yusoff. "Geosocial Formations and the Anthropocene." *Theory, Culture and Society* 34, no.2–3 (2017): 3–23.

Cocker, Mark. *Birders: Tales of a Tribe*. London: Jonathan Cape, 2001.

Collier, Stephen, and Andrew Lakoff. "Vital Systems Security: Reflexive Biopolitics and the Government of Emergency." *Theory, Culture & Society* 32, no.2 (2015): 19–51.

Council of Canadian Academies. *Canada's Top Climate Change Risk.*
Ottawa *(ON): The Expert Panel on Climate Change Risks and Adaptation Potential, Council of Canadian Academies.* 2019.

Courage, Rebecca. "The Physical, Social and Economic Impacts of Hurricane Igor on Newfoundland." Appendix: Contact information, Questions and Answers. Undergraduate Project. Memorial University, 2013.

Cowen, Deborah. *The Deadly Life of Logistics: Mapping Violence in Global Trade.* Minneapolis: University of Minnesota Press, 2014.

Cresswell, Tim. "Mobilities III: Moving On." *Progress in Human Geography* 38, no. 5 (2014): 712–21.

– "Mobility: The Lifeblood of Modernity and the Virus that Threatens to Undo It." Mobile Lives Forum (website). 20 March 2020. https://en. forumviesmobiles.org/2020/03/18/mobility-lifeblood-modernity-and-virus-threatens-undo-it-13266?fbclid=IwAR2E502wPtjTBuATtx-Qj14f7aX9m-rpaJxsu8fjMSaCjgJSgWoXsWqJn4mo.

– *Plastiglomerate.* London: Penned in the Margins, 2020.

– "Towards a Politics of Mobility." *Environment and Planning D: Society and Space.* 28, no. 1 (2010): 17–31.

Cresswell, Tim, and Craig Martin. "On Turbulence: Entanglements of Disorder and Order on a Devon Beach." *Tijdschrift voor economische en sociale geografie* 103, no. 5 (2012): 516–29.

Cunsolo, Ashlee, and Neville Ellis. "Ecological Grief as a Mental Health Response to Climate Change-Related Loss." *Nature Climate Change,* no. 8 (2018): 275–81.

Davidson, Debra, and Eva Bogdan. "Reflexive Modernization at the Source: Local Media Coverage of Bovine Spongiform Encephalopathy in Rural Alberta." *Canadian Review of Sociology* 47, no. 4 (2010): 359–80.

Davis, Lauren, Irem Sengul, Julie Ivy, Luther Brock, and Lastella Miles. "Scheduling Food Bank Collections and Deliveries to Ensure Food Safety and Improve Access." *Socio-Economic Planning Sciences,* no. 48 (2014): 175–88.

de Certeau, *The Practice of Everyday Life.* Translated by Steven Rendall. Berkeley: University of California Press, 1984.

El Akkad, Omar. *American War.* New York: Alfred A. Knopf, 2017.

Elliott, Anthony, and John Urry. *Mobile Lives.* London: Routledge, 2010.

Fardink, Paul. "The Helicopter Response to Hurricane Katrina." *Vertiflite* 57, no. 2 (2011): 48–58.

Fink, Sheri. *Five Days at Memorial: Life and Death in a Storm-Ravaged Hospital.* New York: Random House, 2013.

Finnis, Joel. *Projected Impacts of Climate Change for the Province of Newfoundland and Labrador*. St. John's, NL: Memorial University, 2013.

Fleming, Michael. "'Roads Less travelled': Dependency and Resilience in Locally-Owned Trucking Companies on the Great Northern Peninsula of Newfoundland and Labrador and the Acadian Peninsula of New Brunswick." PhD thesis, Memorial University of Newfoundland, 2019.

Folke, Carl, Stephen Carpenter, Brian Walker, Marten Scheffer, Terry Chapin, and Johan Rockström. "Resilience Thinking: Integrating Resilience, Adaptability and Transformability." *Ecology and Society* 15, no. 4 (2010): 20.

Folke, Carl, Johan Colding, and Fikret Berkes. "Synthesis: Building Resilience and Adaptive Capacity in Social-Ecological Systems." *Ecology and Society* 11, no. 1 (2003): 352–87.

Ford, James, Nicole Couture, Trevor Bell, and Dylan Clark. "Climate Change and Canada's North Coast: Research Trends, Progress, and Future Directions." *Environmental Reviews* 26, no.1 (2018): 82–93.

Fothergill, Alice, and Lori Peek. *Children of Katrina*. Austin: University of Texas Press, 2015.

Foucault, Michel. "Governmentality." In *The Foucault Effect: Studies in Governmentality*, edited by Graham Burchell, Colin Gordon, and Peter Miller, 87–104. Chicago: University of Chicago Press, 1991.

– "Governmentality." In *The Essential Foucault: Selections from The Essential Works of Foucault 1954–1984*. New York: The New Press, 1994.

– *Security, Territory, Population: Lectures at the College de France, 1977–1978*. New York: Palgrave MacMillan, 2014.

Frantzeskaki, Niki, Jill Slinger, Heleen Vreugdenhil, and Els van Daalen. "Social-Ecological Systems Governance: From Paradigm to Management Approach." *Nature and Culture* 5, no. 1 (2010): 84–98.

Freudenburg, William, and Margarita Alario. "Weapons of Mass Distraction: Magicianship, Misdirection, and the Dark Side of Legitimation." *Sociological Forum* 22, no. 2 (2007): 146–73.

Freudenburg, William, Robert Gramling, Shirley Laska, and Kai Erikson. *Catastrophe in the Making: The Engineering of Katrina and the Disasters of Tomorrow*. Washington, DC: Island Press, 2011.

– "Organizing Hazards, Engineering Disasters?: Improving the Recognition of Political-Economic Factors in the Creation of Disasters." *Social Forces* 87, no. 2 (2008): 1015–38.

Fulmore, Cynthia, and Sunny Russell. "After the Flood: Surviving
    Hurricane Juan." *Canadian Operating Room Nursing Journal* 23, no. 2
    (2005): 6, 8–10, 35–6.
Giddens, Anthony. *Runaway World: How Globalization is Reshaping our
    Lives*. New York: Routledge, 2003.
Glauser, Wendy. "Blood-Delivering Drones Saving Lives in Africa and
    Maybe Soon in Canada." *Canadian Medical Association Journal* 22,
    no. 190 (2018): E88–9.
Government of Newfoundland and Labrador. *Charting Our Course:
    Climate Change Action Plan 2011*. St. John's: Newfoundland, 2011.
    https://www.turnbackthetide.ca/files/government-action/climate_
    change.pdf.
– "The Development of a Sustainable Transportation Plan for Labrador."
    2006. https://www.google.com/url?sa=t&rct=j&q=&esrc=s&-
    source=web&cd=&ved=2ahUKEwjU79aPpaD3AhVKZcAKHQSO
    BIoQFnoECAgQAQ&url=https%3A%2F%2Fwww.gov.nl.
    ca%2Fti%2Ffiles%2Fpublications-ltp-consultation.pdf&usg=
    AOvVaw26ZFS7myiB7dfmCj4hodTb.
– *Uncommon Potential – A Vision for Newfoundland and Labrador
    Tourism*. St. John's: Newfoundland, 2009.
Government of Nova Scotia. *Choose How You Move: Sustainable
    Transport Strategy*. Halifax: Nova Scotia, 2013.
– *Climate Change Progress Report*. 2019. https://climatechange.
    novascotia.ca/sites/default/files/Climate-Change-Progress-Report-
    October-2019.pdf.
– *Environmental Goals and Sustainable Prosperity Act*. 2013.
    https://climatechange.novascotia.ca/sites/default/files/uploads/
    environmental%20goals%20and%20sustainable%20prosperity.pdf.
– *Toward a Greener Future: Nova Scotia Climate Change Action Plan*.
    Halifax: Nova Scotia, 2009.
Goyette, Sue. *Ocean*. Kentville: Gaspereau Press, 2013.
Graham, Stephen, ed. *Disrupted Cities: When Infrastructure Fails*.
    New York: Routledge, 2010.
– "Disruptions." In *The Routledge Handbook of Mobilities*, edited by
    Peter Adey, David Bissell, Kevin Hannam, Peter Merriman, and Mimi
    Sheller, 468–71. New York: Routledge, 2014.
– *Vertical: The City from Satellites to Bunkers*. London: Verso, 2016.
Gramling, Robert, and William Freudenburg. "A Century of Macondo:
    United States Energy Policy and the BP Blowout Catastrophe."
    American Behavioral Scientist 56, no. 1 (2012): 48–75.

Grieve, Malcom, and Lori Turnbull. "Emergency Planning in Nova Scotia." In *Multilevel Governance and Emergency Management in Canadian Municipalities*, edited by Daniel Henstra, 62–90. Montreal & Kingston: McGill-Queen's University Press, 2013.

Hage, Ghassan. *Waiting*, edited by Ghassan Hage, 97–106. Melbourne: Melbourne University Publishing, 2009.

Halifax Regional Municipality, *Urban Forest Master Plan*. 2013.

Hannam, Kevin, Mimi Sheller, and John Urry. "Editorial: Mobilities, Immobilities and Moorings." *Mobilities* 1, no. 1 (2006): 1–22.

Harvey, David. *The Condition of Postmodernity*. Oxford: Blackwell: 1989.

Hesse, Markus. "Cities and Flow: Re-asserting a Relationship as Fundamental as it is Delicate." *Journal of Transport Geography*, no. 29 (2013): 33–42.

Hodgetts, Timothy, and Jamie Lorimer. "Animals' Mobilities." *Progress in Human Geography*. Published online (2019): 1–23.

Holling, Crawford. "Engineering Resilience versus Ecological Resilience." In *Engineering with Ecological Constraints*. National Academy of Engineering, 1996.

– "Resilience and Stability of Ecological Systems." *Annual Review of Ecology and Systematics*, no. 4 (1973): 1–23.

Hussain, Akhtar and Pitr Musilek. "Resilience Enhancement Strategies For and Through Electric Vehicles." *Sustainable Cities and Society*, 80 (2022): 1–18.

Hyndman, Donald, David Hyndman, and Norman Catto. *Natural Hazards and Disasters*. Belmont, CA: Brook/Cole, 2008.

Ikeya, Nozomi. "Practical Management of Mobility: The Case of the Emergency Medical System." *Environment and Planning A*, no. 35, (2003): 1537–64.

Ingold, Tim. "Earth, Sky, Wind, and Weather." *Journal of the Royal Anthropological Institute*, no. 13 (2007): 19–38.

IPCC. "Climate Change: New Dimensions in Disaster Risk, Exposure, Vulnerability, and Resilience." Managing the Risks of Extreme Events and Disasters to Advance Climate Change Adaptation. A Special Report of Working Groups I and II of the Intergovernmental Panel on Climate Change, edited by C.B. Field, V. Barros, T.F. Stocker, D. Qin, D.J. Dokken, K.L. Ebi, M.D. Mastrandrea, K.J. Mach, G.-K. Plattner, S.K. Allen et al. Cambridge, UK: Cambridge University Press, 2012.

– "Sea Level Change." In *Climate Change 2013: The Physical Science Basis. Contribution of Working Group I to the Fifth Assessment Report of the Intergovernmental Panel on Climate Change.* Cambridge, UK: Cambridge University Press, 2013.

– "Summary for Policymakers." In *Climate Change 2014: Mitigation of Climate Change. Contribution of Working Group III to the Fifth Assessment Report of the Intergovernmental Panel on Climate Change.* Cambridge, UK: Cambridge University Press, 2014.

– "Summary for Policymakers." In *Global Warming of 1.5°C. An IPCC Special Report on the Impacts of Global Warming of 1.5°C above Pre-industrial Levels and Related Global Greenhouse Gas Emission Pathways, in the Context of Strengthening the Global Response to the Threat of Climate Change, Sustainable Development, and Efforts to Eradicate Poverty.* Geneva: World Meteorological Organization, 2018.

– "Summary for Policymakers." In *Managing the Risks of Extreme Events and Disasters to Advance Climate Change Adaptation (A Special Report of Working Groups I and II of the Intergovernmental Panel on Climate Change).* Cambridge, UK: Cambridge University Press, 2012.

– "Summary for Policymakers." In *Climate Change 2021: The Physical Science Basis. Contribution of Working Group I to the Sixth Assessment Report of the Intergovernmental Panel on Climate Change,* edited by V. Masson-Delmotte, P. Zhai, A. Pirani, S.L. Connors, C. Péan, S. Berger, N. Caud, Y. Chen, L. Goldfarb, M.I. Gomis et al. Cambridge, UK: Cambridge University Press, 2021.

International Federation of Red Cross and Red Crescent Societies, *Cost of Doing.* 2019. https://oldmedia.ifrc.org/ifrc/the-cost-of-doing-nothing/.

Jensen, Ole. "Emotional Eruptions, Volcanic Activity and Global Mobilities: A Field Account from a European in the US during the Eruption of Eyjafjallajökull." *Mobilities* 6, no. 1 (2011): 67–75.

Keil, Roger. "Diseased." In *The Routledge Handbook of Mobilities,* edited by Peter Adey, David Bissell, Kevin Hannam, Peter Merriman, and Mimi Sheller, 388–97, New York: Routledge, 2014.

Kelman, Ilan. *Disaster by Choice: How Our Actions Turn Natural Hazards Into Catastrophes.* Oxford: Oxford University Press, 2020.

Klein, Naomi. *The Battle for Paradise: Puerto Rico Takes on the Disaster Capitalists.* Chicago: Haymarket Books, 2018.

– *On Fire: The Burning Case for a Green New Deal.* London: Allen Lane, 2019.

– *This Changes Everything: Capitalism vs the Climate.* New York: Simon and Schuster, 2014.

Klinenberg, Eric. *Heat Wave: A Social Autopsy of Disaster in Chicago.* Chicago: Chicago University Press, 2002.

Kochanoff, Stan. "Trees versus Power Lines: Priorities and Implications in Nova Scotia." *Plan Canada* 44, no. 1 (2004): 43–5.

Latour, Bruno. *Aramis, or the Love of Technology.* Cambridge, MA: Harvard University Press, 1996.

– "From Multiculturalism to Multinaturalism: What Rules of Method for the New Socio-scientific Experiments?" *Nature and Culture* 6, no. 1 (2011): 1–17.

– *Politics of Nature: How to Bring the Sciences into Democracy.* Translated by Catherine Porter. New Delhi: Orient Longman, 2004.

– "What are the Optimal Interrelations of Art, Science and Politics in the Anthropocene?" *Bifrost Insights.* 20 November 2017. https://bifrostonline.org/bruno-latour-what-are-the-optimal-interrelations-of-art-science-and-politics-in-the-anthropocene/.

Lavau, Stephanie. 2014. "Viruses." In *The Routledge Handbook of Mobilities*, edited by Peter Adey, David Bissell, Kevin Hannam, Peter Merriman, and Mimi Sheller, 298–305. New York: Routledge, 2014.

Lefebvre, Henri. *Rhythmanalysis: Space, Time and Everyday Life.* Translated by Stuart Elden and Gerald Moore. New York: Continuum, 2004.

Levitas, Ruth. *Utopia as Method: The Imaginary Reconstitution of Society.* New York: Palgrave MacMillan, 2013.

Liboiron, Max. *Pollution Is Colonialism.* Durham: Duke University Press, 2021.

Lin, Weiqiang. "Flying through Ash Clouds: Improvising Aeromobilities in Singapore and Australasia." *Mobilities* 9, no. 2 (2013): 220–37.

Lindroth, Marjo, and Heidi Sinevaara-Niskanen. "Colonialism Invigorated? The Manufacture of Resilient Indigeneity." *Resilience: International Policies, Practices and Discourses* 7, no. 3 (2019): 240–54.

Lockie, Stewart. "Why Environmental Sociology?" *Environmental Sociology* 1, no.1 (2015): 1–3.

Lorimer, Jamie. "Nonhuman Charisma." *Environment and Planning D: Society and Space*, no. 25 (2007): 911–32.

Luke, Timothy. "On the Political Economy of Clayoquot Sound: The Uneasy Transition from Extractive to Attractive Models of Development." In *A Political Space: Reading the Global through Clayoquot Sound*, edited by Warren Magnusson and Karena Shaw, 91-112 Minneapolis: University of Minnesota Press, 2003.

MacIntyre, John. *Deep Freeze Winter 2015.* Halifax: MacIntyre Purcell Publishing, 2015.

Manderscheid, Katharina, Tim Schwanen, and David Tyfield.
"Introduction to Special Issue on 'Mobilities and Foucault.'" *Mobilities*
9, no. 4 (2014): 479–92.

Markolf, Samuel, Christopher Hoehne, Andrew Fraser, Mikhail Chester,
and B. Shane Underwood. "Transportation Resilience to Climate
Change and Extreme Weather Events – Beyond Risk and Robustness."
Transport Policy, no. 74 (2019): 174–86.

Marshall, Stephen. "The Challenge of Sustainable Transport." In *Planning
for a Sustainable Future*, edited by Antonia Layard, Simin Davoudi and
Susan Batty, 131–48. London and New York: Taylor & Francis, 2001.

Masson, Athena. "The Extratropical Transition of Hurricane Igor and the
Impacts on Newfoundland." *Natural Hazards* 72, no. 2 (2014): 617–32.

McLeod, Donald. *Hurricane Juan: The Unforgettable Storm*. Halifax:
Formac Publishing, 2004.

Milnes, Travis, and Timothy Haney. "'There's Always Winners and
Losers': Traditional Masculinity, Resource Dependence, and Post-
Disaster Environmental Complacency." *Environmental Sociology* 3, no.
3 (2017): 260–73.

Milton, Kay. 2002. *Nature: Towards an Ecology of Emotion*. London:
Routledge, 2002.

Morgan, Stephen, Richard Rackham, Stuart Penny, J.R. Lawson, Robert
Walsh, and Sue Ismay. "Business Continuity in Blood Services: Two Case
Studies from Events with Potentially Catastrophic Effect on the National
Provision of Blood Components." *VoxSanguinis* 108, no. 2 (2015): 150–9.

Morrison, Catherine. "In Crisis, Under Control: 9/11 and Newfoundland's
Emergency Procurement Response." *Summit* 6, no. 1 (2003): 3–6.

Murdoch, Jonathan. "Ecologising the Social: Actor-Network Theory,
Co-construction and the Problem of Human Exemptionalism."
Sociology 35, no. 1 (2001): 111–33.

Murphy, Raymond. "Catastrophism in Canada: Emancipatory of
Sclerotic?" Conference Presentation, Ottawa, Annual Meeting of the
Canadian Sociological Association, June 2015.

– "Disaster or Sustainability: The Dance of Human Agents with Nature's
Actants." *Canadian Review of Sociology and Anthropology* 41, no. 3
(2004): 249–66.

– *Leadership in Disaster: Learning for a Future with Global Climate
Change*. Montreal & Kingston: McGill-Queen's University Press,
2009.

Nail, Thomas. "Forum 1: Migrant Climate in the Kinocene." *Mobilities*
14, no. 3 (2019): 375–80.

Normark, Daniel. "Tending to Mobility: Intensities of Staying at the Petrol
    Station." *Environment and Planning A* 38, no. 2 (2006): 241–52.
Ommer, Rosemary. *Coasts Under Stress: Restructuring and Social-
    Ecological Health.* Montreal & Kingston: McGill-Queen's University
    Press, 2007.
O'Regan, Michael. "On the Edge of Chaos: European Aviation and
    Disrupted Mobilities." *Mobilities* 6, no. 1 (2011): 21–30.
Peréz, Louis. *Winds of Change: Hurricanes and the Transformation of
    Nineteenth-Century Cuba.* Chapel Hill: University of North Carolina
    Press, 2001.
Perrow, Charles. *Normal Accidents: Living with High-Risk Technologies.*
    Princeton: Princeton University Press, 1984.
Pezzullo, Phaedra. "Tourists and/as Disasters: Rebuilding, Remembering,
    and Responsibility in New Orleans." *Tourist Studies* 9 (2009): 23–41.
Potter, Claire Bond, and Renee C. Romano. *Doing Recent History: On
    Privacy, Copyright, Video Games, Institutional Review Boards, Activist
    Scholarship, and History That Talks Back.* Athens: University of
    Georgia Press, 2012.
Redfield, Peter. "Fluid Technologies: The Bush Pump, the LifeStraw and
    Microworlds of Humanitarian Design." *Social Studies of Science* 46,
    no. 2 (2016): 159–83.
– "Vital Mobility and the Humanitarian Kit." In *Biosecurity Interventions:
    Global Health and Security in Question*, edited by Andrew Lakoff and
    Stephen Collier, 147–72. New York: Columbia University Press, 2008.
Reggiani, Aura, Peter Nijkamp, and Diego Lanzi. "Transport Resilience
    and Vulnerability: The Role of Connectivity." *Transportation Research
    Part A*, no. 81 (2015): 4–15.
Remes, Jacob. *Disaster Citizenship: Survivors, Solidarity, and Power in the
    Progressive Era.* Urbana: University of Illinois Press, 2016.
Risseeuw, Carla. *The Fish Don't Talk About the Water: Gender
    Transformation Power and Resistance Among Women in Sri Lanka.*
    Leiden: Brill Academic Publishing, 1989. Quoted in Tim Cresswell.
    In Place/Out of Place: Geography, Ideology, and Transgression.
    Minneapolis: University of Minnesota Press, 1996.
Robinson, Mary. *Climate Justice: A Man-Made Problem with a Feminist
    Solution.* London: Bloomsbury, 2018.
Rutland, Ted, and Alex Aylett. "The Work of Policy: Actor Networks,
    Governmentality, and Local Action on Climate Change in Portland,
    Oregon." *Environment and Planning D: Society and Space*, no. 26
    (2008): 627–46.

Salter, Mark. "To Make Move and Let Stop: Mobility and the Assemblage
of Circulation." *Mobilities* 8, no. 1 (2013): 7–19.

Sassen, Saskia. *Expulsions: Brutality and Complexity in the Global
Economy.* Cambridge, MA: Harvard University Press, 2014.

Savitzky, Satya. "Scrambled Systems: The (Im)mobilities of 'Storm
Desmond.'" *Mobilities* 13, no. 5 (2018): 662–84.

Scarry, Elaine. *Thinking in an Emergency. (Amnesty International Global
Ethics Series).* New York: W.W. Norton & Company, 2011.

Schwanen, Tim, David Banister, and Jillian Anable. "Scientific Research
about Climate Change Mitigation in Transport: A Critical Review."
Transportation Research Part A, no. 45 (2011): 993–1006.

Sell, Rebecca, Mikel Rothenberg, and Charles Chapman. "Vital Signs."
In *Dictionary of Medical Terms*, 6th ed. Hauppauge, NY: Barron's
Educational Series, 2012.

Sheller, Mimi. *Aluminum Dreams: The Making of Light Modernity.*
Boston: MIT Press, 2014.

– *Island Futures: Caribbean Survival in the Anthropocene.* Durham: Duke
University Press, 2020.

– "Islanding Effects: Post-Disaster Mobility Systems and Humanitarian
Logistics in Haiti." *Cultural Geographies* 20, no. 2 (2013): 185–204.

– "Mobility." *Sociopedia.isa* (2011):1–12.

– *Mobility Justice: The Politics of Movement in an Age of Extremes.*
London: Verso, 2018.

Sheller, Mimi, and John Urry. "The New Mobilities Paradigm."
Environment and Planning A 38, no. 2 (2006): 207–26.

Silver, Amber, and Catherine Conrad. "Public Perception of and Response
to Severe Weather Warnings in Nova Scotia, Canada." *Meteorological
Applications* 17, no. 2 (2010): 173–9.

Simpson, Jamie. *Journeys through Eastern Old-Growth Forests:
A Narrative Guide.* Halifax: Nimbus Publishing, 2015.

Sobel, Adam. *Storm Surge: Hurricane Sandy, Our Changing Climate, and
Extreme Weather of the Past and Future.* New York: Harper Collins, 2014.

Sodero, Stephanie. "Blood Drones: Using Utopia as Method to Imagine
Future Vital Mobilities." *Mobilities* 15, no. 1 (2020): 11–24.

– "Greenhouse Gases, Pine Beetles, and Humans: The Ecologically-
Mediated Development of British Columbia's Carbon Tax." *Canadian
Journal of Sociology* 40, no. 3 (2015): 309–30.

– "Policy in Motion: Reassembling Carbon Pricing Policy Development in
the Personal Transport Sector in British Columbia." *Journal of
Transport Geography*, no. 19 (2011): 1471–81.

Sodero, Stephanie, and Richard Rackham. "Vital Mobilities." In *Vital Mobilities in Handbook on Methods and Applications for Mobilities Research*, edited by Monika Büscher, Malene Freudendal-Pedersen, Sven Kesselring, and Nikolaj Grauslund Kristensen, 172–81. Cheltenham, UK: Edward Elgar Publishing, 2020.

Sodero, Stephanie, and Mark CJ Stoddart. "A Typology of Diversion: Legitimating Discourses of Tourism Attraction, Oil Extraction and Climate Action in Newfoundland and Labrador." *Environmental Sociology* 1, no. 1 (2015): 59–68.

Sou, Gemma, and John Douglas. "After Maria: Everyday Recovery from Disaster." N.d. https://www.hcri.manchester.ac.uk/research/projects/after-maria/.

Spaargaren, Gert, Arthur Mol, and Hans Bruyninckx. "Introduction: Governing Environmental Flows in Global Modernity." In *Governing Environmental Flows: Global Challenges to Social Theory*, edited by Gert Spaargaren, Arthur Mol, and Frederick Buttel, 1–37. Cambridge, MA: MIT Press, 2006.

Steinmetz, George. "Ceasarism and Parliamentarism." 2009. Review of *Caesarism, Charisma, and Fate – Historical Sources and Modern Resonances in the Work of Max Weber*. Edited by Peter Baehr. New Brunswick, NJ: Transaction Publishers, 2008.

Suliman, Samid, Carol Farbotko, Hedda Ransan-Cooper, Karen McNamara, Fanny Thornton, Celia McMichael, and Taukiei Kitara. "Indigenous (Im)mobilities in the Anthropocene." *Mobilities* 14, no. 3(2019): 298–318.

Szerszynski, Bronislaw. "Planetary Mobilities: Movement, Memory and Emergence in the Body of the Earth." *Mobilities* 11, no. 4 (2016): 614–28.

The Telegram. *Hurricane Igor: In the Eye of the Storm*. St. John's: Creative Publishers, 2010.

Trainor, Sarah Fleisher, Anna Godduhn, Lawrence K. Duffy, F. Stuart Chapin III, David C. Natcher, Gary Kofinas, and Henry P. Huntington. "Environmental Injustice in the Canadian Far North: Persistent Organic Pollutants and Arctic Climate Impacts." In *Speaking for Ourselves: Environmental Justice in Canada*, edited by Julian Agyeman, Peter Cole, Randolph Haluza-DeLay, and Pat O'Riley, 144–162. Vancouver: UBC Press: 2010.

Tsing, Anna Lowenhaupt. *The Mushroom at the End of the World: On the Possibility of Life in Capitalist Ruins*. Princeton: Princeton University Press, 2015.

Uexküll, Jakob von. *A Foray into the Worlds of Animals and Humans: With A Theory of Meaning.* Translated by Joseph D. O'Neil. Minneapolis: Minnesota University Press, 2010.

United Kingdom Department for Transport. *Transport Resilience Review.* 2014. https://www.gov.uk/government/uploads/system/uploads/attachment_data/file/335115/transport-resilience-review-web.pdf.

United Nations Environment Programme, *Eco-System Based Disaster Risk Reduction.* n.d. https://www.unep.org/explore-topics/disasters-conflicts/what-we-do/disaster-risk-reduction/ecosystem-based-disaster-risk.

United Nations Environment Programme. *Frontiers 2018/19 Emerging Issues of Environmental Concern. Chapter 5: Maladaptation to Climate Change: Avoiding Pitfalls on the Evolvability Pathway.* Nairobi: UNEP, 2019.

United Nations Sustainable Development Goals. *Nature's Dangerous Decline 'Unprecedented'; Species Extinction Rates 'Accelerating.'* 2019. https://www.un.org/sustainabledevelopment/blog/2019/05/nature-decline-unprecedented-report/.

United States House of Representatives. "Recognizing the Duty of the Federal Government to create a Green New Deal." 2019. https://www.congress.gov/bill/116th-congress/house-resolution/109/text.

Urry, John. "Climate Change, Travel and Complex Futures." *British Journal of Sociology* 59, no. 2 (2008): 261–79.

– *Mobilities.* Cambridge: Polity Press, 2007.

– "Mobility and Proximity." *Sociology* 32, no. 2 (2002): 255–74.

– *Societies Beyond Oil: Oil Dregs and Social Futures.* London: Zed Books, 2013.

– "Sociology and Climate Change." *Sociological Review* 57, no. s2 (2010): 84–100.

– "The System of Automobility." *Theory, Culture and Society* 21, no. 4/5 (2004): 25–39.

Usher, Mark. "Veins of Concrete, Cities of Flow: Reasserting the Centrality of Circulation in Foucault's Analytics of Government." *Mobilities* 9, no. 4 (2014): 550–69.

Valdivia, Gabriella. "'Petro-Capitalism.'" In *Green Politics: An A-to-Z Guide*, edited by Dustin Mulvaney and Paul Robbins, 312–14. London: Sage, 2011.

Weber, Max. *The Vocation Lectures.* Illinois: Hackett Books, 2004.

Whyte, Kyle, Jared Talley, and Julia Gibson. "Indigenous Mobility Traditions, Colonialism, and the Anthropocene." *Mobilities* 14, no. 3 (2019): 319–35.

Wiersma, Yolanda, Troy Davis, Elizabeth Eberendu, Ian Gidge, Maria Jewison, Hiliary Martin, Kaylah Parsons et al. "Hurricane Igor Impacts at Northern Latitudes: Factors Influencing Tree Fall in an Urban Setting." *Arboriculture and Urban Forestry* 38, no. 3 (2012): 92–8.

Wilson, Edward O. *Biophilia*. Cambridge, MA: Harvard University Press, 1984.

Yarwood, Richard. "One Moor Night: Emergencies, Training and Rural Space." *Area* 44, no. 1 (2012): 22–8.

Index

accessibility, 8, 48, 148–9
actor-network theory, 41
adaptation, 18, 113–17, 155–6,
    167, 181
Adey, Peter, 14, 24, 136, 142, 166,
    179, 189
aging, 74, 99, 122; elderly, 26,
    112; senior citizens, 13, 119–22,
    169, 191
airport, 23–4, 40, 47, 57–62,
    99, 105
air quality, 35, 139–40
Alario, Margarita, 114
Alberta, 29, 44, 70, 136–8, 154,
    180, 191
all-hands-on-deck, 110
all-hazards approach, 58, 74
allocating, 114, 131–2, 137,
    142–3, 192
all-terrain vehicles, 193.
    See also quads
Anable, Jillian, 14, 23, 167, 185
Anderson, Ben, 14, 136, 142,
    179, 189
animals, 6, 13, 31, 37, 44, 79–80,
    136, 140–1
Anthropocene, 22, 54, 81, 95, 175

anxiety, 15, 46, 125, 136, 140, 184
Appleyard, Donald, 50
assemblages, 41, 174
atmosphere, 18–22, 27–8, 36, 41–6,
    53, 171–5
automobility, 32, 77, 95, 108–9,
    121–6; car-oriented, 50–1
autonomous vehicles, 177; driver-
    less cars, 52

back-up, 15, 28, 75, 126–8, 134–6,
    176–7. See also redundancy
Bærenholdt, Jørgen Ole, 87
Baldwin, Andrew, 38, 52–4, 92–5
Banister, David, 14, 23, 48,
    167, 185
Barbados (Ichi-rougan-aim), 96
Barnes, Barry, 42
Barton, David, 46
batten down the hatches, 58–60,
    73, 147–8
Bauman, Zygmunt, 23, 187
Beatley, Timothy, 36, 173
Beck, Ulrich, 5, 18, 28, 40, 71, 121,
    171, 185
Bendell, Jem, 167
Bennett, Jane, 33, 41, 82, 169–70

biodiversity, 22, 27–31, 65, 80,
    106, 171
Birtchnell, Thomas, 19, 107
Bissell, David, 37
blame, 114
blockages, 62, 84, 123
blue urbanism, 167, 173, 187
Boas, Ingrid, 94–5
body, 41, 55, 167–70, 186, 191;
    bodies, 26, 33, 162–8
bridges, 40–4,105–8, 151–6,
    176–8, 184; Bailey, 108, 151
British Columbia, 7, 20, 44, 69,
    138, 141, 154, 168, 175, 191
Brown, Hillary, 145–6, 156,
    173, 183
Budd, Lucy, 24, 47
Büscher, Monika, 19, 107

Canadian Association of Physicians
    for the Environment (CAPE),
    139, 140, 143
Canadian Forces, 65, 102, 109,
    150, 167
Canadian Hurricane Centre,
    58, 101
Canadian Red Cross, 9–10, 62, 150
canals, 27–8
canoes, 39
carbon dioxide, 11, 36, 41, 66, 81,
    96, 175
carbon pricing, 121; carbon tax,
    164, 168; climate action tax, 142
care, 4, 6, 21, 39, 41, 62, 133–4,
    139–44, 165–71, 176, 189; care-
    givers, 122; caring, 190–2
Castells, Manuel, 23
catastrophic mobilities, 13, 80,
    89–90, 161
Catto, Norm, 110, 116, 121, 166

Chariandy, David, 25
charisma, 13, 79–86, 93–7, 156;
    charismatic immobility, 84–8,
    148–51, 185
circulations, 23–7, 33, 116–17,
    152, 158, 169, 174
Clam Harbour, NS, 86
Climate Change Action Plan, 76,
    120
Climate Change Reduction Act, 77
climate crisis, 7, 18, 22, 27, 33, 38,
    55, 72–3, 94–101, 184
climate emergency, 4–9, 15, 40, 71,
    139–44
climate migrant, 94–5. See also cli-
    mate mobilities
climate mobilities, 12, 81, 94–7
climate refugee, 38, 94–5. See also
    climate mobilities
climate routing, 5, 15, 156–63,
    189–91
colonialism, 38, 56; climate colo-
    niality, 96, 190; settler colonial-
    ism, 11–12, 96–8
Colville, Alex, 14–19, 187–8
community resilience, 161, 165,
    181–4, 190
commuting, 17, 37, 57, 123
contingency, 127, 133
COVID-19, 38, 80, 164, 180
Cowen, Deborah, 22, 129
Cresswell, Tim, 13–16, 19–25,
    32–8, 99–107, 187
Cunsolo, Ashlee, 72, 140
cycling, 8, 22, 38, 47, 51, 85, 140

Daniel's Harbour, NL, 84, 117
Dartmouth, NS, 59, 76, 130, 140
Davis, Paul, 116
Dean-Simmons, Barb, 104

decarbonize, 20
diesel, 123, 128–33, 137–9
disability, 13, 191
disaster capitalism, 93
Disaster Financial Assistance
    Arrangements, 86, 103, 117–18
disaster management, 33, 44,
    73–4, 116
disaster sociology, 45
discipline, 33–4
disease, 20, 69–71, 87, 94–7, 122,
    136, 139–43; Lyme, 139–40,
    180; vector-borne, 139, 143, 180
disrupt(ion), 32, 94–5, 106–10,
    170, 178–9; disruption to cli-
    mate, 50, 138, 162, 190; disrup-
    tion to mobility, 3–5, 18, 84,
    139; mess, 64
diversion, 27
driving, 45–51, 89, 120, 151,
    178; bus(es), 25–9, 46–7, 66–8,
    126–7; car, 33, 48–55, 84–5,
    133–4, 179
drones, 43, 105, 171, 177
Dunderdale, Kathy, 135
dystopia, 49, 162

early warning systems, 147,
    170, 175
ecological approach to mobilities,
    4, 12–15, 38–43, 48–9, 53, 80,
    157–61, 185–9; ecological
    mobilities, 13–14, 29–33, 35–9,
    171, 188
Ecology Action Centre, 8, 172
El Akkad, Omar, 162
electricity grid, 138
Elliott, Anthony, 42
Ellis, Neville, 73
Elliston, NL, 178

emancipatory catastrophism, 5, 28,
    71, 121
embrace green and blue, 4, 15, 160,
    171, 182, 187, 189
Emergency Management
    Organisation (EMO), 58, 73, 75,
    83, 88, 151, 181
emergency mobilities, 14, 24, 136,
    142, 150, 189
energy, 27–8, 37–40, 74–7, 137–40,
    180, 188; Energy Supplies
    Emergency Act, 137, 143, 177
enjoy, 57, 82, 140; joy, 51
entanglement, 11–13, 63, 85–7
Epstein, Howard, 73
evacuation, 44, 89–91, 160,
    180–1, 190
extreme weather, 3–4, 45–7, 54,
    89–92, 119–21, 155–6, 180;
    weather forecasting, 61,
    102, 174

ferry, 67–8, 85, 106–7, 124–5;
    Halifax-Dartmouth, 59; Marine
    Atlantic, 99
:15 CITY, 163, 178
Finnis, Joel, 151
fire, 59, 64–7, 101–5, 110, 133–4,
    150–2, 181; forest fire, 29, 191;
    wildfire, 139
fisheries, 114–16, 177
flex/ibility, 135, 153, 160, 180;
    think flex, 4, 15, 160, 179–82,
    187–9
floodwater, 34, 41, 117, 150, 172
flows, 14, 48–9, 53–4, 129, 169–74
flying, 45, 59, 67, 180
food, 20–4, 62–6, 97–100, 108,
    128–33, 150, 163, 177–8; gro-
    ceries, 62

fossil fuel, 55, 134–8, 140–4
Fothergill, Alice, 90
Foucault, Michel, 23, 33–5, 87
Freudenburg, William, 12, 27, 34, 45, 114
Fröhlich, Christiane, 38, 52
Fry, Hannah, 175
future-proofed, 14, 157; future-proofing, 185

gas, 28, 116–20, 123–9, 131–6, 176
gender, 25–6, 50, 89, 92
generators, 44, 62, 74, 106, 119, 126–9, 135, 142, 146–9, 160, 177
geoecological, 129; geoecologies, 33
Giddens, Anthony, 27–8, 44, 68
global heating, 15, 19–22, 28, 37, 52, 161, 165
global warming, 141. *See also* global heating
governmentality, 87
Government of Canada, 137, 154
Government of Newfoundland and Labrador, 120–1
Government of Nova Scotia, 77
governmobility, 87–9, 106–8
Graham, Stephen, 14, 156
Gramling, Robert, 27
greenhouse gases, 15, 18, 40
Green New Deal, 164–7
grief, 65, 73, 84
Grieve, Malcolm, 72
Gulf Stream, 41

Haiti (Ayiti), 38
Halifax Explosion, 71–2, 116
Halifax Port Authority, 59, 66, 70–2, 131

Halifax Regional Municipality (K'jipuktuk), 66, 85, 127, 149
Hannam, Kevin, 22
harbour, 35, 59–61, 64–6, 84–6, 130; Halifax Harbour, 3, 62, 71, 174; St. John's Harbour, 100–1, 142, 151, 186, 194
health, 62–3, 122–4, 133–8, 140–4, 168, 189–92; health care, 62, 70, 133–6, 165, 170–6, 186; health emergency, 138; mental health, 21–6, 53–7, 68, 80, 94, 133–8, 139–44, 189
heat, 20–1, 25–6, 31, 37, 40, 45, 134; Chicago heat wave (1995), 26; extreme heat, 20–1, 40; heat dome, 7, 141; heat wave, 15–19, 21–6, 40, 81, 92, 139–41
Hedderson, Tom, 111
helicopters, 5, 13, 29, 105–8, 122, 150
Holling, C.S. (Buzz), 39, 155
Hurricane Arthur (New Brunswick, 2016), 9
Hurricane Dorian (Nova Scotia, 2019), 6, 96, 185
Hurricane Earl (Newfoundland, 2010), 102
Hurricane Katrina (New Orleans, 2005), 6–10, 23–7, 34, 84, 90–2, 129, 186
Hurricane Maria (Puerto Rico, 2017), 10–14, 90–3, 124–8, 144, 168, 186–9
Hurricane Sandy (New York, 2012), 10–14, 35–6, 102, 124–7, 156, 174, 186
hyper-mobility, 25

ice, 18–19, 30, 44, 80–1, 105, 117, 154; iceberg, 32, 42, 84; ice storm, 33, 45–7, 55, 65, 76, 186
Icelandic ash cloud, 23, 33, 43, 46, 55, 186
income, 65, 97, 168, 191–2; high-income, 95, 169; low-income, 11, 26, 62–3
Indigenous, 38, 78, 96, 138, 162, 178
Industrial Revolution, 20, 36, 54
inequity, 97, 170
infrastructure, 14, 105, 118–23, 143–8, 154–8
Ingold, Tim, 81–2
insects, 31, 79; mosquitoes, 54, 139; ticks, 31, 139
insurance, 51, 91, 103
Intergovernmental Panel on Climate Change (IPCC), 20–1, 52, 141–3, 164, 174
International Organization for Migration (IOM), 94, 110, 119, 148, 172
Irving, 131, 135, 155
islanded, 92, 139
isolation, 6, 12–13, 121, 149, 171

Jensen, Ole B., 46, 145
Jones, Yvonne, 113
just-in-time, 38, 129–31, 134, 138, 177–8
just transition, 160, 164–6, 189–92

Keefe, Douglas, 131–2, 135
Kelly, Peter, xii, 85
kinetic elite, 25
Klein, Naomi 25, 36, 93, 128, 137, 165
Klinenberg, Eric, 26

Knights Cove, NL, 108
Kolbert, Elizabeth, 22, 34

Lanzi, Diego, 153
Latour, Bruno, 29, 40–1
Levitas, Ruth, 162
Liboiron, Max, xii–xiii
livability, 48
Lockie, Stewart, 54
Lorimer, Jamie, 13, 79–80
Luke, Timothy, 156
Luscher, Dan, 163

MacDonell, John, 73
MacIsaac, Angus, 62
MacNeil, Alphonse, 131–5
maladaptation, 111
Marine Environmental Observation, Prediction and Response Network, 13
Markolf, Samuel, 138, 153, 180
Marshall, Stephen, 48–9, 118, 160
Marystown, NL, 107, 109, 111
Massey, Joan, 76
materialism, 169
materiality, 41
McLeod, Donald, 65, 85
medical supplies, 15, 62, 108, 130, 139
Meyer, Robinson, 168
Mi'kma'ki (land/territory), 56–7; Mi'kmaw, 57; Mi'kmaw intellectual traditions, 78
Million Trees Initiative, 35, 172
mingling, 82
mitigation, 68–73, 113–19, 142–7, 167, 185–9
mobility justice, 37, 89, 95, 187
Montreal (Tiohti), 8, 44–5, 57, 132
moorings, 3, 18, 59, 174, 178

mundane, 51, 81–2, 90, 125, 130–5, 148, 168
Murphy, Raymond, 43, 45, 59

Nail, Thomas, 95
nature, 12, 33–4, 41–5, 71–4, 81, 101–3, 111, 157, 173
neighbourhoods, 26, 180
neighbours, 50, 51, 85, 93. *See also* neighbourhoods
Netherlands, 33–5, 53, 157–8, 173–4
net-negative, 142
Netukulimk, 78
never seen anything like it, 101, 111, 150, 184
New Brunswick (home of the Wolastoqiyik, Mi'kmaq, and Peskotomuhkati peoples), 9, 43, 57, 65, 89, 131, 139
new normal, 58, 68, 180
New Orleans (Bulbancha), 10, 27–8, 33–5, 81–4, 90–3, 186
New York (Lanape territory), 124
Nijkamp, Peter, 153
1951 Refugee Convention, 94
Nova Scotia Power/Emera, 61–5, 73–6

Ocasio-Cortez, Alexandria, 165
ocean acidification, 22
oil, 27–32, 99–102, 113–18, 129–33, 135–8; BP oil spill, 27, 132; peak oil, 12, 38, 188
O'Regan, Michael, 46
over-dependency, 24, 47, 167
oysters, 35–6, 172

Paris Agreement, 52, 143, 164
Parsons, Kelvin, 118

Peek, Lori, 90
Peggys Cove, NS, 69, 83
Perrow, Charles, 130, 174
Point Pleasant Park (Amntu'kati), 8, 65–6, 70
post-carbon, 14, 50, 123, 136, 155
Potter, Claire Bond, 22
power outages, 44, 61, 90, 123–6, 133, 154, 168; blackouts, 170; rolling blackouts, 134, 169
praise, 114, 121
Prince Edward Island (Epekwitk), 57, 60, 127
public transit, 66–8, 73–8, 121–6, 161–5, 179
Puerto Rico (Boriken), 36, 90–3, 124–8, 144, 168, 186

quads, 5, 13, 106, 108, 122, 124, 151

race, 25–6, 50, 89, 92, 168, 186
rail, 57, 61–2, 153–4; Lac-Mégantic, 138
Random Island, NL, 101, 103–4, 112
ration, 44, 189
Redfield, Peter, 170
Red Rebel Brigade, 183
redundancy, 15, 100, 160, 182–7, 189–90; rebrand redundancy, 4, 15, 176–7, 187–90
reflexive modernization, 27, 68
Reggiani, Aura, 153
resilience, 14, 110–14, 144–9, 151–6, 177; infrastructure resilience, 14, 145–56; social-ecological resilience, 14, 152, 158; transport resilience, 14, 77, 145–9, 151–8

revolutionize mobility, 15, 160–1, 182–9

rhythm, 59, 67, 109

ride sharing, 52, 163; Lyft, 52; Uber, 52

risk, 26–8, 62, 68, 139, 154; manufactured risk, 28, 44

Romano, Renee, 22

Room for the River, 34–5, 53, 173

root cellar, 160, 177–8

Rothe, Delf, 38, 52–4, 92, 95

routine, 40, 82, 87, 178

safety, 47–50, 74, 131, 167

Sambro, NS, 86

Savitzky, Satya, 13, 107, 188

scenario-building, 143, 151, 162

Schwanen, Tim, 14, 23, 167, 185

scrambled mobilities, 52, 106–8, 122, 151, 176, 188

sea level rise, 21, 34, 42, 48, 54, 151–4, 162, 172–4

security, 28, 34–5, 73, 94–5, 118, 164–9

Sheller, Mimi, 18, 22–6, 37–8, 95–7, 129, 161

shipping, 31–4, 49, 53, 66, 106, 155

Skaggs, Beverley, 50

Sloane, Dawn, 65

Slow, 46–9, 53, 60, 84, 94, 96, 179

snow, 21, 40, 105, 176–80; Snowmageddon, 6, 185; White Juan, 8, 68–70, 149

Solnit, Rebecca, 15

Sou, Gemma, 93

speed, 21–3, 48, 130, 179–80

state of emergency, 44, 85–9, 137, 142–3, 149

status quo, 12–15, 114–18, 153, 158–9, 184–8

Stephenville, NL, 116–17

St. John's, NL, 99–101, 142, 151, 186

storm surge, 36, 61, 116–17, 127

stormwater, 35, 66, 146–9, 157

stress, 71, 89, 107, 112, 127, 139–40

subway, 36; underground/tube, 36

supply chains, 32, 122–4, 129–34, 136, 143, 177–9

sustainable transport, 12, 33, 39, 49, 57, 160

Sustainable Transportation Strategy, 51, 77, 121, 178

Swissair crash, 13, 68–71, 185

Synard, Sam, 111

taxis, 100, 127

"the resilient Newfoundlander," 113–14, 149, 180

tides, 53–7

tipping points, 6, 141

Titanic, 42, 174

Tomblin, Stephen, 110, 116, 121, 166

tourism, 22, 84, 99, 115, 155; tourists, 25, 31, 83, 152

traffic, 12, 23, 33, 48–53, 86, 105, 127, 157

transboundary, 68

Trans-Canada Highway, 57, 100, 109

transformation, 54, 153, 166, 180; transformative, 77, 121, 155, 163–4, 189

Trans Mountain pipeline, 138, 141

Tsing, Anna Lowenhaupt, 15, 28–31, 162

turbulence, 9, 23–4, 49, 53–4, 107, 168, 179–80
Turnbull, Lori, 72

Uexküll, Jakob von, 31, 55
Urban Forest Master Plan, 66, 142
urban plan, 5, 172
Urry, John, 12, 22–3, 38–42, 123, 129, 162–3
Usher, Mark, 34
utopia, 162. *See also* dystopia

Vancouver (K'emk'emelay), 171, 191
violence, 89, 95–6
vital mobilities, 15, 32, 103, 169–71, 189; prioritize vital mobilities, 4, 15, 160, 168, 182, 187–9
vulnerability, 10, 73–4

walking, 38, 45–7, 51, 57, 85, 140, 151, 163, 180
Weber, Max, 79, 97
Williams, Danny, 112, 149
Wilson, E.O., 81
window of opportunity, 128, 148
World War I, 71, 79, 108
World War II, 164

Yusoff, Kathryn, 53

zero-carbon, 142, 179
zero-emission vehicles, 6, 20, 52, 137–8, 141, 164; electric vehicles, 20, 142